Trade unions

TRADE UNIONS

Michael P. Jackson

LONGMAN
London and New York

LONGMAN GROUP LIMITED
Longman House, Burnt Mill,
Harlow, Essex CM20 2JE, England.
and Associated Companies throughout the World.

Published in the United States of America
by Longman Inc., New York

First published 1982
Second impression 1983

BRITISH LIBRARY CATALOGUING IN PUBLICATION DATA

Jackson, Michael P.
  Trade unions.
  1. Trade-unions
  I. Title
  331.88   HD6483   80–42054

  ISBN 0–582–29580–7

Printed in Hong Kong by
Wilture Printing Co. Ltd.

CONTENTS

Preface   vi

1. Introduction   1
2. Trade union growth and development   10
3. White collar and non-manual trade unionism   31
4. Internal democracy   53
5. The challenge from the shop floor   86
6. Collective bargaining and economic objectives   104
7. Trade unions: conflict or compromise   122
8. Trade unions and governments: new directions?   148
9. Conclusions: trade unions as mature organisations   170

Bibliography   181
Index   193

PREFACE

This book is an introduction to the study of trade unions. It is designed for students who may have little previous knowledge of the academic study of industrial relations. Necessarily, some issues are not followed through as far as I would like, but I hope that at least I have been able to convey a flavour of the debate.

I am grateful for the help and encouragement received in the preparation of this book from a wide range of people. Members of staff from Stirling and elsewhere, and students who have taken industrial relations courses I have taught, have all made different but important contributions. Of course, I remain responsible for any errors.

As always, I am particularly indebted to my wife and family for their help and encouragement.

We are grateful to the following for permission to reproduce copyright material:

The author's agents for extracts from *Power in Trade Unions* by V.L. Allen, published by Longman Group Ltd 1954; George Allen & Unwin Ltd and Macmillan Publishing Co. Inc for extracts from *The Government of a British Trade Union* by J. Goldstein (1952 by The Free Press); British Journal of Industrial Relations for our Tables 6 and 8 from *Union Growth Revisited: 1948–1975 in Perspective*, Volume XIV, November 1976 Tables 5 and 7 by R. Price and G.S. Bain; Cassell Ltd for extracts (some slightly adapted) from *Trade Unionism* by J.A. Banks; Fontana Paperbacks for our Diagram 1 from p 179 of *The Politics of Industrial Relations* by Colin Crouch; Her Majesty's Stationery Office for our Table 3 from p 1242 of the *Department of Employment Gazette* December 1979, by permission of the Controller of Her Majesty's Stationery Office; The London School of Economics & Political Science for extracts from *Industrial Democracy* by Beatrice Webb published by Longman Group Ltd 1920; Macmillan, London & Basingstoke for our Table 10 from p 62 of *Trade Unions & the Economy* by Michael P. Jackson and for extracts from *Political Parties* by Robert Michels, trans. by Eden & Cedar Paul (Copyright © 1962 by The Crowell-Collier Publishing Company) and *Union Democracy* by Seymour M. Lipset, et al (Copyright © 1956 by The Free Press, a Corporation); Oxford University Press for extracts (one slightly adapted) from *The Growth of White Collar Unionism* by G.S. Bain 1970; Sage Publications Ltd for our Table 7 from Table 3, p 42 of *Challenge to Power* by Klaus von Beyme; Supply & Services Canada for our Table 2 from *Canada Year Book 1979* reproduced by permission of the Minister of Supply & Services Canada.

Trade unions are a feature of all industrial societies. In most countries they are important and influential bodies. Clegg has referred to them as 'one of the most powerful forces shaping our society and determining our future'.[1] In many countries they organise a majority of the working population. This is the case, for example, in Australia, Belgium, Great Britain and Sweden. They organise a smaller but significant proportion in New Zealand, Italy, Ireland, Norway, West Germany and the Netherlands and about 30 per cent or less of the working population in Canada, France, and the USA (see Table 1).

However, even the industrial influence of unions cannot be measured by the extent of their membership alone. For example, while a union may organise only, say, 50 per cent of workers in any particular factory, because they have bargaining rights for that factory, effectively they may be able to determine the wages and working conditions for the whole of the workforce. Thus, in the USA unions only organise about 20 per cent of the workforce but determine the terms and conditions of employment of double that number.

If one looks beyond the industrial sphere then this point is reinforced. Trade unions are one of the most influential pressure groups in many countries. They are able to command the attention of the media and governments over a range of social, political and economic matters.

At a very basic level there are some fairly obvious similarities between trade unions. For example, many definitions suggest that unions must bargain over wages and working conditions on behalf of their members. The Webbs described a trade union as 'a continuous association of wage-earners for the purpose of maintaining or improving the conditions of their working lives'.[2] Many would

1

Table 1:   Trade union membership in selected countries

Country	Year	Number of members	Density (per cent)*
Australia	1977	2,794,400	57.0
Belgium	1977	2,400,000	63.2
Canada	1978	3,298,000	31.4
France	1976	5,245,000	30.9
Germany (West)	1977	8,600,000	38.0
Ireland (Republic)	1977	367,290	34.8
Italy	1977	7,500,000	38.4
Netherlands	1977	1,650,000	39.0
New Zealand	1977	473,432	44.5
Norway	1977	692,209	37.9
Sweden	1979	3,364,824	81.8
U.K.	1978	13,112,000	54.3
U.S.A.	1976	21,006,000	20.1

* Calculated as a percentage of the working population.

Note: The accuracy of some of the membership figures is uncertain. Many commentators would claim that the Italian and French figures are an overestimate. The Norwegian figure only refers to the main union federation (the LO): if other unions are included then the total rises to well above 50 per cent.

Sources: Various

argue that this is not an adequate definition of a trade union: for example, unions are not now restricted to wage-earners but have been extended to all those who have to sell their labour, and unions do far more than simply bargain over wages (they have always also provided friendly society benefits, and some unions stress political and social as well as industrial aims).[3] However, at least the Webbs definition allows us to note that seeking to bargain over terms and conditions of employment is a common feature of trade unions.

From the earliest days there have also been strong links between trade unions in different countries. In some instances unions in one country have been directly influenced by developments in another. The earliest trade unions in Australia, for example, were established by British immigrants who modelled their new organisations on their British experience. The Australian trade union movement's path began to seriously diverge from its British counterpart in the late nineteenth century, though the early links are still important for they helped to influence the structure of the movement. The strong links between the Canadian and USA trade union movements do not reach as far back as those between unions in Britain and Australia (in fact, the British and French trade union movements had as much influence as the USA's on Canadian unions in the early stages of their development) but they have been more enduring. Today about half of Canadian trade unionists are members of unions that have their headquarters in the USA. Table 2 shows that 49.0 per cent of Canadian unionists are members of what are termed 'international unions': in this context essentially unions based in the USA. The majority of these organisations 40.6 are affiliated to both the central union organisation in the USA (the American Federation of Labor/Congress of Industrial Organisation) and the central union organisation in Canada, the Canadian Labour Council (CLC) Jamieson[4] in his review of Canadian industrial relations notes the importance of these links and that Ross and Hartman[5] saw them as being so strong that they classified Canada and the USA as one 'industrial relations system'.

While the similarities and links between unions are important, so are the differences. There are crucial differences between union

Table 2:   Union membership in Canada, 1977

Type and affiliation	Number of unions	Membership	
		Number	Percentage
International Unions			
AFL-CIO/CLC	71	1,278,834	40.6
CLC only	5	166,359	5.3
AFL-CIO only	6	3,857	0.1
Unaffiliated unions	7	95,667	3.0
Total	89	1,544,717	49.0
National unions	103	1,492,093	47.4
Directly chartered local unions	259	30,883	1.0
Independent local organisations	141	81,520	2.6
Total	592	3,149,213	100.0

Source: Canada Year Book, 1979

movements in different countries and between individual unions in the same country.

The British trade union movement, for example, is relatively unified. The vast majority of union members are in unions which are affiliated to the Trades Union Congress (TUC). In 1978 112 unions were affiliated to the TUC and they claimed 11,865,300 members or about 92 per cent of the total British trade union membership. Although the TUC's powers are limited it has been able to prevent the major rifts developing between sections of the union movement that are a characteristic of some other countries. The British trade union movement is also dominated by a small number of large unions. Table 3 shows that 80 per cent of union members are in the 26 largest unions, all of which have over 100,000 members each. However, a relatively large number of very small unions still operate: 255 unions have less than 1,000 members and account for less than 1 per cent of all members. By contrast many other trade union movements in Western Europe are divided internally with separate co-ordinating bodies for catholic, protestant, communist and socialist unions. In countries like France this has seriously weakened the union movement and is one of the reasons why unionisation is so low. In the USA the current internal divisions are less serious, but

Table 3:   Trade union membership in Britain, 1978, by size of union

Number of members	Number of unions	Total membership (000s)	Percentage of total membership of all unions
Under 100	72	4	0.0
100–499	135	34	0.3
500–999	48	34	0.3
1,000–2,499	62	103	0.8
2,500–4,999	37	134	1.0
5,000–9,999	26	169	1.3
10,000–14,999	9	112	0.9
15,000–24,999	14	267	2.1
25,000–49,999	19	711	5.5
50,000–199,999	14	947	7.3
100,000–249,999	15	2,263	17.3
250,000 +	11	8,335	63.6
Total	462	13,112	100.0

Source: Department of Employment *Gazette*, December 1979

there is a history of division, most importantly between the AFL and the CIO (in fact it was not until 1955 that the two bodies settled their differences and joined together to form the AFL/CIO) and a substantial proportion of unions (accounting for over 20 per cent of the membership) are not affiliated to the AFL/CIO. The pattern of union membership in the USA is similar to that in Britain. In both countries a small number of large unions dominate. In Britain the largest union is the Transport and General Workers' Union (T&GWU) with about two million members, whereas in the USA the largest union is the Teamsters' with about 1,900,000 members: in the USA 48 unions have over 100,000 members and they account for 88.8 per cent of total union membership (if the 26 largest unions were taken to allow direct comparison with the figures quoted for Britain this would show that they accounted for 73.3 per cent of total union membership). At the same time both countries have a large number of unions with small memberships (in the USA 127 unions have less than 100,000 members and account for less than 12 per cent of all members).

A similar pattern of membership can be seen in Australia: for example, in 1977 only 16 unions had more than 50,000 members each but they accounted together for over 54 per cent of total union membership, whereas 229 unions had less than 10,000 members and only accounted for 13 per cent of total union membership. A different pattern exists though in some Western European and some Scandinavian countries. In West Germany the main trade union federation, the Deutscher Gewerkschaftsbund (DGB), which covers 82 per cent of all union members, is composed of just 17 unions. As in Britain, USA and Australia there are a number of large unions: the largest, the Metalworkers' has over 2.5 million members and the largest three unions have almost 60 per cent of the total DGB membership. However, because there are fewer unions in total there are far fewer unions with smaller memberships. A similar situation exists in Sweden where the main trade union federation, the Landsorganisationen Sverige (LO) (which covers 62 per cent of all union members) is composed of just 25 unions.

There are also important differences between the structure of trade union movements in different countries. In Britain the structure is complex to say the least. Most authors[6] distinguish three and sometimes four different organising bases. One is the craft union, where entry is restricted to workers who have been apprenticed in a particular occupation; another is the industrial union where recruitment and organisation is restricted to a particular industry; and a third is the general union where recruitment is unrestricted by trade, grade or geographical region. Sometimes a fourth category is described, the occupational union. This has a similar basis to the craft union (sometimes occupational unions are seen as a type of craft union) but is not restricted to apprenticed occupations. However, in practice, union structure in Britain is more complex than this, for no union fits the above categorisation exactly. For example, most craft unions, like the Amalgamated Engineering Union, have now opened up their ranks to non-craft members; similarly, most general unions concentrate on sections of industry (T&GWU concentrates particularly on transport industries) and no union organises all of the workers in an industry (some like the National Union of Miners (NUM) restrict their recruitment to one industry, but by some definitions this would not allow them to be classified as an industrial union because they are not the only union operating in that industry).

The best contrast to the structure of trade unionism in Britain can be seen in West Germany. Each of the seventeen trade unions in the main union federation (the DGB) covers one fairly well defined industry or group of industries. For example, one union, the Industrial Union of Metal Workers, covers the whole of the iron and steel industry. In Sweden the position is somewhat similar, but differs a little to that in West Germany: trade unionism is structured broadly on industrial lines, but white collar workers are more frequently organised separately and some unions cut across industrial boundaries.

In other countries the picture is less complex than in Britain but is by no means as clear as in West Germany or Sweden. For example, the main trade union federation in France, the Confédération Générale du Travail (CGT) has for many years organised on industrial lines, but because of the religious and political divisions (in practice the CGT only organises about half of French trade unionists) there is considerable competition between unions in particular industries. Trade unionism in the USA and Canada is not seriously divided by religious and political differences and there has been a general predisposition in favour of industrial unions. Nevertheless, the picture is still fairly complex as many unions have organised beyond industrial boundaries.

Another level at which variations can be noted between trade union movements in different countries is that of internal government. In some countries union government is highly centralised. In Sweden, for example, not only do union officials and presidents have considerable power, but the main trade union confederation, the LO, also has extensive powers, particularly over wage bargaining. Broadly, the same is true of the trade union movement in West Germany. The main trade union federation, the DGB, has less powers than its Swedish counterpart, but the individual unions are strongly centralised. A different model operates in Australia where the national officials of unions have relatively little power. The federal nature of the country is important and is reflected in the trade unions through the extent of the independence given to the state organisations. In the USA, similarly a federal country, trade union government is not as strongly influenced by state boundaries. However, government in USA unions is still much more decentralised than in West Germany and Sweden because of the independence of the branch organisation.

The position in Britain is more complicated and, though it is more exaggerated than elsewhere, it illustrates well the considerable differences that often exist over internal government between different trade unions in the same country. Virtually all major British unions have a common basic level of constitutional machinery. For example, the supreme policy-making body is normally the delegate conference, which meets either annually or bi-annually. The day-to-day running of affairs is left in the hands of a national executive committee and a number of full-time officers (in many cases the General Secretary is the most important full-time officer, but sometimes the President has equal or greater authority). Nearly all unions also have some kind of branch organisation at the local level and many also have district and regional organisation as well. When one looks beyond this very basic level, though, the picture is far more complicated. This can be illustrated by simply referring to some of the contrasts between the position in the two major general unions, the T&GWU and the General and Municipal Workers Union (GMWU).[7]

The differences between the unions can be seen at each level of the organisation. The delegate conference of the T&GWU is held every two years, whereas in the GMWU it is held every year. The full-time officials play a larger role in the GMWU than in the T&GWU conference: for example, in the GMWU the regional secretaries act as leaders of the important 'district delegations'. The executive committee of the T&GWU is composed of 39 members, 28 of whom are elected by the members through the regions and 11 of whom represent the trade groups. All executive committee members are 'lay' representatives. The executive committee of the

GMWU on the other hand is composed of 30 members, 3 from each region, but a third (one from each region) are full-time officials (the regional secretaries). The General Secretaries of both unions are elected for life by the membership, but the appointment of other full-time officials differs between the unions. The full-time officers in the T&GWU are appointed by the executive whereas those of the GMWU are initially selected by the Regional Committees but after two years have to stand for election (though in practice they have never been defeated). The two unions are also organised very differently in terms of their internal structure. The T&GWU is organised on both a regional and trade group basis (the former deals with administrative and the latter with industrial issues) whereas in the GMWU the regions have a dominant role (even though since 1969 there have been some moves to strengthen the industrial machinery through the introduction of industrial conferences).

If one extended the coverage beyond these two unions then the differences would multiply: the variations in internal government are enormous. Some British unions are highly centralised, others are decentralised, some allow full-time officials to have a direct say in decision-making, others preclude it. One could continue the list indefinitely.

However, for the moment probably sufficient has been said to illustrate the differences between British unions and the variations between union movements in different countries. Such differences do not call into question the important basic similarities and points of contact between unions, but they cannot be ignored. They are of considerable significance and need to be taken into account in a more detailed analysis of the growth, development and implications of trade unions.

NOTES

1. H.A. Clegg, *Trade Unionism under Collective Bargaining*, Blackwell, Oxford, 1976, p. 11.
2. S. and B. Webb, *The History of Trade Unionism*, Longmans, London, 1924, p. 1.
3. For a fuller examination of the aims and objectives of trade unions, see M.P. Jackson, *Industrial Relations*, Croom Helm, London, 1977.
4. S. Jamieson, *Industrial Relations in Canada*, Macmillan, Toronto, 1973.

5. A.M. Ross, P.T. Hartman, *Changing Patterns of Industrial Conflict*, Wiley, New York, 1960, quoted in *ibid.*, p. 2.
6. See, for example, J.H. Richardson, *An Introduction to the Study of Industrial Relations*, Allen & Unwin, London, 1965.
7. Based on review by H.A. Clegg, *The Changing System of Industrial Relations in Great Britain*, Blackwell, Oxford, 1979.

Chapter two

TRADE UNION GROWTH AND DEVELOPMENT

The growth of trade unions over the past hundred years or so has been one of the most spectacular developments evident in Western industrialised nations. While it is fair to point out that in a number of countries the existence of trade unions as long ago as the seventeenth century can be noted (the Webbs[1] referred to traces of sporadic combinations and associations of workers in Britain by the end of the seventeenth century), such organisations tended to have relatively short lives and it was not until the middle of the nineteenth century that stable, national trade unions were established on a significant scale. Even then, development was concentrated amongst skilled workers. In Britain, the 'new model' unions were established from the 1850s onwards, following the lead of the Amalgamated Society of Engineers, Machinists, Smiths, Millwrights and Pattern Makers (that union was formed in 1851 and later became known as the Amalgamated Society of Engineers), but they restricted entry to skilled workers and trod a cautious, conservative path, concentrating on building up a stable organisation rather than furthering broader political objectives. Similarly in the USA the first stable development of trade unions occurred with the founding of the American Federation of Labor in 1886, an alliance of craft-based unions.

In most countries the development of unions amongst unskilled manual workers occurred later than it did amongst skilled workers. In Britain it started in the 1880s following strikes at Bryant and May (matchmakers), the South Metropolitan Gas Company and the London Docks. 'New unionism' as it became known, differed significantly from the 'model unionism' of the skilled workers. The 'new unionism' workers were less well paid and consequently could not afford the high subscriptions demanded by the skilled unions; their unions were less conservative in administrative terms, building on numbers rather than stable organisation, and in political terms being closely linked to socialist ideals and the strike weapon.

However, although unions had started to organise British unskilled manual workers by the end of the nineteenth century, it was not until the First World War period that the major expansion of unskilled manual worker unionism occurred in Britain. Table 4 shows that at the beginning of the century there were about two million union members; by 1920 there were over eight million. Subsequently the number of union members declined, especially in the inter-war years, during the Depression, but the major step forward had been taken, and although it was not until during the Second World War that membership figures reached the 1920 heights again, trade unionism had been established as a major political, social and economic force.

The growth and development of trade unions in other Western nations shows some similarities to the British model but also some contrasts. Australia provides the closest parallel to the British experience. The union movement had started to organise unskilled manual workers before the beginning of the twentieth century and subsequently grew steadily, embracing almost half of the workforce by the beginning of the Second World War.

In the USA unions took much longer than those in Britain or Australia to become established amongst unskilled manual workers. In fact it was not until the 1930s that they made significant inroads into unskilled manual occupations and mass production industries (the major extension of unionism in the USA in this sector came after the New Deal legislation when the industrial unions developed and mass production workers in industries like steel, textiles and automobiles were unionised).[2]

In many continental Western European countries although skilled workers' unions had been established by the nineteenth century, the subsequent history of unionism and its development to a mass movement embracing unskilled manual workers has been much more chequered than was the case in Britain. For example, in Germany trade unions developed strongly in the late nineteenth and early twentieth centuries. They began to penetrate the unskilled manual sector and by the beginning of the First World War they had attracted about three million members: this total had risen to more than nine million by 1922. However, they suffered reverses during the economic crisis of the 1920s and by the early 1930s

Table 4:   Unionisation in the United Kingdom 1901–78

Year	Union membership	Union density	Year	Union membership	Union density
1901	2,025,000	12.4	1950	9,289,000	44.0
1911	3,139,000	17.1	1951	9,535,000	44.9
1921	6,633,000	34.3	1952	9,583,000	45.0
1923	5,429,000	32.9	1953	9,523,000	44.3
1924	5,544,000	33.1	1954	9,556,000	43.9
1925	5,506,000	32.4	1955	9,741,000	44.2
1926	5,212,000	30.4	1956	9,778,000	43.9
1927	4,919,000	28.4	1957	9,829,000	44.1
1928	4,806,000	27.5	1958	9,639,000	43.1
1929	4,858,000	27.2	1959	9,623,000	42.6
1930	4,842,000	26.5	1960	9,835,000	42.8
1931	4,624,000	25.0	1961	9,916,000	42.5
1932	4,444,000	23.9	1962	10,014,000	42.1
1933	4,392,000	23.5	1963	10,067,000	42.0
1934	4,590,000	24.4	1964	10,216,000	42.3
1935	4,867,000	25.0	1965	10,323,000	42.2
1936	5,295,000	27.2	*1966	10,260,000	42.6
1937	5,842,000	29.3	1967	10,188,000	42.8
1938	6,053,000	29.8	1968	10,189,000	43.1
1939	6,298,000	31.6	1969	10,468,000	44.4
1940	6,613,000	33.9	1970	11,174,000	47.7
1941	7,165,000	36.3	1971	11,120,000	47.9
1942	7,867,000	39.3	1972	11,391,000	48.7
1943	8,174,000	43.1	1973	11,570,000	48.5
1944	8,087,000	44.2	1974	11,755,000	49.6
1945	7,875,000	41.5	1975	12,184,000	51.7
1946	8,803,000	43.5	1976	12,376,000	51.8
1947	9,145,000	44.4	1977	12,846,000	53.3
1948	9,319,000	45.1	1978	13,112,000	54.3
1949	9,274,000	44.5			

* Prior to 1966, union density based on total occupied/economically active population. After 1966, union density based on number of employees (employed/unemployed) at June. 1966 figures calculated on both bases. The first figure based on occupied/economically active population.

Source: *Historical Abstract of British Labour Statistics, 1886–1968* HMSO, London, 1971; Department of Employment *Gazette*.

faced strong political opposition: in 1933 the free trade union movement was dissolved by the Hitler regime. The present-day West German trade union movement, therefore, really only dates from 1949 when the Allies encouraged the establishment of national federations.

The German case is an extreme one but in other European countries trade unions have had a similarly chequered history. For instance, although French workers embraced trade unionism in the late nineteenth century and French trade unions were able to claim a million members before the First World War, the movement went into decline in the post-First World War years, partly as a result of internal divisions. In fact, it was not until 1936 (following the Matignon Agreement) that French trade unionism could claim to be a mass movement. Membership of the largest trade union federation, the CGT, leapt from one million to five million: the impact was particularly strongly felt in the mass production industries. The Catholic trade unions also increased their membership from about 100,000 to over 400,000.

The growth of trade unions, then, has been a universal phenomenon in Western industrialised nations over the past hundred years. However, as has been noted, and as Table 5 shows, the pattern and intensity of the growth has varied. The relatively consistent trend noted in some countries has to be compared with the much more volatile trend in others. If one looked beyond the broad national contexts then, again, while certain broad consistencies would be noted, important variations would need to be recognised. As a result, explanations for the growth of trade unions have to be able to account not only for broad similarities but also for significant differences.

EXPLANATIONS FOR UNION GROWTH

Industrialisation and functionalism

Clearly one of the most important spurs to the development and growth of trade unions has been industralisation. The decline of the domestic and the growth of the factory system meant that workers increasingly became isolated from their employers. The individual worker had relatively little power to represent his own interests but had a great deal in common with his fellow workers.

Table 5: Unionisation in selected countries

Year	Australia		Canada		USA		West Germany*		UK	
	No. of members	% union-isation	No. of members	% union-isation	No. of members	% union-isation	No. of members	% union-isation	No. of members	% union-isation
1891	54,888	4.1					343,000	—	1,572,000†	11.2
1901	97,174	6.1			1,125,000	3.0	857,100	5.7	2,025,000	12.4
1911	364,732	27.9	133,000	4.7	2,343,000	5.9	2,788,500	15.6	3,139,000	17.1
1921	703,009	51.6	351,000	10.6	4,781,000	11.9	8,779,000	42.6	6,638,000	34.3
1931	769,006	47.0	366,000	8.8	3,310,000	6.2	5,177,000	23.5	4,624,000	25.0
1941	1,075,680	49.9	540,000	12.1	8,944,000	15.0		—	7,165,000	36.3
1951	1,690,300	57.0	1,215,000	23.5	15,000,000	23.8	7,569,400	36.7	9,535,000	44.9
1961	1,894,600	53.6	1,826,000	28.5	17,328,000	21.1	8,105,500	36.8	9,916,000	42.5
1971	2,436,600	51.4	2,597,000	30.9	20,752,000	22.3			11,120,000	47.9

* Figures for Germany as a whole before 1941
† Figure for 1892

Note: The figures are taken from a variety of different sources. They are not, therefore, directly comparable and should be taken as a broad guide only.

Thus industralisation meant that there were fairly obvious benefits to be gained from unionism.

Some writers would see industrialisation as the crucial element in the development of trade unions. For them industrialisation created a new need and this need had to be filled: trade unions, then, almost had to be created. This kind of functionalist analysis[3] sees society as having certain basic needs, which have to be met in one way or another. An agrarian economy may have one set of needs, an industrial economy another.

Such a view can be seen in the writing of Tannenbaum.[4] He views trade unions essentially as groups of people with a community of interest. In the middle ages trade unions were not needed. The important community of interest was the particular trade in which people worked. The need produced by this community of interests was filled by the craft guilds. The industrial revolution, Tannenbaum argues, destroyed the traditional work community. The crucial division became that between employer and employee, rather than between one trade and another. Thus employees' community of interest created a new need, the need for a new type of organisation. Trade unions were a response to this new need. According to Tannenbaum 'the organisation of workers is essential in a modern industrial society, and if unionism did not exist it would have to be invented'.[5]

This approach to the growth and development of trade unions brought Tannenbaum into direct conflict with the Webbs. Tannenbaum argued that the medieval craft guilds were the real origins of present-day trade unions. The Webbs vehemently disputed this. They wrote, 'we assert, indeed with some confidence, that in no case did any Trade Union in the United Kingdom arise, either directly or indirectly, from a Craft Guild'.[6] As far as they were concerned there were major differences between the craft guild and the trade union. Craft guilds, they said, were dominated by the master craftsmen, who owned the means of production and the product. On the other hand, trade unions were entirely associations of workers who owned neither the means of production nor the product.

The functionalist approach is probably best developed in systems theory.[7] Essentially systems theorists view society as being made up of a variety of interrelated parts. As a result, if changes take place to one part of the system, then changes have to be made to another to restore the balance. From this point of view industrialisation can be seen as an important change to part of the system. Trade unions, then, are seen as the response, the change needed to another part of the system to restore the balance.

Such analysis need not simply be undertaken on a societal scale: it can also be used to look at individual industries and groupings. Thus Smelser[8] used systems theory for his study of the late eighteenth and early nineteenth century Lancashire cotton industry. He isolated a number of changes concerned with the industry and the society in which it operated, and argued that these were the cause of the developments he noted in trade unions. Centrally he argued that changes took place to the nature of the cotton industry (the 'putting out' system declined, to be replaced by the factory system) and to the operation of the family (in particular the separation of home from work). This led trade unions in the cotton industry to develop into something like their present-day equivalents.

The development of capitalism

The view that the development of trade unions is linked to industrialisation is different in its specific form but nevertheless has something in common with the view that trade unions are essentially a reaction to the development of capitalism. An economy based on capitalism leads to a division between those who own the means of production and those who have to sell their labour. It leads to the development of a community of interests between those who have to sell their labour and the development of trade unions as organisations to represent and defend them. Such a point of view suggests that trade unions are a development dependent on the capitalist system and without capitalism would not be necessary.

In some ways the existence of trade unions in Eastern European countries might be taken as a challenge to this point of view. If trade unions are only necessary in, and are a direct response to, capitalist societies, then why do they exist in societies based on socialism? One answer would be that Eastern European societies, like the USSR, are not truly socialist, but are simply examples of state capitalism. There is still a wage labour system and still a community of interests between those who have to sell their labour. Another answer would be to suggest that trade unions in Eastern European countries are really different kinds of bodies than their Western European counterparts and fulfil a different function. Brown's[9] analysis of trade unions in the USSR, for example, suggests that their main function at the national level is to work with the government to implement the national plan. They do not bargain with employers in the same way as do trade unions in Western capitalist nations. At the local level they help to interpret national guidelines, modify them to local needs, and deal with individual grievances. The position in Poland with the development of independent trade unions in 1980, is rather more complicated. These unions have broken the traditional pattern of trade unions in Eastern Europe, but in doing so they have illustrated the difficulty of accommodating trade unions which aspire to many of the features of their Western counterparts in a socialist system.

Another problem which faces explanations based on either industrialisation or capitalism is how to account for the differential development of trade unions in different countries, in different industries and in different localities. One answer might be to say that such differences are simply a response to different rates of industrialisation or differences in the development of capitalism. This kind of explanation might help to show why trade unions developed later in the USA than in Britain, and why they have developed in some industries more quickly than in others. Certainly large-scale units of production have been established at different periods of time in different industries and countries and there is some link between the size of the enterprise and the degree of unionisation. Price and Bain[10] have shown that the larger the enterprise the more likely it is that the workforce will be unionised. For example, in 1974 union density in manufacturing industries in Britain was 62.2 per cent, but union density in manufacturing establishments with 200 workers or more was 89.2 per cent.

However, this argument does not seem to offer a complete explanation for all of the variations noted. Another possible explanation suggested by Marxists centres on the idea of consciousness. For example, Allen[11] argues that although capitalism is a necessary precondition for the development of trade unions, it is not in itself sufficient to determine their existence. An important factor is 'consciousness': whether workers are aware of their class position and where their true interests lie. Thus, although he argues that the existence of a free labour market is a necessary condition for the growth of trade unions, he states that the actual emergence of unions is determined by social values. 'All members of a free labour market are in the same basic economic position but whether or not they realise this will depend on their social images which are in turn a product either of traditional values or social class position.'[12]

In the original Marxist formulation consciousness was to be encouraged by industrialisation and the development of the urban community. Workers who had previously been spread out and often worked in small groups, if not in isolation, were brought together. Initially there might be conflict between workers as each strove for higher wages but eventually they would realise that they had a common interest in raising wage levels in general. Their consciousness would be further heightened when they found that the trade unions they formed to represent their interests were attacked by the judiciary, and as a result they would be forced to form political parties. Eventually they would realise that traditional political action was insufficient and determine on a revolutionary course.

Banks notes that in practice 'the history of Marxist movements since Lenin... would seem to provide evidence that this growing class consciousness on the part of the proletariat has not been the crucial factor in social change. Rather does it appear that revolutions have been made in advance of the development of class consciousness.'[13] Looking at the lessons to be learnt from the Cuban revolution, he recognises that 'it is not necessary to wait until all conditions for revolution exist: the insurrection can create them'.[14] Of course, men cannot make revolutions as they please, in simply any situation, and ignore altogether the social circumstances of their time and place, but nevertheless they can make them.

Banks also mentions that in practice the leading members in revolutions have often been not members of the working class but members of the intelligensia, men whose occupations are not associated with the series of events previously described. In this context it is worth noting that the British trade union and labour movements received support during their formative stages from a number of people who might be classified as members of the interlligentsia. Thus, the lessons Banks draws for the generation of revolutions may also apply in other less dramatic situations.

Economic conditions

A further but still related possible explanation for the growth and development of trade unions involves a discussion of economic costs and benefits. If the costs of union membership are greater than the benefits then a potential member will not join, whereas if the reverse is true he will join. The costs might include subscriptions, employer displeasure, diminution of promotion prospects and the like, while the benefits might include higher wages and greater job security. Of course, costs and benefits are not static over time. For example, workers may believe union membership to have additional benefits during an inflationary period: inflation may be seen as a threat to their standard of living and union membership as an important way of guarding against this threat. Neither are they necessarily the same at any particular time in different countries or industries.

This line of thinking has led some writers to put forward what has been termed a 'prosperity theory' of union growth. Thus, it might be argued that the level of economic activity and the corresponding level of prosperity can be related to the rate of union growth. In relatively prosperous times workers may be able to take the risk of joining unions because with a strong demand for labour a variety of jobs will be available; they might also better be able to afford union subscriptions and any financial sacrifice called for during strike action (say to establish bargaining rights for the union). Such lines of thought led writers like Wolman to argue that 'union growth is positively correlated with prosperity, rising when business is good and falling when business is bad'.[15]

There is some empirical evidence to support such claims. For example, the level of union activity increased substantially in the early part of the twentieth century in many countries: the 'boom' period that followed the First World War was matched by a growth in unionisation rates in both Britain and the USA (in 1911 unionisation levels were at about 17 per cent in Britain and 6 per cent in the USA whereas by 1921 they had been increased to 34 per cent and 12 per cent). Similarly, union activity decreased in both Britain and the USA during the Depression. By 1931 the level of unionisation had fallen to 25 per cent in Britain and 6 per cent in the USA.

However, some writers note that a crude 'prosperity theory' of union growth needs to be modified. For example, Davis[16] compared the movement of union membership with a condition of 'prosperity' in sixty-one cases, covering four major countries (England, France, Germany and the USA). He found that although in two-thirds of the cases in which the year was classified as one of prosperity there were marked rises (more than 3 per cent) in union membership, in 25 per cent of such cases union membership declined. Davis argued that a more sophisticated theory of union growth is necessary: he suggests that as a starting point the following theory might be examined:

Under conditions of 'liberal capitalism' when labor has major new grievances and an improving position in the labor market, unions tend to grow. When labor has no major new grievances or when its position in the labor market is not improving, conditions for organisation are not especially favorable; and when labor is economically weak or losing ground in the labor market, though grievances exist and give rise to organisation movements, these movements are not likely to result in a general increase in union membership, which tends to decline.[17]

Davis has also taken the discussion a stage further than other writers from this school by recognising that even this theory needs to be modified. In particular he notes that the growth of unions has been affected by the quality of union leadership and the reaction of the state. For example, he argues that unionism failed to develop to the extent it might have in the USA during the First World War, despite the favourable economic conditions, because of the poor quality of the leadership of the American Federation of Labor (the major trade union organisation at the time). On the other hand, the successful organising campaign of the Committee for Industrial Organisation, which broke away from and challenged the AFL in the late 1930s, owed a great deal to the positive leadership and the lessons learnt from the mistakes of the past. Similarly, Davis points to the importance of state support for the development of trade unionism in France in the 1930s. Particular reference might be made to the Matignon Agreement of 1936 which followed a period of industrial strife that culminated in a national strike: it recognised the freedom to organise and belong to a trade union and to conclude labour contracts. However, Davis adds the caveat that it is by no means always possible to see a direct correlation between a socialist government and union growth.

Davis' emphasis on the importance of the attitude of the state for union growth might be extended by referring to the British experience. The early growth of British unions was hampered on a number of occasions, initially by restrictive legislation (most spectacularly through the Combination Acts of 1799 and 1800) and then by restrictive interpretation of legislation by the judiciary (again, most spectacularly seen in the *Quinn* v. *Leatham* case of 1900[18] and the *Taff Vale Railway Company* v. *Amalgamated Society of Railway Servants* case of 1901[19]). However, the position was eased later when trade union and labour pressure persuaded the state to take a different line. In the early twentieth century the state was persuaded to reverse the restrictive interpretations of the judiciary in the instance of the two cases referred to, through the Trade Disputes Act of 1906, and later concerning the right of unions to make donations to political parties (restricted by the Osborne judgment of 1911)[20] through the Trade Unions Act of 1913. A crucial point to be made in these cases is that the state did not take action conducive to union growth in a vacuum, it did so largely as a reaction to working-class power. The extension of the franchise and the development of the Labour Party meant that working-class votes had to be cultivated: the Liberal Party still nursed the hope that it could retain working-class support and was willing to take parliamentary action to this end.

A similar line of thought is pursued by Price and Bain[21]. Looking at the development of trade unions in Britain in a later period they note that although union membership increased between 1970 and 1974, it increased less and in a different sequence than might have been expected: on the basis of economic conditions alone one would have expected membership to have increased faster between 1971 to 1974 than it did between 1969 and 1970, whereas in fact the reverse was true. They argue that the explanation is that the hostile government attitude towards trade unions between 1971 and 1974 to some extent counterbalanced the favourable economic conditions.

One of these authors, Bain[22], also uses the same line of thinking in his discussion of trade unionism in Canada. He argues that one of the ways in which unionisation in Canada could be increased from its historic relatively low levels is by government action: the government would need to design and administer its labour legislation so that employers were less able to resist unionisation and unions were more able to obtain recognition from them. For example, the government (or if action were taken by the provinces, governments) could introduce legislation so that a union could get access to the names, addresses and telephone numbers of employees it sought to organise, and it (or they) could relax the rules relating to recognition (Bain argues that the rules on representativeness, which state the amount of support the union must have in a bargaining unit before it can be given recognition by the labour relations board, are too harsh: one of the reasons for this belief is that frequently workers will not join or support a union until it is recognised, so that, in some circumstances, recognition can be a precondition for representativeness).

In another study, Bain, this time with Elsheikh,[23] has attempted a more sophisticated analysis of union growth using many of the variables already discussed. A model is presented using the following equation:

$$\triangle T_t = \beta_0 + \beta_1 \triangle P_t - 1 + \beta_2 \triangle W_t + \beta_3 \triangle U_t + + \beta_4 \triangle U_t^-$$
$$+ \beta_5 \triangle (D_t - 1)^{-1} + \beta_6 G_t + \mathcal{E}_t$$

'Where $\triangle T_t$ is the current rate of change of union membership;
$\triangle P_t - 1$ is the rate of change of prices lagged one year;
$\triangle W_t$ is the current rate of change of money wages;
$\triangle U_t^+$ and $\triangle U_t^-$ represent respectively the positive and negative changes in the current rate of unemployment;

$(D_t - 1)^{-1}$ is the inverse of the level of union density lagged one year; G_t is a dummy variable which takes the value of unity for the period 1937–47 and zero for all other years and represents the impact of government action upon union growth; $\mathcal{E}_t$ is a random disturbance term; and the expected signs of all the coefficients are positive except those for $\triangle U_t+$ and for the constant term.'[24]

In one of their articles Bain and Elsheikh show how this model can be used to explain the rate of change of union density in the United States between 1897 and 1970.[25] They argue that their model enables them to explain 69 per cent of the variation in union density over this period. Further they suggest that the value of the model is not significantly reduced if sections rather than the whole of the time period are studied. This is particularly important as earlier research by Moore and Pearce[26] indicated that existing models might be able to explain pre- better than post-1945 union growth: that there was a structural shift in 1945 so that the same factors did not explain union growth before and after that date. Bain and Elsheikh challenge this assumption. In another work they show how their model can be applied also to the United Kingdom, Australia and Sweden.[27]

The Bain and Elsheikh model, though, is not without its critics: for instance, it has been criticised by Richardson[28] on a variety of grounds (this criticism stimulated a short debate in the journals).[29] For example, he attacks the quality of their theoretical analysis: he calls it 'shallow' and 'ad hoc'. He also attacks the quality of their data, in particular their union density series, and argues that they should have considered other relevant explanatory variables, such as the changing composition of the labour force. Further he discusses (Bain and Elsheikh claim that they did as well) the possibility of a two-way relationship: changes in wages, prices and unemployment may affect the level of union growth but may also be affected by it.

Criticism of structuralist explanations

The kinds of explanation for union growth looked at so far can all be developed from their rather straightforward and crude bases: they all can be formulated in a sophisticated fashion taking account of a number of variables and interactions.

At their extreme, however, they can all be subject to one major criticism: that they are too determinist. They suggest that unions grow and develop in reaction to say, industrialisation, capitalism or economic prosperity. The development of unions is seen as inevitable given certain other conditions. Essentially, then, at their extreme all three are structuralist explanations. Of course, none need be taken to its extreme, and many of the writers we have referred to have recognised the need for modification. While it is not acceptable to say that, for example, industrialisation 'caused' trade unions, it is certainly reasonable to argue that industrialisation had an effect on union development.

Some of the writers we have referred to have also recognised the need to appreciate that it is not enough simply to say a factor exists: one also needs to know whether the people concerned appreciate its existence. This is explicitly recognised in the Marxist notion of consciousness and could be extended to other theoretical approaches. For example, it is not sufficient to say that industrialisation created conditions conducive to the growth of trade unions; one also needs to show that the people likely to set up and join trade unions recognised this new potential.

This line of thought can be taken even further. It might be argued that if you need to ensure, for example, that potential trade union members recognise the importance of new conditions resulting from industrialisation before you can say industrialisation affects the growth of trade unions, then it might be wise to dispense with the notion that industrialisation affects the growth of unions altogether. The result would be to concentrate entirely on the individual, what he feels and what he believes.

Such an approach comes close to ethnomethodology and phenomenology. Accepting this view one needs to examine the 'taken for granted assumptions' and concentrate on the variety of meanings held by different people.[30] The centre of attention is clearly the individual and the meaning he attaches to aspects of social life. Thus, the search for regular patterns is abandoned in favour of the detailed examination of differences in meaning.

Few people would argue with the view that different people

attach different meanings to similar phenomena and social situations. However, it is important to question the extent of the variations noted and to see whether there is any pattern to the variations. If, for example, one can argue that all workers who have had a similar kind of industrial background hold similar (but not the same) views on industrialisation, and that the differences between these views are substantially less than the differences between the views of the group as a whole and those held by other people with a different industrial background, then it might be reasonable to talk about categories of people holding certain types of view on industrialisation. To talk about one view or type of view being held might be an approximation, but it might be an approximation worth making to aid understanding and further enquiry.

Another related kind of criticism of the three theories looked at so far is that they do not make sufficient allowance for individual initiative and influence. This criticism could be taken to the extreme of the 'great men' theory of history: the history of trade unionism could be told in terms of the actions and ideas of its leaders. However, one need not take this line of thought so far: one could simply say that while individuals do not by themselves determine history, they nevertheless at certain points can influence it. The Webbs, for example, in their history of British trade unions,[31] argued that trade union activity was legalised in the 1870s partly at least because of the way that the five leading trade unionists of the time (whom they refer to as the 'Junta') presented their case to the Royal Commission on Trade Unions (established in 1867). The 'Junta' played down the militant side and political role of trade unions (which was uppermost in people's minds and the real reason for the establishment of the Royal Commission following the 'Sheffield Outrages'[32]) and concentrated on their role as friendly societies. The result was the introduction of two pieces of legislation, the Trade Union Act of 1871 and the Conspiracy and Protection of Property Act of 1875, which effectively legalised trade unions.

The emphasis the Webbs placed on the role of individuals like the 'Junta' in the development of trade unions in Britain has been criticised by writers like Allen. He argues that 'Persons respond to situations rather than create them; they may influence timing and intensity but rarely direction.'[33] In fact, Allen may have been unduly harsh on the Webbs on this count, for they certainly did not see the 'Junta' as acting completely independently or reversing the direction of history. The Webbs seem to have argued that if the unions' case had been put differently then the development of unionism in Britain might have been affected: the 'Junta' dealt with a difficult period in a particular way. However, it is clear that they were only able to point to the friendly society role of trade unions because it was, in fact, a major function of the skilled workers' unions at the time. The 'Junta' chose a particular emphasis, they did not create the conditions which allowed a choice to be made.

The importance of the role of individual trade union leaders can possibly best be seen by looking below the simple numerical growth in union membership, and concentrating on the kind of union structure established. It has already been noted, for example, that Britain has a particularly complex trade union structure when compared to many other countries. In Britain trade unions are organised on a variety of different bases. If one wants to explain the development of trade unionism in Britain, as compared say to West Germany, then one of the first pre-requisites is to appreciate that the structure of trade unionism in Britain was never planned centrally in the way it was in West Germany. In Britain the structure grew up piecemeal as a reaction to particular circumstances and needs: in West Germany the structure reflects decisions of the occupying powers after the Second World War. However, one also needs to recognise that the British structure in part reflects the strategic choices, the preferences and the aspirations of individual union leaders. It is reasonable to argue, for example, that the Transport and General Workers Union would have developed in a different fashion had Bevin not been its leader for its first twenty years.[34]

This is not to say that the Union would not have existed had it not been for Bevin: it is to argue, though, that Bevin was such a dominant figure in the Union that its history and current structure would have been different if there had been a different leader. For example, without his leadership the trade group structure might have developed in a different way, certain unions which were encouraged to amalgamate might not have done so, and other unions with whom amalgamation talks broke down might now have been part of the T&GWU. Bevin was careful to ensure that he always carried his executive committee with him in any decisions he made: yet clearly he was a strong influence over them and the knowledge that Bevin, a nationally known figure with well-publicised views, was leader of the Union undoubtedly affected attitudes towards it. Further, the T&GWU is such a large part of the British union jigsaw that had it developed in a different way there could not but have been consequences for many other British unions. Of course, this does not mean that the British union structure would not still have been complex but the detail would have been different.

Banks[35] has attempted to provide an approach to understanding the growth and development of trade unions which enables one to integrate some of the different and often competing influences outlined above. His aim is to produce an approach which enables us to see 'how much of history is determined by processes beyond human control and how much is consciously willed'.[36] To use the terms of the discussion so far, how much of trade union growth and development is determined by factors like industrialisation, economic prosperity and the development of capitalism, and how much is the result of the interpretations, ideas and will of individual workers and union leaders. He proposes that we should adopt a 'step-by-step' approach to explanation. This would enable us to appreciate the way in which unions have developed through trial and error: workers have tried to construct unions in certain ways and at certain times but have been frustrated, partly because the conditions under which they have had to work have not been conducive to such development, whereas at other times their efforts to construct unions and expand them have been successful, partly as a result of their own efforts, and partly because they have been operating in a sympathetic environment. Thus Banks says: 'From this point of view a trade union movement is a "socially constructive" grouping of organisations whose activities may be defined in terms of objectives, shared by their members, provided it is understood that sometimes these objectives are achieved, but also that others are given up when they are seen as no longer relevant or no longer desirable in the new circumstances which have arisen.'[37]

The example Banks presents to illustrate his approach is taken from the history of British trade unions, and compares the attempts to establish general unionism with the emergence of new model unions. The notion of general unionism had its greatest appeal during the 1830s (the Webbs[38] defined the period 1829 to 1842 as the 'revolutionary period' for trade unions and concentrated on the attempt to establish general unions). The most spectacular manifestation of general unionism was Robert Owen's Grant National Consolidated Trade Union. The Union, of which Owen eventually became President, was established in 1834, ostensibly to support workers involved in a dispute at Derby, but it quickly expanded its aims: it proposed to rationalise the existing structure of trade unions and to provide assistance for all workers on strike. Although the union was an immediate success (the Webbs argued that it quickly attracted half a million members)[39] its success was short-lived. Following government prosecutions (the most spectacular was in 1834 when six labourers from the village of Tolpuddle, Dorset, were prosecuted for taking unlawful oaths and sentenced to transportation to Australia for seven years – they became known as the 'Tolpuddle Martyrs') and failure to provide the level of assistance strikers expected, support for it faded. The union eventually collapsed when the treasurer absconded with its funds.

The story of events surrounding the development of new model unions is a very different one. It was noted earlier that new model unions were essentially cautious, conservative bodies concerned to establish their organisation amongst skilled workers. As the Webbs noted,[40] the generation of union leaders that succeeded those who had attempted to establish general unionism had much more limited aims than their predecessors. They abandoned broad political objectives in favour of stability: 'Laying aside all projects of social revolution, they set themselves resolutely to resist the worst of the legal and industrial oppressions from which they suffered, and slowly built up for this purpose organisations which have become integral parts of the structure of a modern industrial state.'[41] According to the Webbs, the more limited aims were much more realistic and in the environment of the time were the only ones which stood a chance of success. Again, earlier we noted the Webbs' argument that it was only because these new union leaders were able to point to the non-political nature of the unions when appearing before the Royal Commission on Trade Unions that trade unions were accepted and given essential legal status.

For Banks the contrasting histories of general unionism and new model unions can only be understood if one accepts that in the former case the aims and aspirations of the leaders could never have been met in the social circumstances of the time, while in the latter case the leaders chose the method most conducive to success in the environment in which they had to operate. Thus he says that the failure of general unionism may 'be symptomatic of the fact that desire alone will not result in a revolutionary new order' while the success of new model unions 'indicates how innovation in the social, as in the material world, takes its point of departure from the nature of the circumstances in which men have to cope'.[42]

CONCLUSIONS

It is clear that trade unions flourish in certain conditions rather than others. A number of writers have successfully highlighted important variables in this context. One of the most crucial may be the economic conditions in which unions operate and try to recruit members. Bain and Elsheikh have been able to specify these conditions and show how they affect union growth with some precision.

However, while the environment in which unions operate is important it is not by itself a sufficient explanation for the growth and development of trade unions. The reactions of union members, and probably crucially union leaders, to these conditions, is also important. Unions may or may not take advantage of favourable environmental conditions: favourable conditions do not make union growth inevitable, simply possible or, at the most, likely.

Banks has provided a useful way of bringing together the influence of environmental conditions and the reactions of union leaders to them. The way in which such factors interrelate needs more examination, but work in this area is probably the most fruitful way of proceeding.

NOTES

1. S. and B. Webb, *History of Trade Unions*, Longman, London, 1896.
2. The emergence of the CIO was an important factor in this development.
3. Essentially functionalist analysis stresses certain needs within society which have to be fulfilled and the interelationship of different parts of society.
4. F. Tannenbaum, *The True Society : A Philosophy of Labour*, Cape, London, 1964.
5. Quoted by J.A. Banks, *Trade Unionism*, Collier-MacMillan, London, 1974, p. 51.
6. Quoted *ibid.*, p. 3.
7. Its application to sociology was pioneered in the work of Parsons and Smelser.
8. N.J. Smelser, *Social Change in the Industrial Revolution*, Routledge & Kegan Paul, London, 1959.
9. E.C. Brown, *Soviet Trade Unions and Labor Relations*, Harvard

U.P., Cambridge (Mass.), 1966.
See also, J.L. Porkett, 'Industrial relations and participation in management in the Soviet-type communist system', *British Journal of Industrial Relations*, vol. XVI (1978), no. 1, pp. 70–85; B. Ruble, 'Dual functioning trade unions in the USSR', *British Journal of Industrial Relations*, vol. XVII (1979), no. 2, pp. 255–41.

10. R. Price, G.S. Bain, 'Union growth revisited : 1948–1974 in perspective', *British Journal of Industrial Relations*, vol. XIV (1976), no. 3, pp. 339–55.

11. V.L. Allen, 'Trade unions : An analytical framework', in B. Barrett *et al.* (eds), *Industrial Relations in the Wider Society*, Collier-MacMillan, London, 1975.

12. *Ibid.*, p. 61.

13. J.A. Banks, *Social Movements*, Macmillan, London, 1972, pp. 46–7.

14. Quoted in Banks (Ibid) from C. Guevara, *Guerilla Warfare*, p. 13.

15. Quoted by H.B. Davis, 'The theory of union growth' in W.E.J. McCarthy (ed.) *Trade Unions*, Penguin, Harmondsworth, 1972, p. 214.

16. *Ibid.*

17. *Ibid.*, pp. 219–20.

18. *Quinn* v. *Leatham* [1901] A.C. 495; 70 L.J. (P.C.) 76; 85 L.T. 289; 65 J.P. 708; 50 W.R. 139; 17 T.L.R. 749, H.L.; 45 Digest (Repl.) 280, 33.

19 *Taff Vale Railway Co.* v. *Amalgamated Society of Railway Servants* [1901] A.C. 426; 70 L.J. (K.B.) 905, n; 83 L.T. 474; 50 W.R. 44; 44 Sol. Jo. 714; 45 Digest (Repl.) 528.

20. *Osborne* v. *Amalgamated Society of Railway Servants* [1911] 1 Ch. 540; [1911–13] All E.R. Rep. 102; 80 L.J. (Ch.) 315, 104 L.T. 267; 27 T.L.R. 289, C.A.; 45 Digest (Repl.) 530, 1132.

21. Op. cit.

22. G.S. Bain 'Union growth and public policy in Canada', *The Labour Gazette*, Nov./Dec. 1978, vol. LXXVIII, pp. 529–37.

23. See G.S. Bain, F. Elsheikh, *Union Growth and the Business Cycle: An Econometric Analysis*, Blackwell, Oxford, 1976; and F. Elsheikh, G.S. Bain, 'American trade union growth : an alternative model' in *Industrial Relations*, vol. 17 (1978), no. 1, pp. 95–9.

24. F. Elsheikh, G.S. Bain (1978), *op cit.*, pp. 75–6.

25. *Ibid.*

26. W.J. Moore, D.F. Pearce, 'Union growth : a test of the Ashenfelter–Pencavel model', *Industrial Relations*, vol. 15 (1976), no. 2, pp. 244–7.
27. G.S. Bain, F. Elsheikh (1976), *op. cit.*
28. R. Richardson, 'Trade union growth', *British Journal of Industrial Relations*, vol. XV (1977), no. 2, pp. 279–82.
29. See, F. Elsheikh, G.S. Bain, 'Trade union growth: a reply', *British Journal of Industrial Relations*, vol. XVI (1978), no. 1, pp. 99–102; R. Richardson, 'Trade union growth : a rejoinder', *British Journal of Industrial Relations*, vol. XVII, (1978) no. 1, pp. 103–5.
30. See D. Silverman, *The Theory of Organisations*, Heinemann, London, 1970. In this book Silverman stresses the importance of such questions though not at that time explicitly putting forward an ethnomethodological or phenomenological approach.
31. *Op. cit.*
32. A series of measures taken by trade unionists against non-unionists in the Sheffield cutlery trade which culminated in an explosion at the house of a worker who refused to join a union.
33. V.L. Allen, *The Sociology of Industrial Relations*, Longmans, London, 1971.
34. For a discussion of Bevin's role in the Transport and General Workers Union see A. Bullock, *The Life and Times of Ernest Bevin*, Heinemann, London, 1960.
35. J.A. Banks (1974), *op cit.*
36. *Ibid.*, p. 54.
37. *Ibid.*, p. 55.
38. *Op. cit.*
39. Note that this is the Webbs' figure and their assessment has since been challenged.
40. S. & B. Webb, *op. cit.*, p. 180.
41. *Ibid.*, p. 180.
42. J.A. Banks (1974), *op. cit.*, p. 56.

Chapter Three

WHITE COLLAR AND NON-MANUAL TRADE UNIONISM

CHANGES IN THE STRUCTURE OF THE LABOUR FORCE

Part of Kerr's[1] logic of industrialisation thesis is that industrialisation has been accompanied by a change in the composition of the labour force. Initially the movement was from emphasis on the primary to emphasis on the secondary sector: later the movement was towards the tertiary sector. Many aspects of Kerr's thesis have been challenged[2] but his analysis of the change in the composition in the labour force (although still open to debate in detail) has some general validity as far as Western nations are concerned. In most Western industrialised nations employment in the primary sector has declined (in the USA currently only about 4 per cent of the employed population are engaged in agriculture and in Britain the figure is only about 2 per cent, although in France it is still 13 per cent, Italy 19 per cent and the Republic of Ireland 25 per cent) and employment in the tertiary sector has increased (in the USA about 60 per cent of the employed population are engaged in service industries, and in Britain the figure is about 50 per cent, although in West Germany and the Republic of Ireland it is still only about 40 per cent and in Italy it is 35 per cent).

The growth of the white collar sector of the labour force is a related phenomenon. It is difficult to define this sector adequately or precisely,[3] yet the trends are so significant that they can be discussed without having to be too concerned with detailed boundaries. Table 6 shows the percentage of the occupied population in Britain in the main occupational groups between 1911 and 1971. From this table it can be seen that white collar workers increased as a percentage of the total workforce from 18.7 in 1911 to 30.9 in 1951 and to 42.7 in 1971. Direct comparisons

Table 6: Major occupational groups in Britain 1911–71, as a percentage of total employed population

Occupational groups	1911	1921	1931	1951	1961	1966	1971
Employers and proprietors	6.7	2.8	6.7	5.0	4.8	3.4	2.6
All white collar workers	18.7	21.2	23.0	30.9	35.9	38.3	42.7
Managers and administrators	3.4	3.6	3.7	5.5	5.4	6.1	8.6
Higher professionals	1.0	1.0	1.1	1.9	3.0	3.4	3.8
Lower professionals and technicians	3.1	3.5	3.5	4.7	6.0	6.5	7.7
Foremen and inspectors	1.3	1.4	1.5	2.6	2.9	3.0	3.0
Clerks	4.5	6.5	6.7	10.4	12.7	13.2	14.0
Salesmen and shop assistants	5.4	5.1	6.5	5.7	5.9	6.1	5.6
All manual workers	74.6	72.0	70.3	64.2	59.3	58.3	54.7
Total occupied population	100.0	100.0	100.0	100.0	100.0	100.0	100.0

Source: R. Price, G.S. Bain, 'Union growth revisited: 1948–1974 in perspective', in *British Journal of Industrial Relations*, vol. XIV (1976) No. 3, p. 348.

with the position in other countries is difficult, yet some guide can be obtained by looking at the percentage of the workforce in professional, managerial, administrative, clerical and sales occupations. If this figure is taken then it shows that 47 per cent were in such occupations in the USA (1977), 45 per cent in Canada (1978), 41 per cent in Japan (1977), 43 per cent in New Zealand (1976), 59 per cent in Austria (1977) and 44 per cent in Sweden (1975).[4]

Elliott[5] has pointed out that this growth in white collar employment has been particularly important as far as female workers are concerned. He has also noted that in Britain white collar employment has increased in a variety of different industries, drawn from all sectors of the economy. The increase, according to this argument, is not simply a result of changes in the distribution of employment between the major sectors of economic activity, but is also a result of the substitution of white collar for blue collar employment in the same industries. For example, he suggests that 'in the primary and tertiary sector there has been a substitution out of male manual employment into female white collar employment'.[6]

Changes in the structure of employment and the extent of white collar employment have considerable significance. For example, studies have pointed to the implications for social stratification and social change.[7] Such developments are also particularly important for trade unions. Traditionally trade unions have found recruitment much more difficult in some industries than in others. In many instances it appears that traditionally highly unionised areas are in decline, whereas traditionally lowly unionised areas are expanding. Price and Bain[8] note that in Britain employment in education increased by 185 per cent between 1948 and 1971, in insurance, banking and finance by 131 per cent and in professional and scientific services by 88 per cent over the same period. The same trends continued between 1971 and 1978; employment in education increased by 24 per cent, in insurance, banking and finance by 15 per cent and in professional and scientific services by 22 per cent.[9]

While employment in these areas showed a significant increase, employment in certain others showed a significant decrease. Price and Bain's figures for 1948 to 1971 show a decrease of 47 per cent for mining, 54 per cent for railways and 58 per cent for agriculture, forestry and fishing. If the 1971 to 1978 period is examined then the decrease is 12 per cent for mining, 13 per cent for railways and 10 per cent for agriculture, forestry and fishing. Union density levels have traditionally been relatively low in education, insurance, banking and finance and professional and scientific services (in 1974 the figures were about 50 per cent, 45 per cent and 20 per cent respectively) whereas they have been relatively high in mining and railways (in 1974 the figures were 96 per cent and 97 per cent respectively) although they have been low in agriculture.

Similar comments can be made about developments in other countries. For example, in France and West Germany employment in highly unionised areas like mining has decreased significantly (between 1968 and 1977 by about 27 per cent in France and 7 per cent in West Germany) while employment in lowly unionised areas, like finance, insurance and business services has increased significantly (between 1968 and 1977 by about 47 per cent in France and 22 per cent in West Germany).[10]

Price and Bain[11] have attempted to give a precise indication of the effect of changes in the occupational structure on union membership in Britain. They have argued that if the distribution of industrial employment had not changed between 1948 and 1974, then union membershipship would have been about 8 per cent higher than it was. However, the problem for trade unions is not restricted to changes in occupational structure. Trade unions, traditionally, have not found it easy to recruit white collar workers, irrespective of occupation. In Britain, whereas 58 per cent of blue collar workers are members of a trade union, the figure for white collar workers is 39 per cent; in the USA the comparable figures are 39 per cent for blue collar and 10 per cent for white collar workers. This argument is reinforced if trade union membership in one particular industry is looked at. In Britain in the manufacturing industries, blue collar union density was about 73 per cent in 1974, whereas white collar union density was less then half that figure in the same year, at 32 per cent.[12]

Some writers have argued that changes in the occupational structure and the growth of white collar employment might not simply affect the density of union membership, but might also affect the ability of unions to act as radical or protest organisations.[13] The thinking behind this idea is that white collar employees not only have less affinity towards trade unionism but also have a different orientation and social outlook from the rest of the labour force. They are far less likely to be keen to engage in protest or to press for significant social change. Loveridge notes that at one time this view was taken so far as to question whether, given the increase in white collar employment, unions could 'survive as a "force majeure" in the modern pluralistic state'.[14]

Such views have less support today than they had in the 1950s. One of the reasons is that it has been shown that in certain circumstances white collar and non-manual workers, despite their reservations, have been willing to join trade unions and have been willing to take militant action in support of their claims.

WHITE COLLAR UNIONISATION

The level of action membership amongst white collar workers varies considerably between countries. Table 7 shows that in the USA only about 10 per cent of white collar workers are members of trade unions whereas the comparable figure for Sweden is 70 per cent. In many countries white collar unionisation has increased

Table 7:   White collar unionisation in selected countries

Country	Percentage of white collar workers unionised
Sweden	70
Denmark	55–60
Austria	60
Norway	50
Great Britain	39.4
Belgium	35–38
Australia	30
West Germany	24★
Netherlands	20★
France	15
USA	10†
Italy (CGIL)	10.4 (public sector)

★ Approximate figures   † Updated figure (1976)

Note: Figures relate to the early or mid-1970s. They should be treated with some caution and used as a guide only.

Source: Klaus von Beyme, *Challenge to Power*, Sage, London, 1980, p. 42.

since the end of the Second World War but this trend has by no means been uniform or consistent.

For example, in Britain although there has been a general increase in union membership amongst white collar workers since the end of the Second World War, in part this simply has been a reflection of the growth in the size of the white collar labour force. As a result when changes in the labour force are taken into account and white collar union density is considered rather than just white collar union membership, the trend is less consistent. From Table 8 it can be seen that although white collar union membership increased between 1948 and 1964, white collar union density actually declined over the same period. It is only since 1964 that there has been a fairly consistent increase in both white collar union membership and density.

Similarly in the USA although white collar union membership has increased since the end of the Second World War, the trends have not been consistent. For example, between 1955 and 1960 white collar union membership declined from 2,463,000 to 2,192,000 whereas subsequently membership increased (by 1970 it stood at 3,353,000 and by 1976 at 4,068,000: for consistency,

Table 8: White collar union membership in Britain and USA

Britain	White collar membership (000s)	Density (%)	Manual worker membership (000s)	Density (%)
1948	1,964	30.2	7,398	50.7
1964	2,684	29.6	7,534	52.9
1970	3,592	35.2	7,587	56.0
1974	4,263	39.4	7,491	57.9

USA	White collar union membership (000s)	White collar employees (000s)	White collar union density (%)
1955	2,463,000	24,585,000	10.0
1960	2,192,000	28,522,000	7.7
1970	3,353,000	37,997,000	8.8
1976	4,068,000	43,700,000	9.3

Source: R. Price, G.S. Bain, 'Union growth revisited: 1948–1974 in perspective', *British Journal of Industrial Relations*, vol. XIV (1976) No. 3, pp. 339–55; *Statistical Abstract of the United States of America*.

membership of independent unions has been excluded). If union density were considered, rather than just membership, then the variations in the trends would be even more complex.

White collar union membership also varies considerably from industry to industry. For example, in Britain today approximately 87 per cent of all employees in the public sector are union members and if white collar employees alone are considered then the figure is a little lower, but still about 80 per cent. Traditionally white collar unionisation has been considerably lower in private industry. In Britain the distributive trades and the business sector have always had low union densities (in the distributive trades about 13 per cent and in the business sector about 38 per cent). However, there has been an increase in union membership amongst white collar workers in private industry in recent years. The best documented increase is amongst white collar employees in manufacturing industry. Union density amongst this group rose from 12.1 per cent in 1964 to 32 per cent in 1974.[15] Female white collar unionisation, though, remains an area where relatively little has been achieved in Britain: certainly the increase in unionisation amongst female white collar workers has been less than the increase amongst male white collar workers.

There is some consistency in the areas of greatest and least white collar unionisation between different countries. As a generalisation, employees in the public sector are relatively highly unionised in all countries (for example, in West Germany about 76 per cent of public sector employees are unionised, in the USA about 53 per cent and in Australia about 72 per cent) and white collar employees in the private sector are lowly unionised (for example, in West Germany only about 24 per cent of white collar private sector workers are unionised, in the USA about 7 per cent and in Australia about 26 per cent). Similarly, in most countries unionisation is very low in the distributive trades (for example, in the USA 16 per cent and in Australia 27 per cent) though some sections of the distributive trades are relatively better unionised in France, particularly the Paris department stores.

There are major differences in the way in which white collar employees are organised between different industries. In some industries what in effect are white collar unions have been established, whereas in others white collar employees are members of unions that also organise manual workers. In Britain the National and Local Government Officers Association and the Association of Scientific, Technical and Management Staffs only organise white collar workers whereas the Transport and General Workers Union and the General and Municipal Workers Union organise white collar workers alongside manual workers (though the former union has a separate white collar section). In other countries the position similarly varies. In most countries public sector workers are organised separately in white collar unions but in other sectors a mixed pattern holds with some white collar workers organised separately but others members of general or industrial unions.

A note of caution needs to be sounded about any discussion of white collar union membership trends. Such discussion is sometimes confused because of the difficulty of distinguishing between white collar trade unions and professional associations. Lumley[16] suggests four basic types of professional association: the 'Prestige Association', the 'Study Association', the 'Qualifying Association' and the 'Occupational Association', which itself can be subdivided into the 'Co-ordinating Association and the 'Protective Association'. He argues that the protective association and to a lesser extent the co-ordinating association, have the protection of the occupational interest of their members as their main concern, and that the qualifying association, because it controls entry to a profession, has influence in the employment field. Consequently he classifies these kinds of professional associations as white collar unions, but not the prestige or the study association.

Blackburn[17] is not only concerned to distinguish between trade unions and professional associations but also between trade unions which accept traditional union values and those which do not. He argues that many white collar unions do not accept traditional union values which in the present British context he defines as:

1. viewing collective bargaining and the protection of members' interests against employers as their main function;
2. ensuring that they maintain their independence from employers as far as negotiation is concerned;
3. accepting that strikes and other forms of industrial action may be used;
4. declaring itself to be a trade union;
5. registering as a trade union;
6. affiliating to the Trades Union Congress;
7. affiliating to the Labour Party.

Blackburn uses these factors to assess what he terms 'unionateness'. He clearly has a view of a trade union as being more than simply an expression of co-operation between employees in the same trade or industry: he views a trade union as being part of a social movement. Also his discussion of unionateness need not simply be constrained to white collar unions. However, his discussion is particularly applicable to them and was originally developed in this context.

EXPLANATIONS FOR THE GROWTH OF WHITE COLLAR UNIONS

One of the most persistent explanations for the growth of white collar unionisation centres on the size of the employing establishment.[18] Broadly it is argued that the larger the employing unit, the more likely it is that white collar workers will join trade unions.

David Lockwood in his study of clerks used this as the basis for his explanation of unionisation.[19] As the size of the employing organisation increased so the clerks' jobs became more routinised and repetitive. At the same time the close contact between the clerk and his superiors began to disappear and the personal bond that had developed between the two broke down. Crucially, clerks in large-scale organisations developed a different kind of attitude towards their employer and their employment, a kind of attitude which was more sympathetic to the development of unionisation.

According to Lockwood this helps to explain why unionisation has developed most quickly amongst white collar workers employed in the predominantly large scale public sector, while it has developed most slowly in private industry where employment concentration is far less.

Support for this point of view can be gained from a variety of studies in different national contexts. For example, Sturmthal, like Lockwood, after reviewing evidence from eight different national studies concluded that unionisation had proceeded fastest amongst white collar employees in the public sector because they tend to be concentrated in large groups and employed in bureaucratic organisations.[20]

A similar line of thought has been followed by Seglow in his study of unions in the broadcasting industry.[21] He argued that the Association of Broadcasting Staff changed from being essentially a moderate staff association into a much more militant trade union because of developments in the British Broadcasting Corporation, where its main membership lay. One of the most important changes referred to was the bureaucraticisation of the Corporation's organisation.

In some instances bureaucratic organisations can be linked to the restriction of promotion opportunities or at least a belief that this is the case. Kelsall, Lockwood and Tropp's study of the British civil service[22] showed how non-graduates were often effectively prevented from obtaining promotion because of the structure of the organisation. One result was that they turned their energies to forming associations to exert pressure for their own interests. On a more general level, other authors have linked the blockage of promotion opportunities to the development of white collar unions.

Looked at from the trade union point of view, there is also reason to believe that they might concentrate their recruiting efforts on white collar workers in large-scale organisations. There are fairly obvious economies of scale to be gained from concentrating recruitment on large-scale organisations. Subsequently union members employed in large scale organisations are also likely to be easier to service and administer.

There are, of course, a number of terms used in such a discussion which are interrelated but not the same. For example, large-scale organisation does not necessarily mean that employment of white collar workers is highly concentrated, nor is large-scale organisation necessarily highly bureaucraticised. Some studies confuse the issue by measuring one factor and discussing another.

Nevertheless, the general notion that increased concentration of employment of white collar workers is one of the reasons for their increasing unionisation has fairly widespread acceptance. However, it is usually intertwined with another notion: that is, that increased concentration of employment of white collar workers has proceeded alongside a change in their economic position. For example, Lockwood's analysis pointed to the general deterioration in the economic position of the clerk as compared to other workers.[23] He noted that between 1905 and 1955 the average earnings of British manual workers increased by 674 per cent while the average earnings of clerks increased by between 265 and 463 per cent depending on the type of work undertaken. Lenski[24], has shown that similar trends can be discovered in the USA. Looking simply at male workers, he shows that between 1939 and 1959 the average income of clerical workers increased from $1421 to $4785 a year whereas the average income of craftsmen and kindred workers increased from $1309 to $5240 and the average income of operatives increased from $1007 to $4299. Thus the incomes of craftsmen overtook those of clerical workers and the gap between the income of clerical workers and operatives narrowed. The evidence suggests that such trends have continued. In Britain between 1960 and 1970 manual workers' earnings increased by 8 per cent more than white collar workers' earnings. Table 9 shows that between 1970 and 1975 again manual workers' earnings

Table 9: Index of average earnings, manual and non-manual, Britain, 1970–77.

Year	Non-manual adults	Manual adults*	
		Male	Female
1970	100.0	100.0	100.0
1971	111.7	110.3	112.9
1972	124.5	127.8	130.8
1973	138.0	145.9	151.3
1974	157.0	173.4	193.1
1975	202.9	212.4	244.4
1976	244.5	238.8	290.3
1977	267.3	259.9	316.7

* Males over 21, females over 18.

Source: Department of Employment *Gazette*.

increased by more than non-manual workers' earnings (non-manual earnings increased by 102 per cent while manual male earnings increased by 112 per cent and manual female earnings increased by 144 per cent). The position was a little more complicated between 1975 and 1977 when, partly because of public sector wage rises, non-manual wages increased by more than male manual wages but by less than female manual wages.

White collar workers have suffered other similar setbacks. Traditionally their working conditions, pension and sickness arrangements, holiday entitlement and other fringe benefits have been better than those of manual workers. However, in the years since the Second World War this gap in particular has also been narrowed as manual workers have successfully claimed such benefits themselves.

Lumley argues that on the surface such factors may be seen as crucial in persuading white collar workers that it would be in their own economic interests for them to join a trade union. However, he argues that on further analysis, while this may be an important background factor, it may not in itself determine the growth of unionisation amongst white collar workers. Thus he says: '... pay and fringe benefits will remain a general background factor leading to the growth of white collar unionism but will not, by themselves, act as a stimulus to this growth or distinguish the relative growth between and within industries'.[25]

Loveridge has put forward a rather more sophisticated version of the theory that white collar unionisation is determined by the economic position of such workers.[26] He argues that white collar workers will join trade unions (and professional associations will start to act like trade unions) if they maintain high and increasing aspirations and if it becomes clear (because of bureaucraticisation, rationalisation or redundancy) that these aspirations are not being fulfilled. There are two crucial elements to this argument. The first is that white collar workers must have expectations which are not being met. As an example, Loveridge quotes the position of a number of groups who held a strategic position within the technical control function during the early stages of industrialisation. This allowed them 'to acquire first an occupational language and then an occupational identity, which is defined by them in terms of a high status position in the "traditional" occupational hierarchy'.[27] This self-assessment is maintained despite the fact that their position has changed and they are no longer central to the industrial process, with the result that their market position fails to match their expectations and aspirations. The second crucial element is that the shortfall between aspirations and the true position must be made clear to the workers concerned. 'So long as the market and work situation remains relatively ambiguous it is possible to deceive others and even oneself as to the true nature of the position one occupies. If however the system of rewards is both changed and made clear to all, say through a productivity deal between the employers and a manual union, then self deception is no longer possible.'[28]

Walker's explanation for the development of white collar unionism in Australia is a modification and amalgamation of a number of the explanations discussed so far.[29] He argues that the crucial factor in determining union membership is the development of what he calls a 'union attitude'. He notes that a 'union attitude' developed amongst Australian white collar public sector and bank and insurance company employees partly because of the bureaucraticisation of their employment and the fact that there were a large number of workers undertaking very similar tasks for a small number of employers. A union attitude developed amongst other white collar workers as, following inflation and the success of manual workers in gaining fringe benefits, not only did the economic position of white collar workers suffer, but so also did their status.

Moore's discussion of the unionisation of school teachers in the USA similarly mixes economic with other factors.[30] One of the principal factors encouraging teacher unionisation, according to Moore, is the rate of inflation. He suggests that because public school revenues are derived from property taxes which change slowly over the business cycle 'rapid increases in the price level tend to decrease teachers' real income, thus strengthening their interest in joining unions'.[31] In his analysis of teacher unionisation in the USA between 1919 and 1970, Moore suggested that an increase of one percentage point in prices was associated with almost a one percentage point increase in the rate of change of union membership (the increase in prices was measured using a two year moving average and was lagged for one year because it was assumed that teachers would be reluctant to join a union because of a temporary decline in their economic position). However, Moore also mentioned a number of other factors which he saw as important in encouraging union membership amongst teachers. These included the general climate towards unionisation (in his study he defined this in terms of the percentage of union membership in a particular state) and government encouragement or discouragement of collective bargaining.

Crompton's[32] discussion of the increase in the unionisation of the British insurance clerk since the 1960s has some links with the work of Walker and Moore, in that like them she examines the way in which changes in the position of an occupational group have affected their attitude towards unionisation. Crompton's thesis, however, has a different, more specific, emphasis in that her discussion centres on the class position of the group of workers she studies.

Her initial concern is to examine the class position of white collar workers in general which, as she recognises, traditionally has been ambiguous. In summary she suggests that 'to the extent that white-collar workers carry out the functions of capital then their class situation may be associated with that of the bourgeoisie. To the extent that they carry out the functions of labour their class position resembles that of the proletariat.'[33] In the case of the insurance clerk, Crompton suggests that changes which have occurred in work organisation, in particular the rationalisation of the industry and the resulting introduction of 'modern managerial techniques' and computer technology, have taken them much closer to the position of the proletariat than used to be the case. In her own words, they have been subject to 'double proletarianisation'. This means that the work they have been doing has been de-skilled and their direct links to the function of capital have been reduced. These changes to the class position of the insurance clerk, in their train, have brought changes to the market and work situations: the opportunities for career advancement have declined, relative earnings have decreased, as has security of employment.

According to Crompton these changes to the class (and related changes to the market and work) situation of the insurance clerk help to explain the increase in unionisation. In particular, they help to explain why between 1965 and 1975 the proportion of insurance clerks who were members of a TUC-affiliated union rose from 13 per cent to 28 per cent. She does not rule out other factors, like the effect of government policy, as providing at least part of the explanation for the unionisation of this group of workers, but she argues forcefully that these other factors have not been as important as the change in the class situation.

Underlying this discussion is Crompton's belief that her concern with the class position of white collar workers is an example of a distinctive sociological approach to the subject. She contrasts this with what she terms an industrial relations approach, a perspective which she claims denies the relevance of class factors as a basis for the exploration of union growth and behaviour.[34] Such a distinction is open to debate on a number of levels:[35] at least, even if this distinction is used it should not be taken so far that the discussion of white collar unionisation is rigidly compartmentalised, for a single theory or approach is unlikely to prove totally satisfactory in this area.

One of the authors Crompton classifies (and if her classification is to be used, then with reason) as exemplifying the industrial relations approach is Bain.[36] He has put forward what is probably the most comprehensive and sophisticated attempt to explain the growth of white collar unions. He reviewed a number of explanations put forward by other authors, including many of those looked at here. Among them were the suggestion that union membership might be a reflection of the socio-demographic characteristics of the employee (for example, age or sex); of their economic position (for example, earnings, terms of employment, and employment security); of their work situation (for example, proximity to manual workers or opportunities for promotion); and of the public image of the union concerned or their recruitment policies. While not rejecting these explanations completely, all, according to Bain, had their drawbacks and were of 'negligible importance'.

As an alternative he suggested that an explanation for the growth of white collar unions should be based on three factors: the degree of employment concentration, the extent to which employers are prepared to accept and recognise white collar unions, and the extent to which such recognition is encouraged by the government. Bain suggested that the 'relationship between these key independent variables and between them and the dependent variable can be usefully summarised in a two equation descriptive model.

$$D = f(C,R)$$

$$R = g(D,G)$$

where D = the density of white-collar unionism
       C = the degree of employment concentration
       R = the degree to which employers are prepared to recognise unions representing white collar employees; and
       G = the extent of government action which promotes union recognition.'[37]

The first equation suggests that the degree of white collar unionism is related to the degree of employment concentration and the degree to which employers are willing to recognise white collar unions. 'The more concentrated their employment the more likely employees are to feel the need to join trade unions because of "bureaucratization", and the more easily trade unions can meet this need because of the economies of scale characteristic of union recruitment and administration.' However, although employment concentration is a condition that is favourable for the growth of white collar unions it is not in itself sufficient. It must be accompanied by a willingness on the part of employers to recognise such unions. 'The greater the degree to which employers are willing to do this the more likely white collar employees are to join unions. This is because they are less likely to jeopardise their career prospects by joining, they can more easily reconcile union membership with their loyalty to the company, and they will obtain a better service as their unions will be more effective in the process of job regulation.'

At the same time it needs to be recognised that the degree to which employers are prepared to recognise unions representing white collar workers is partly dependent on the membership density of these unions, and on pressure from government to do so. This is shown in the second equation. 'Employers generally do not concede recognition to a union before it has some membership in their establishment. The only exception to this is when employers recognise a union prior to it having obtained any membership in order to encourage its growth at the expense of other 'less desirable' unions', and even in these cases recognition is in part a result of membership density (the density of the less desirable union). 'But while a certain density of membership is a necessary condition for any degree of recognition to be granted . . . it is generally not a sufficient condition. The industrial strength of white collar unions as determined by the size of their membership and their willingness and ability to engage in industrial warfare, has generally not been sufficient in itself to force employers to concede recognition. This has also required the introduction of government policies which have made it easier for unions to exert pressure for recognition and harder for employers to resist it.'[38]

In a series of articles Adams[39] recognises the importance of Bain's work but nevertheless is critical of it. At one level he is critical of the quality of the theory. For example, he claims that Bain explains future growth of white collar unions by reference to present union density, but gives no adequate explanation of the causes of present density. Thus, he says, 'the model is circular. For density to advance, density must first exist but the factors responsible for the original attainment of membership by unions are not explicated.'[40] Similarly Adams argues that when Bain discusses the factor likely to encourage white collar unionism he refers to bureaucratisation, but in fact when he operationalises his model he uses employment concentration instead. Adams suggests that bureaucratisation and employment concentration are not the same thing. 'If employees in a large enterprise are not administered in a bureaucratic fashion would we still expect them to be more union prone than employees in a small enterprise who are administered bureaucratically?'[41]

Adams also suggests that Bain places too much emphasis on the importance of the role of the government in persuading employers to recognise white collar unions. He refers to a number of instances from the British experience where a union's own recruiting efforts have been more important than government policy: for example, the London Clearing Banks gave recognition to the National Union of Bank Employees in 1967 as a result of pressure from the union itself, which culminated in strike action.

Adams most detailed attack on Bain's thesis, however, follows an examination of the growth of white collar unionism in Sweden.[42] White collar employees had already begun to turn to union methods in Sweden before the beginning of the First World War. The first real expansion of union membership, though, occurred during the 1915 to 1923 period. Between 1915 and 1921 'membership in the major foremen's association more than tripled; the Bank Employees Association went from 950 members in 1915 to 5,500 in 1920; the commercial workers jumped from 827 to 7,358'.[43] Many new organisations came into existence including those for insurance employees, non-commissioned officers, telephone employees, school mistresses, and engineers and technicians in industry. White collar union membership subsequently suffered a setback in the 1920s: few new organisations were formed and few existing ones established new bargaining rights. According to Adams, Bain's theory is not very helpful in explaining events related so far. The government did nothing to encourage the recognition of trade unions during the First World War period. Rather white collar union recognition was the result of discontent amongst employees brought about by the decline in their standard of living. Then, looking at the 1920s, he says that the 'turnaround in white collar unionisation of the early twenties was, beyond any reasonable doubt, produced by the depression. Although the white collar workers had sufficient cause to demand union services, they had little reason to expect that unions would be effective on their behalf. There was no major change in government policy, or in employment concentration, as one might expect from the Bain model.'[44]

The growth of white collar unionism in Sweden re-started in the late 1920s and early 1930s. In 1931 white collar associations in the private sector formed the Central Organisation of Employees and although initially it tried to distance itself from manual unionism eventually it adopted a more militant posture. Membership of the organisation grew from 20,000 in 1931 to 47,000 by 1937. Other white collar unions similarly expanded. The Swedish union of Clerical and Technical Employees in Industry, for example, increased its membership from 318 in 1929 to 11,000 by 1937. According to Adams, although Bain's theory provides some insight into union growth during this period it falls short of providing an adequate explanation. The Right of Association and Negotiation Act of 1936 gave assistance to unions claiming recognition from employers and there is little doubt that this was an important factor in encouraging union recognition and membership. As such, this appears to be consistent with Bain's theory. However, Bain argued that unions would be powerless to affect recognition themselves while in practice the 1936 law can be directly traced to action initiated by white collar associations. Further, Adams claims that Bain's theory is of little help in explaining union growth prior to the 1936 Act. During this period, white collar workers joined trade unions in the hope that this would be of assistance in enhancing their economic position rather than because there was any certainty of the effectiveness of recognised unions.

The growth and development of white collar unions continued fairly steadily after the Second World War. In 1950 approximately 53 per cent of the Swedish non-manual labour force was unionised: by 1970 the figure had increased to 63 per cent. Many white collar organisations which had previously thought of themselves as 'something other than trade unions' began to change their attitude and to accept that they were part of the broad union movement (this is true even of the professional associations, who held out longest against the notion that they were unions, but who participated in a strike in 1971 for the first time). Adams concedes that of all the periods discussed, Bain's model provides the most insight into the post-war years. The establishment of bargaining procedures enabled white collar unions to prove their value and was a major factor in their expansion. 'However, again contrary to Bain, the unions themselves must be given substantial credit. The original fears of employers have to a large extent, disappeared. Although white collar groups have resorted to strikes on occasions, massive conflict has not resulted . . . Although Swedish employers would probably prefer to deal with no union, one does not find the level of animosity that is common between labour and management in many other countries. Instead, there is an aura of genuine respect and acceptance.'[45]

Throughout Adams' review of the growth of white collar unions in Sweden a number of points recur. One is that Bain's emphasis on the importance of government policy to encourage union recognition has been misplaced. While in certain instances government policy on such matters has been an aid, it has not generally been critical, and anyway government policy has often been a response to union pressure. A second point that might be highlighted is that Adams claims that Swedish white collar workers have joined trade unions because they have suffered economic reversals, and they have hoped that union membership might be able to counter this trend. However, Adams stresses that they hoped rather than believed that this would be the case. Finally, Adams emphasised the role that unions themselves can play in persuading white collar workers to join and in persuading employers to bargain with them.

One of Bain's co-authors in some of his work on white collar unions, Price, has offered a rejoinder to Adams' criticisms. His rejoinder attacks both Adams' criticisms of Bain's theory, and Adams' own analysis. Considering Adams' criticisms of Bain's theory, Price argues that he misrepresents crucial elements of that theory. 'It is, for example, quite bizarre to ascribe to Bain the view that "bureaucracy is the prime, negative motivating factor driving white collar workers to adopt trade union methods"; or that "government action is both a necessary and a sufficient condition for white collar union growth".' When looking at Adams' own explanation for the growth of white collar unions, Price argues that the suggestion that industrial action by white collar unions was a crucial factor in their gaining recognition is not borne out by the facts. 'While it is true that many of these bodies took industrial action prior to recognition, Adams fails to present any evidence to refute Bain's proposition that, in isolation, and without the support of a generally favourable government policy, industrial action would not have resulted in recognition.'[46]

CONCLUSION

The growth of the white collar labour force has been of major importance for trade unions. They have had to make strenuous efforts to unionise a sector which traditionally has not easily embraced them. Increasingly they have succeeded, though in most countries white collar workers are still significantly less unionised than blue collar workers.

The literature shows a number of factors which help to account for white collar unionisation. For example, reference has been made to the relative decline in the white collar workers' economic position, to the increasing bureaucratisation of his job, to growth in the distance between him and his employer, and to government policy on the recognition of trade unions. Studies vary in the emphasis they place on such factors, yet few deny that all could and, in certain circumstances, have had a role to play.

The central question then is not whether a deteriorating economic position, or increasing employment concentration, encourages the growth of white collar unions or not: rather it is whether such factors could be said to be so important that they actually determine union growth. Disagreement over this question is greatest. Adams is one of the authors who has added another dimension to this issue: he has raised the question as to whether trade unions themselves can affect the growth in their own membership or whether they are simply the prisoners of external conditions.

Possibly the most useful approach to this question is to follow a similar line to that proposed for the study of union growth in general. The argument then was that individual action was constrained but not determined by external conditions. Thus, individuals could affect what happened but had to recognise the bounds of possibility.

Applying this line of thinking to white collar unions one might argue then that union recruiting policies aimed at groups of white collar workers in, for example, small establishments enjoying close relationships with employers, or against a background of government hostility, may stand very little chance of success. On the other hand, given the 'right conditions', unions may or may not be able to exploit them and recruit white collar workers into membership depending on the strategy they adopt, the image they portray and the vigour of the leadership. The 'right conditions', then, do not determine success in recruitment, but they are a prerequisite for it.

One also needs to recognise, however, that while the ability of individual unions may be limited in the short term, in the longer term it may be less constrained for they may be able to affect 'external conditions' themselves. As Adams pointed out in his study of Swedish white collar unions, they can affect issues like government policy on recognition, which itself might be characterised as an 'external condition'. Of course, they can also affect other matters to some extent, like the economic position of white collar workers and the bureaucratisation of employment. Their degree of influence over matters like these will vary but they clearly should not be entirely excluded from consideration.

NOTES

1. C. Kerr, J.T. Dunlop, F.H. Harbison, C.A. Myers, *Industrialism and Industrial Man*, Heinemann, London, 1962.
2. See, for example, J.H. Goldthorpe, 'Social stratification in industrial society' in P. Halmos (ed.) *The Development of Industrial Societies*. Sociological Review Monograph No. 8, University of Keele, 1964.
3. See G.S. Bain, R. Price, 'Who is a white collar employee?', *British Journal of Industrial Relations*, vol. x (1972), no. 3, pp. 325–39.
4. Source, *International Labour Organisation Yearbook, 1978*.
5. F. Elliott, 'The growth of white collar employment in Great Britain 1951–1971', *British Journal of Industrial Relations*, vol. XV (1977), no. 1 pp. 39–44.
6. *Ibid.* p. 40.
7. See for example, C. Wright Mills, *White Collar*, Oxford U.P., London, 1959.
8. R. Price, G.S. Bain, 'Union growth revisited: 1948–1974 in perspective', *British Journal of Industrial Relations*, vol. XIV (1976) no. 3, p. 344.
9. Source, *Annual Abstract of Statistics*.
10. Source, *International Labour Organisation Yearbook, 1978*.
11. *Op. cit.*
12. Source, R. Price, G.S. Bain, *op. cit.*

13. See for example, D. Bell 'Union growth and structural cycles' in W. Galenson, S.M. Lipset (eds), *Labour and Trade Unionism*, Wiley, New York, 1960, pp. 89–93; C.A.R. Crosland, *The Future of Socialism*, Cape, London, 1956.
14. R. Loveridge, 'Occupational change and the development of interest groups among white collar workers in the UK: a long-term model', *British Journal of Industrial Relations*, vol. X (1972) no. 3, pp. 340–65.
15. See R. Price, G.S. Bain, op. cit.
16. R. Lumley, *White Collar Unionism in Britain*, Methuen, London, 1973.
17. R.M. Blackburn, *Union Character and Social Class: A Study of White Collar Unionism*, Batsford, London, 1967.
18. Elements of this explanation can be traced back to the writing of Marx.
19. D. Lockwood, *The Blackcoated Worker*, Allen & Unwin, London, 1958.
20. A. Sturmthal (ed.), *White Collar Trade Unions*, University of Illinois Press, London, 1966.
21. P. Seglow, *Trade Unionism in Television*, Saxon House, Farnborough, 1978.
22. R.K. Kelsall, D. Lockwood, A. Tropp, 'The new middle class in the power structure of Great Britain', *Transactions of the Third World Congress of Sociology*, 1956.
23. D. Lockwood, *op. cit.*
24. G.E. Lenski, *Power and Privilege*, McGraw-Hill, New York, 1966.
25. *Op. cit.*, p. 51.
26. R. Loveridge, *op. cit.*
27. *Ibid.* p. 365.
28. *Ibid.* pp. 351–2.
29. K.F. Walker, 'White collar unionism in Australia' in A. Strumthal (ed.), *op. cit.*, pp. 1–36.
30. W.J. Moore, 'An analysis of teacher union growth', *Industrial Relations*, vol. 17 (1978), no. 2, pp. 204–15.
31. *Op. cit.*, p. 205.
32. R. Crompton, 'Trade unionism and the insurance clerk', *Sociology*, vol. 13 (1979), no. 3, pp. 403–25.
33. *Ibid.* p. 407.
34. See, also, R. Crompton, 'Approaches to the study of white collar unionsim', *Sociology*, vol. 10 (1976), no. 3, pp. 407–24

35. For example, is her description of a sociological approach one which covers all of sociological endeavour in this area; is there such a clear distinction between sociology and industrial relations?

36. G.S. Bain, *The Growth of White Collor Unionism*, Oxford U.P., London, 1970.

37. *Ibid.*, p. 183.

38. *Ibid.*, p. 184.

39. See, for example, R.J. Adams, 'Bain's theory of white collar union growth: a conceptual critique', *British Journal of Industrial Relations*, vol. XV (1977), no. 3, pp. 317–21; R.J. Adams, 'The recognition of white collar unions'. *British Journal of Industrial Relations*, vol. XIII (1975), no. 1, pp. 102–106.

40. R.J. Adams, 1977, p. 318.

41. *Ibid.*, p. 319.

42. R.J. Adams, 'White collar union growth: the case of Sweden', *Industrial Relations*, vol. 13 (May 1974) pp. 164–176. See also R.J. Adams, *The Growth of White Collar Unionism in Britain and Sweden: A Comparative Investigation*, Industrial Relations Research Institute, University of Wisconsin, 1975.

43. *Ibid.*, p. 168.

44. *Ibid.*, p. 170.

45. *Ibid.*, p. 175.

46. Book review by R.J. Price in *British Journal of Industrial Relations*, vol. XIV (1976), no. 3, p. 369.

Chapter four
INTERNAL DEMOCRACY

THE WEBBS' VIEW OF THE TRANSITION FROM PRIMITIVE TO REPRESENTATIVE DEMOCRACY

As long ago as the end of the nineteenth century, the Webbs[1] recognised that policy-making in trade unions had passed from the hands of the membership directly, to representative bodies and organisations. They discussed this change in terms of primitive and representative democracy. Primitive democracy existed in the local trade clubs of the eighteenth century. Policy was made directly by all members: 'The members in each trade, in general meeting assembled, themselves made the regulations, applied them to particular cases, voted the expenditure of funds, and decided on such action by individual members as seemed necessary for the common weal.'[2] Sometimes such clubs appointed officers, but when they did so they were chosen in rotation and for particular meetings only. When it became necessary to appoint a committee to carry out certain important tasks, again the members of the committee were chosen in rotation.

The Webbs summarised the operation of primitive democracy in the early trade clubs in the following way:

The early trade club was thus a democracy of the most rudimentary type, free alike from permanently differentiated officials, executive council or representative assembly. The general meeting strove itself to transact all the business and grudgingly delegated any of its functions either to officers or to committees. When this delegation could no longer be avoided, the expedients of rotation and short periods of service were used 'to prevent imposition' or any undue influence by particular members. In this earliest type of trade union democracy we find, in fact, the most childlike faith not only that 'all men are equal', but also that 'what concerns all should be decided by all'.[3]

Such a method of decision and policy-making was obviously only compatible with small-scale operation.[4] However, the Webbs argued that it was not so much the scale of operation as the 'exigencies of their warfare with the employers'[5] that led trade unions to depart from their model of primitive democracy. The Webbs also noted, though, the great reluctance with which trade unions moved from the earlier model. In most cases the development was far from deliberate but evolved unconsciously out of piecemeal decisions designed to deal with particular situations. Throughout the nineteenth century trade unions tried to devise ways of ensuring that officials gained only very restricted power; one such way was the use of the referendum to determine all important questions. Ironically, the Webbs argued that it was the impracticability of devices like the referendum that led to the final break with primitive democracy.

The Webbs, thus, were able to note that by the end of the nineteenth century, although the 'old theory of democracy is still an article of faith, and constantly comes to the front when any organisation has to be formed for brand-new purposes', trade union constitutions 'have undergone a silent revolution. The old ideal of the Rotation of Office among all members in succession has been practically abandoned. Resort to the aggregate meeting diminishes steadily in frequency and importance. The use of the Initiative and the Referendum has been tacitly given up in all complicated issues, and gradually limited to a few special questions on particular emergencies.' In their place 'we have the appearance in the Trade Union world of the typically modern form of democracy, the elected representative assembly, appointing and controlling an executive committee under whose direction the permanent official staff performs its work'.[6]

The Webbs spent some time looking in detail at the way 'representative democracy' had been established in one union, the Amalgamated Association of Operative Cotton-Spinners. They described the way that legislative power was vested in a Parliament, comprised of representatives from the various provinces and districts. This Parliament elected the General Secretary (the senior executive officer) and an executive council of thirteen members, of whom seven had to be working spinners and six were usually permanent officials. The six permanent officials, in turn, formed a sub-council and undertook most of the daily administration of the union.

The Webbs spent so long examining the workings of this particular union because they believed that it provided a model for representative democracy in trade unions. They said: 'We have watched the working of this remarkable constitution during the last seven years, and we can testify to the success with which both efficiency and popular control are secured.' Efficiency was secured by the employment of highly trained staff while popular control was ensured by

the real supremacy of the elected representatives. For the 'Cotton-Spinners' Parliament' is no formal gathering of casual members to register the decrees of a dominant bureaucracy. It is, on the contrary, a highly organised deliberative assembly, with active representatives from the different localities, each alive to the distinct, and sometimes divergent, interests of his own constituents. Their eager participation shows itself in constant 'party meetings' of the different sections, in which the officers and workmen from each district consult together as to the line of policy to be pressed upon the assembly.[7]

The Webbs contrasted the organisation adopted by the Cotton Spinners with that adopted by other unions. Many permitted the membership to elect officers and the executive council directly, not through an intermediate agency, such as the Cotton Spinners' Parliament. The Webbs argued that direct election led either to constant fighting between members of the executive and officers or to a coalition between executive members and officers against the rank and file. In the case of the former, the union suffered because of inefficiency: in the case of the latter, the union suffered because it became little more than a dictatorship of the officers.[8]

The Webbs' review of the transition from primitive to representative democracy, then, was a cautionary tale, but essentially an optimistic one.[9] Size meant that it was no longer possible in the majority of cases for union members directly to make all decisions and policy of the union; however, providing certain guidelines were adhered to, representative institutions could be established which would enable the members to gain the benefits of scale, yet retain an important degree of influence over general union policy, if not detailed decision-making.

A MORE PESSIMISTIC VIEW

The essential optimism of the Webbs contrasts starkly with the pessimism of another major writer of the same period. Michels examined the workings of voluntary associations, including trade unions, and concluded that they were dominated by small cliques or by oligarchy.[10] Rank and file members, Michels argued, had little or no say in policy-making in trade unions: policy was made by and for the benefit of a small group of permanent officials and leaders.

Michels' thesis was developed after a study of the German Social Democratic Party. The choice of this organisation was not accidental; Michels aimed to see the extent to which an organisation that had the extension of democracy as one of its principal aims operated internally on a democratic basis.

The development which is central to Michels' thesis is 'the need for organisation'. Michels argued that in order to achieve their aims organisations like political parties and trade unions needed to do more than merely collect large numbers of members. They needed to operate efficiently and this inevitably meant the development of some kind of organisation, the election or appointment of leaders and officials.

The Webbs' and Michels' accounts do not differ substantially up to this point. However, they diverge dramatically later, for, while the Webbs believed that it was possible, providing certain procedures were adopted, for the rank and file member to control officials and leaders (and thus ultimately to control policy), Michels argued that such a position was untenable. The leaders and officials have at their disposal a whole armoury of weapons which enables them to dominate the rank and file members and determine policy irrespective of the members' wishes. Thus, Michels argued: 'The leaders possess many resources which give them an almost insurmountable advantage over members who try to change policies. Among their assets can be counted (a) superior knowledge, e.g. they are privy to much information which can be used to secure assent for their programme; (b) control over the formal means of communication with the membership . . . and (c) skill in the art of politics.'[11]

The domination of the bureaucratic leaders is also facilitated according to Michels by what he termed 'the incompetence of the masses'. Few members attend meetings of the organisation; the 'pulls of work, family, personal leisure activities and the like severely limit the amount of actual time and psychic energy which the average person may invest in membership groups'.[12] Further, few members have the level of education and 'general sophistication' necessary to participate fully in the affairs of the organisation.

According to Michels, then, oligarchy was a natural consequence of organisation. This is summed up in his famous statement: 'It is the organisation which gives birth to the dominion of the elected over the electors, of the mandatories over the mandators, of the delegates over the delegators. Who says organisation, says oligarchy.'[13] Thus, in so far as organisation was essential for a voluntary association to achieve its aims, oligarchy was inevitable in that association, no matter what the intention of the founders or what the philosophy embraced by the association.

However, Michels went further than merely indicating that policy in trade unions would be determined by an oligarchy. He also indicated the factors that would be taken into account in determining that policy. The oligarchy that determines policy develops special interests and aims. 'By a universally applicable law, every organ of the collectivity, brought into existence through the need for the division of labor, creates for itself, as soon as it becomes consolidated, interests peculiar to itself.' These interests are always conservative, 'and in a given political situation these interests may dictate a defensive and even reactionary policy.'[14] Not only will these interests differ from those of the rank and file member ('the interests of the working class demand a bold and aggressive policy'[15]) but the policy adopted will be the opposite of that demanded both by the rank and file and by the original aims of the association.

Interestingly, Michels argued that in the trade union movement 'the authoritative character of the leaders and their tendency to rule democratic organisations on oligarchic lines are even more pronounced than in the political organisations'. As a result, he argues that it is even easier in the trade union than in the political organisation

for the officials to initiate and to pursue a course of action disapproved of by the majority of workers they are supposed to represent. It suffices here to refer to the two famous decisions of the trade union congress at Cologne in 1905. In one of these the leaders declared themselves to be opposed (in opposition to the views of the majority) to the continued observance of the 1st of May as a general labor demonstration of protest. In the second, the discussion of the general strike was absolutely forbidden. By these and similar occurrences the oligarchical practices of the leaders are sufficiently proved, although some writers continue to dispute the fact.[16]

One of the main criticisms of the Michels thesis by subsequent Marxist writers has been that Michels only considered organisations in a capitalist society. It is not surprising, so such critics argue, that the masses are uninterested and unable to participate in the affairs of the organisation for they have never been encouraged to do so. In a capitalist society education and training are linked to wealth, with the result that the mass of people are denied access to them. However, in a socialist society the position will be different; education and training will be available to all, and all will be encouraged to participate in decision-making.[17] This view is probably best expressed by Bukharin:

> (Under socialism) what constitutes an eternal category in Michels' presentation, namely the 'incompetence of the masses' will disappear, for this incompetence is by no means a necessary attribute of every system; it likewise is a product of the economic and technical conditions, expressing themselves in the general cultural being and in the educational conditions. We may say that in the society of the future there will be a colossal overproduction of organisers, which will nullify the 'stability' of the ruling groups.[18]

A similar point has been made more recently by another writer. Lane has argued that the tendency towards oligarchy in trade unions, 'has never been more than a tendency'. Crucially, he states that where oligarchy exists 'it is attributable to the nature of trade unionism in a capitalist environment'.[19]

Michels seems to have anticipated this criticism to some extent. He argues that while socialist parties cannot deny the existence of oligarchy they endeavour to explain it by suggesting that it is 'the outcome of a kind of atavism in the mentality of the masses, characteristic of the youth of the movement'. They go on to argue, he notes, that the socialist regime 'will soon restore them to health, and will furnish them with all the capacity necessary for self-government'.[20] However, Michels argues that this position is built on a misunderstanding of the nature of the problem.

> The objective immaturity of the mass is not a mere transitory phenomenon which will disappear with the progress of democratization 'au lendemain du socialisme'. On the contrary, it derives from the very nature of the mass as mass, for this, even when organized, suffers from an incurable incompetence for the solution of diverse problems which present themselves for solution – because the mass 'per se' is amorphous, and therefore needs division of labor, specialization, and guidance.[21]

SUPPORT FOR MICHELS

The Michels thesis has been re-examined in a number of different contexts. However, perhaps the best known re-examination in a trade union setting is that of Lipset, Trow and Coleman.[22] They deliberately chose to examine in detail a case where Michels' thesis did not seem to fit. 'In this', they said, 'our purpose is not, of course, to "refute" Michels or other previous workers in this area, but rather to refine and build on their insights and findings.'[23] The case study they examined was that of the International Typographical Union (ITU).

In summary Lipset *et al.* argued that democracy had been maintained in the ITU because of the survival of an organised opposition in the union which prevented any one group from gaining control. The organised opposition had survived, they argued, because of a number of unusual circumstances which could be seen by examining the history of the union and the context in which it operated. Five such unusual circumstances might be highlighted. First, members of the ITU were more interested and involved in the work of the union than one might have expected. This was partly because of the nature of the craft of printing: the high status of printers and their irregular hours of work had led to the creation of a strong occupational community, which in turn had fostered the desire of printers to participate in the affairs of their union. Second, the borderline or marginal status of printing between the middle and working class meant that there were different groups with different values within the union. Third, a fairly high proportion of the printing trades were organised before the union was formed and as a result the various sections of the union had a long history of autonomy which led them to resist strongly efforts to create a centralised structure. Fourth, as a result of earlier problems, the union had developed a number of devices designed to enable the whole of the membership to participate in major aspects of decision-making; these include the election of officers by the whole of the membership and provisions for referenda of the membership. Fifth, the results of elections were accepted; ruling groups had not tried to preserve their position after an election defeat by 'illegal means'.

Lipset *et al.* were at pains to point out that the ITU was atypical of most trade unions. Organised opposition had only survived because of 'favourable dice throws'. In most unions such conditions would not exist and unions would be dominated by an oligarchy. They concluded:

This study has not 'disproved' Michels' theory; rather, in a sense, it has given additional empirical support to his analysis of the connection between oligarchy as a political form and the overwhelming power held by the incumbent officers of most private organizations, by demonstrating that where an effective and organized opposition does exist, it does so only because the incumbent administration does not hold a monopoly over the resources of politics.[24]

One of the best known case studies of the internal organisation of a British trade union is Goldstein's analysis of the Transport and General Workers Union.[25] Completed in the early 1950s, it centred on membership participation in union affairs and policy making. Goldstein argued that there was overwhelming evidence that most rank and file members had little or no interest or involvement in the affairs of the T&GWU. One of the pieces of evidence cited was membership turnover. 'A large turnover', he argued, 'is both evidence and a principal cause of apathy within an organisation.'[26] He noted that during the period 1935 to 1947 membership turnover averaged 33.3 per cent of the total national membership of the union. He stated: 'Though impossible to ascertain from the data presented here, a large proportion of these lapses can be attributed to indifference on the part of the individual, i.e. a failure to identify himself with the Union to which he belongs.'[27] A second piece of evidence quoted was the Union's electoral system and record. He noted that few members regularly exercised their right to vote in elections and commented: 'In fact, the T & GWU's electoral system is in practice as much a cause of apathy as election returns are an index of it. The Union is so diseased by apathy that corruption at the ballot box may go unnoticed by a large majority of rank and file members.'[28] He also calculated that because of the high turnover of membership and the extent of arrears of subscriptions about 80 per cent of union members were ineligible to stand for official positions in the Union at any one time.

However, the crucial evidence presented was a case study of participation at branch level. Goldstein argued that: 'The extent to which the union can claim that it is a representative democracy is dependent upon the amount and degree of participation of rank and file members at Branch level. Without participation there can be no democracy. Without democracy the control of this powerful state within a state rests in the hands of an irresponsible few.'[29] When he came to describe branch life in detail Goldstein painted a picture remarkably close to the most pessimistic of the possibilities outlined above. He noted that branch meetings were held regularly for a membership that was so large that if the majority were to attend, full participation would be impossible. In fact, he said, meetings only attracted a handful of members who dominated branch life. The union civil servants, he said, were in a position to, and often did, 'usurp the policy-determining functions assigned in theory to elected representatives'. Goldstein concluded that the 'features of the Branch disclosed by this mass of descriptive material are those of an oligarchy parading in democracy's trappings'.[30]

Elements of the Michels thesis can also be supported by reference to a host of other studies. For example, many writers have referred to the lack of participation of members in branch affairs. Thus Roberts[31] suggested that attendance at branch meetings fell into the range of 3 to 15 per cent with a concentration between 4 and 7 per cent; a Political and Economic Planning survey[32] found that attendance at branch meetings ranged from 2 to 30 per cent of the membership; and Goldthorpe *et al.*[33] discovered that only 7 per cent of their car workers attended branch meetings regularly. Some writers have tried to account for the differences in attendance between unions and between different types of members; Seidman *et al.*[34] drew up a typology of union members, while Lumley[35] has noted that attendance at branch meetings is often greater amongst white collar than blue collar members. Others have suggested ways of increasing membership attendance; for instance, Cole[36] argued that attendance at branch meetings might be greater if more branches were based on the place of work rather than area of residence. However, few have argued that participation in branch affairs is, or in the foreseeable future could be, more than a minority pursuit.

A number of writers have noted not only that branch meetings are attended by a small minority of members but also that the officials who run the branch are elected by a similarly small proportion; thus, Cyriax and Oakeshott stated that branches 'are nearly always dominated by an inner clique which does the work and is voted into office by a small percentage of the membership'.[37] An International Labour Office survey[38] of trade unionism in Britain noted that voting figures can be higher on contentious issues and it is worth recording that recent ballots amongst members of the National Union of Mineworkers on industrial action achieved very high returns.[39] In many cases, though, voting figures are low, especially for the election of officials, at the national as well as at the local level; less than 8 per cent of members voted in the election for the General Secretary of the Amalgamated Engineering Union in both 1957 and 1964.

Writers like Sayles and Strauss[40] and Tannenbaum and Kahn[41] have argued that there is a greater opportunity for democratic processes to operate at the branch than at the national level. At the local level there is a much closer contact between leaders and rank and file members than could ever be the case at the national level of a major union. However, it is also recognised that the major decisions on union policy are taken not at the local, but at the national level.

A number of other studies have concentrated on leadership in trade unions. Wright-Mills[42] has shown how union leaders can divert trade unions from their central aims; union leaders can become 'managers of discontent'. In another study[43] the same author has referred to national union leaders as part of the 'power elite',[44] while Coleman[45] looks at how union leaders manage to maintain the façade of democracy when their organisations have long since ceased to be subject to democratic control. Many studies have highlighted the excesses of American union leaders. Hall[46] shows how bribery, corruption and violence have been used by some American Union leaders to defeat rank and file critics; specific reference is made to the case of Jock Yabloski who was killed in January 1970 after his challenge for the presidency of the United Mineworkers union. Romer has examined the career of Hoffer in the International Brotherhood of Teamsters in a similar fashion, while Roberts has commented that: 'In some unions the rights of members have been flagrantly violated by union leaders intent on keeping power at all costs. In others, the authority, prestige and monopoly of the unions media of communication are combined to make any successful challenge to the established position of union leaders a remote possibility.'[47] Roberts argued in another publication that American union leaders formed a self-perpetuating elite: 'Defeat is not accepted as a risk inherent in the job, as it is by any democratic politician. Not only do incumbents refuse to accept the possibility of personal defeat, but accession to office of their chosen successor has now become a matter of prestige.'[48]

Considerable concern has also been expressed about the internal procedures for arbitrating in disputes between individual members and the union leaders. Kerr[49] has been particularly critical of the ways unions have failed to develop adequate procedures to guarantee the rights of the individual and his concern has been echoed by Summers[50] and Leiserson.[51] All put forward the view that unions have too much power over the work environment to be permitted to operate without adequate procedures guaranteeing individual freedom. Bromwich[52] surveyed the constitutions of seventy American unions and noted deficiencies in their procedures for dealing with the disciplining of members, disputes over election results, and the like.

Nevertheless, it is important to recognise that despite the wealth of evidence available many writers, and even many of the writers already quoted, are not as pessimistic about union democracy and the ability of rank and file members to influence policy as might be imagined. This is true, for instance, of the authors of the case studies of the International Typographical Union and the Transport and General Workers Union. Thus, Lipset argued that although 'the events and conditions in the ITU are unique and are rarely found in trade unions or other voluntary large social organisations generally, it would be foolhardy to predict that democratic processes cannot develop elsewhere. The specific factors which underlie ITU democracy are not likely to be duplicated elsewhere; but the very great variety of factors present in the situation suggests that democratic processes may develop under quite different conditions and take quite different forms.'[53] Lipset concludes by suggesting that the ITU, if it doesn't provide a model, should provide a touchstone against which the internal organisation of other unions can be appraised and criticised. Similarly, Goldstein, despite his criticisms of oligarchical control in the T&GWU, argued that there is 'no justification for concluding that in such a mass organisation government by oligarchy is inevitable.'[54] He argues that 'in general, the apathetic rank and file member is an alert and inquisitive person',[55] and if branch life is made more stimulating and exciting then a transformation could take place. 'What is lacking', he says, 'is that tradition of democracy which only every-day experience, custom and practice can build within the Union.'[56] The building of this tradition may be made easier in the future 'as the ranks of the Union are filled by working men, who, for the first time in Great Britain's history, will have had schooling till the age of 15 or 16 and been given the opportunity not only to think but also to enjoy the leisure which thoughtful reflection requires'.[57]

This final note of optimism of Lipset *et al.* and Goldstein has not only been echoed by other writers, but in recent years has also been extended considerably. Some have argued that both Lipset *et al.* and Goldstein, despite their optimism, followed Michels too closely and failed to appreciate the number of exceptions to Michels' rule.

LIMITED OPTIMISM

One writer whose work suggests that there are more exceptions to Michels' rule than some have recognised is Turner. He argued that by no means all British unions are dominated by oligarchies and suggested that there are three different styles of union government.[58] The first is what he termed the 'executive democracy'; this type comes closest to the concept of primitive democracy for the unions are characterised by high membership participation, few full-time officials and little distinction between membership and leaders. Such a style of government is typical, Turner argued, of 'closed' occupational unions, which have rigid membership controls. The second category was termed the 'aristocracies'. In these unions the officials are still subject to close scrutiny but by one section rather than by the whole of the membership. This situation is typical, for example, of closed craft unions who have expanded their membership recently; the craft section may retain the right and ability to control the leadership but this privilege may not extend to all sections of the union. The third category is that of 'popular bossdoms'; they are characterised by a low level of membership participation and by the greatest difference between the members and the professional officials on which they depend. In such cases senior officials will operate more or less free from control by the bulk of the membership and in effect will be able to appoint their own successors. This style of government is typical of open unions, covering a wide range of occupations.

Using this typology only the third category of unions would bear much resemblance to the kind of oligarchy described by Michels. Unions in the other categories would possess membership or sections of membership with sufficient interest and knowledge to enable them to challenge and control the leadership. It is interesting to note that, taking the case studies by themselves, and leaving out the interpretation and comments of Lipset *et al.* and Goldstein, it would be possible to fit the studies of the ITU and the T&GWU into Turner's scheme. The ITU presumably would be placed in the first category of unions; thus, both Lipset *et al.* and Turner would accept that the union was essentially democratic. The T&GWU presumably would be placed in the third category; thus, both Goldstein and Turner would accept oligarchical tendencies. However, if the reasoning of the different authors were taken into account then the disagreements between them would be clear; for example, Lipset *et al.* believed that democracy in the ITU was primarily the result of organised opposition whereas Turner saw unions of this type as democratic because of their 'closed' nature and the fact that there is little distinction between members and officials or leaders.

Other writers have centred their criticism of the Michels thesis, and the Lipset *et al.* and Goldstein interpretations, not on the number of exceptions to the rule but on the extent to which the mechanisms outlined were described erroneously. In particular there is a belief that the leaders are subject to challenge at all levels more frequently than some writers have recognised.

Edelstein, in a number of publications,[59] has examined the competition for top union posts. He notes that during 'the past few years the presidents of several American unions have been defeated' and that in many British unions close elections are by no means unknown. He concludes that in both America and Britain 'opposition in important elections has been found to be more frequent and more successful than many observers would have thought possible in trade unions'.[60] Edelstein is supported in this view by writers like Barbash.[61] He notes not only that national union presidents and their chosen replacements have been defeated in elections, but also that they have been shaken by widespread protests and secessions and negotiated settlements have been defeated by the rank and file.

Flanders has noted the way in which the union convention or conference can be used to control leaders and officials. 'The constitutional checks on bureaucracy in the British trade unions are, however, relatively strong. Most of them have annual delegate conferences or the equivalent at which the broad lines of union policy are discussed and decided, in unfettered debate. The passing of resolutions contrary to the executive's recommendations is not an infrequent occurrence.'[62] A similar conclusion was reached by Clegg after a detailed study of the General and Municipal Workers Union. He argued that 'organs of popular control exist and are used. Congress has defeated the platform: and a district secretary has been dismissed by his district council.'[63] He added that instances 'of this kind are to be found mainly in recent years, which seems to reveal . . . that the machinery of democracy within the union . . . is not rusting for lack of use, but used more than ever before'.[64]

Other writers have noted the way in which regional and local machinery and factions can provide an alternative power base to the national executive. One writer, Martin,[65] is particularly associated with discussion of this last development. He argues that the survival of faction (rather than the survival of opposition, as suggested by Lipset *et al.*) is the best safeguard of democracy in unions. He goes on to list a number of the circumstances likely to lead to the survival of faction; interestingly there are a number of overlaps between his list and one produced from the work of Lipset *et al.* Support for Martin's thesis can be gained from the work of Nicholas.[66] Still other writers have referred to the challenge from the workshop. McCarthy and Parker, in a survey conducted for the Donovan Commission,[67] noted the crucial role of shop stewards in workplace relations.

40 per cent of union members get their information about what is happening in the union from their steward. Slightly more members get such information from their union journal, but when it is borne in mind that 54 per cent of the members who see a union journal get it from their steward, the steward is clearly the main source of keeping the member informed.[68]

This crucial role in communications enables the shop steward to build an effective power base. Cyriax and Oakeshott[69] referred to the way in which shop stewards at Briggs' Motor Bodies factory at Dagenham were able to use their position to build a power base which rivalled the official union structure. The power of shop stewards has been referred to by other writers in a wide range of studies.[70]

Banks[71] uses evidence such as this to suggest that trade unions are governed and policy is made not by oligarchies but by polyarchies. Union leaders, Banks argues, are regularly challenged at all levels by the members. This does not mean that all members take an active part in all union affairs all the time; however, it does mean that union leaders are subject to checks by active union members and cannot merely wield power as they wish. Commenting specifically on the work of Lipset *et al.*, Banks says that what they

failed to appreciate is that representative democracy works on the principle that between the rank and file member and the top men there are very many aspiring leaders whose challenge must be met and whose political skills are not negligible. A proper study of the mechanisms of representative democracy must include an investigation of the part played by district, regional and national assemblies in the development of such skills amongst the erstwhile rank and file.[72]

Banks also argues that many studies of union democracy have concentrated too much on purely structural factors. He suggests that much more attention needs to be given to the motivation of members to take part in union government. Thus, he says: 'The study of participation . . . can ill afford to ignore the effect of personality and other differences in people and their circumstances which influence the likelihood of their filling participatory roles.' A democratic system of union government is one in which 'institutional barriers that might prevent members from participating or expressing their opinion have been eliminated. It is not one which results in all the members in the system having the same or equal motives for so behaving.'[73]

Banks receives support on this latter issue from Child, Loveridge and Warner[74] when they argue that in the past too much attention has been focused upon characteristics of the union itself in discussions of democracy in unions. They suggest that considerably more attention could be focused on the union member and membership needs (they also draw attention to the importance of the work group as a major reference point for workshop behaviour, the formation of union attachment and the formulation of membership needs).[75] On a more general level, Banks' views are also echoed in the work of Silverman.[76]

However, in many ways the most radical attack on the theory of oligarchy in trade unions has appeared from another direction: it has been linked to the view that an analysis of trade union policy should be based not on the way in which it is made or on an assessment of the extent to which various parties directly impinge on the policy-making process, but on the extent to which trade union policy is framed in accordance with the wishes of union members and is effective. Such a viewpoint is possibly most closely associated with the work of Allen.[77]

A DIFFERENT DEFINITION OF DEMOCRACY

Allen began by attacking the interpretation of union democracy adopted by most earlier writers. They had viewed union democracy, he said, as analogous to state democracy.[78] As a result they had been concerned to examine the internal mechanisms of government, the rights of individuals, and so on. When one is considering state democracy it is quite reasonable to look at such matters. The state, he said, is a compulsory society:

... the government is responsible for the maintenance of law and order in society ... One must pay taxes, respect property rights, conform to certain health standards, and do nothing that is obviously injurious to other members of the community. One must obey the judicial interpretations of Parliamentary legislation. It is important, then, that a mechanism should be provided to enable those who are affected by legislation to have a say in its determination. Further, because one cannot be sure, at any time, that the legislative and administrative organs of a compulsory society can be kept free from manipulation by private interests, there must be some form of popular control.[79]

However, a trade union is not analogous to a state: it is a voluntary not a compulsory society. Consequently it is inappropriate to look at internal mechanisms as a guide to democracy. Such mechanisms are only important when a person cannot leave the society concerned: they are unimportant when people can leave if they disagree with the policy or administration of the society.

Allen does not argue that internal democratic mechanisms have no place within voluntary organisations.[80] He states that the 'greater the degree of "member participation" the more virile the organisation is likely to be' and that activity in voluntary societies should be 'the beginning of training in social responsibility'. Further, such activity enables 'members to lead a full life, for a man is unable to express himself satisfactorily "by the negative process of contriving an environment where few demands are made of him and where he lives detached from the ordinary preoccupations and concerns of his fellows"'. However, while such internal democratic mechanisms are desirable they are not, according to Allen, indispensable. 'It is the voluntary nature of organisations within a state which is essential for the preservation of democracy within these organisations.'[81]

A trade union is an organisation with a very specific aim. Its aim, Allen believes, can succinctly be stated as: 'to protect and improve the general living standards of its members.'[82] It must be judged by the degree to which it achieves this aim. This means that efficiency is as much a prime concern of a trade union as it is of a business organisation.[83] Trade union leaders, Allen argues, like business leaders, have found that efficiency depends on two factors: first, an essentially bureaucratic organisation, and second, size. 'Far from administrative problems being caused by bigness they are reduced by it. The advantages arising out of specialisation of labour apply as much to the field of administration as to the field of technology.'[84]

If trade unions pursue the interests of their members efficiently then they will, according to Allen, be helping to preserve and extend democracy in society. Unions can persuade management to accept the right of workers to combine in an industry or to have a greater say in industrial decisions. Voluntary societies in general, by representing members' interests, will be helping to extend democracy in a state.

Allen does not argue that union leaders should be free to use power as they wish. 'The use of arbitrary power in trade unions would be inconsistent with the aims of trade unionism and could only result in a violation of those aims. Trade unions are a part of the movement towards real state democracy and they can be an effective part of the movement only by using methods not radically inconsistent with democracy.'[85] But how can the power of officials be checked, if it is recognised that it is also important for these officials to be able to exercise authority to ensure that the aims of the organisation are efficiently achieved? This cannot be done by the use of internal mechanisms for even if they were desirable they would not work. 'Where there is an inherent tendency in organisations for control to be vested in the hands of a few individuals it is no safeguard against abuse of authority simply to install democratic checks. For various reasons these checks may not be operative. In all organisations, even the State, democratic checks operate only in so far as the leaders and the rank and file want them to operate.'[86] There is, Allen states, only one way of solving this problem and that is by retaining the voluntary character of trade unions.

So long as trade union members have the right to 'contract out' of membership if they are dissatisfied with the union they belong to, then a continuous impulse will operate to impel trade-union leaders to retain them. Obviously in a free organisation of this nature workers would retain their membership only if they were satisfied with the work the organisation was doing. Dissatisfaction would be reflected in a declining membership, and in the interest of self-preservation union leaders would be compelled to stem the tide. They would have to get a correct impression of the needs of workers. The democratic mechanism would be operated from the top.[87]

However, it is not only through declining membership that union leaders can be forced to ensure that they are in step with the rank and file; it is also the fear that if they take the wrong action in the future, membership may decline. 'Always, therefore, leadership must walk in step with the rank and file.'[88]

One interesting sidelight on Allen's thesis is that it has led him to oppose compulsory unionism, in particular the 'closed shop'. 'Compulsory trade unionism' he says 'would remove from workers that right to move freely within the context of the democratic state which is a measure of democracy. It would also remove the one check on the authority of trade union leaders which operates automatically and which ensures that the democratic mechanism in trade unionism is used to the best advantage.'[89]

A number of writers have supported Allen's contention that it is erroneous to apply the model of state democracy to trade unions. For example, Hughes has argued that 'trade union government involves an electoral situation and underlying social relations simpler than, and in some ways significantly different from, those of our political democracy'. He concludes: 'Trade union democracy cannot be analysed simply by analogy from, or in terms of the accepted norms of, the political democracy of nation states.'[90] Some support can also be seen in the work of McGrath,[91] who argues that the problems of union government cannot be dealt with by looking at union democracy in the traditional way. Democracy of this kind, he feels, is inappropriate and impossible to achieve in organisations like trade unions.

However, Allen's thesis has also attracted a good deal of criticism. This can be narrowed down to four main areas of contention. First, a number of authors have argued that Allen's basic premise is incorrect; trade unions are not voluntary associations. Thus Lipset says: 'The principle premise, in the argument that oligarchic unions may be regarded as democratic, rests, as Allen makes clear, on the assumption that trade unions are voluntary associations which members may leave much as they may quit a stamp club when they object to what it is doing.' However, he argues that this 'assumption clearly does not apply to most American trade unions . . . Under the closed shop, and more recently the union shop, men cannot legally quit their union without losing their jobs.'[92] Even where the member has the legal power to leave a union and keep a job this is relatively meaningless because the union can blacklist the ex-member and deprive him of substantial pension rights and the like. In a similar vein Hall[93] has pointed out how the provisions of the Taft-Hartley Act have been used to strengthen an American union's hold over reluctant members. The Act makes it difficult for dissident members to leave a union and join another, or to establish another, because of the provisions on bargaining rights.[94] Similar comments have been made about the position in Britain. Flanders[95] has referred to McCarthy's[96] estimate that about 3.75 million trade unionists in Britain work in a closed shop and argues that this means that 'unions are assured of their (members') support regardless of their policies and activities'.[97]

The second criticism has centred on the inability of members to challenge or even evaluate official policy because of their lack of knowledge or the lack of open debate. Thus Slichter has argued that the 'great majority of the members do not have much opportunity or desire to consider and discuss alternative policies. Hence they are not to be regarded as making a choice.'[98] Similarly, Cyriax and Oakeshott have noted that even in union elections 'there is rarely a real clash of wills and choice of candidates which would bring out the issues at stake'.[99] As a result, union members may stay in a union not because they agree with the policies being followed or because they accept that the union is being run efficiently but simply because they have no way of finding out about such matters.

This issue is taken a stage further by Moran,[100] who argues that most union members have little or no interest in the affairs of their union. Continued membership is merely an indication of apathy, not contentment or agreement. This is particularly true of certain aspects of union activity and aims. Most unions in Britain and in Western Europe (if not in the USA) have political (specifically socialist) aspirations and a considerable amount of effort is directed to this area. Many union members show little real sympathy for such aims or activity (this is confirmed broadly in Goldthorpe *et al.*'s study);[101] however, they do not react against it, they are merely apathetic towards it.

The third line of criticism concerns the extent to which membership figures can be seen as a good guide to membership satisfaction. Allen, of course, is not alone in arguing that membership figures are a useful measure of membership interest and approval; they were used in a similar fashion by Goldstein in his study of the Transport and General Workers Union.[102] However, their use in such a way has been challenged by a number of writers. Hughes[103] uses a survey of lapsed membership in the Union of Shop Distributive and Allied Workers to show that only a small proportion of members left because they were dissatisfied with the union or because of apathy: thus, whereas 85 per cent left the union because they either gave up employment or took up employment in another trade, only 1.6 per cent left because they were dissatisfied with the union. Eldridge makes a similar point. He says: '. . . membership fluctuations can only in a very guarded sense be treated as an indicator of membership satisfaction or dissatisfaction. The fluctuations may be caused by quite other factors, such as the general level of employment and the particular fortunes of the industries in which the union operates.'[104]

The fourth line of criticism centres on the notion that unions have well defined aims: in particular, that they have aims and objectives subscribed to by all members and officers. There are a vast number of studies which show that such an assumption is difficult to support. For example, Kendall[105] has argued that although in Europe many union leaders see the organisation as having a primarily political role most members view their association in a purely instrumental light. It is also clear in Britain that although some union activists place emphasis on the political role, other groups do not. Clegg, Killick and Adams[106] noted that union officials gave low priority to political objectives even though they were given high priority by the union rule books. Howells and Woodfield[107] in their survey of workers' preferences in New Zealand record the insensitivity of union officers to members' aims and objectives.

At first sight these criticisms appear damning and they certainly have led most writers to reject Allen's thesis in its present form. However, at the same time, many of the writers who reject Allen's thesis as outlined appear to accept a modification of it. A thesis which stated that union leaders will react to and modify policy in the face of criticism from their members (which may be expressed in a variety of different forms, such as strike action, membership lapses, the establishment of rival unions) seems to be accepted by most commentators. Clearly this differs from Allen's original formulation: it says nothing about the ability of members to criticise, or their ability to leave a union. Many writers, as has been seen above, would argue that union members are unlikely to be able to criticise union policy or leave a union as a form of protest. What this hypothesis suggests, however, is that on occasions members may protest, and that if they do so, union leaders will be compelled to take note. It should also be stated that most writers would probably argue that the conditions outlined above are insufficient to enable one to talk about union democracy, but if one is interested in policy-making rather than attaching labels then this may not matter.

The classic example, often quoted, of a situation in which a union leader was forced to alter the policy he pursued because of the reaction of union members concerns John L. Lewis of the United Mineworkers of America. Lewis became President of the mineworkers union in 1919 after the then President, Hayes, had been forced to resign. Initially Lewis assumed the post on a temporary basis but this was converted to a permanent position in an election held the following year. Lewis thus assumed control of 'the largest, the richest, and by far the most powerful union in America'.[108] The first twelve years of Lewis's reign as President, however, were disastrous. He adopted a conservative stance: Finley says that prior to 1933 he 'was regularly called one of the most reactionary men in American labor, with no program, no vision, no concept of the future'.[109] The USA mining industry, like that in other countries, suffered considerably during this period. Lewis's plan was to allow

economic forces to work themselves out. He put forward his programme for the industry in 1923: 'Shut down 4,000 coal mines,
force 200,000 miners into other industries and the coal problem
will settle itself . . . it is better to have half a million men working in
the industry at good wages . . . than to have a million working in
poverty.'[110] Throughout the 1920s Lewis took no action either to
halt the closures in the industry or to recapture lost union members. By the early 1930s disillusionment in the union had reached
such a state that two major attempts were made to form breakaway
unions. The second of these attempts led to the establishment of
the Progressive Miners of America Union, a body which survived
to provide a constant, if less than spectacular, example of the dis-
sension in the miners' ranks.

By 1932 membership of the union had fallen to something between 60,000 and 100,000; when Lewis became President of the
union it had stood at half a million. The union was no longer able
to bargain effectively on behalf of its members or enforce contracts
made. Finley comments that:

'If John L. Lewis had departed the labor movement in 1933, or had met
an untimely death, those scholars of labor's past would indeed have placed
a harsh judgment upon him. His years in office to that point had been
filled with the almost virtual destruction of the United Mineworkers of
America. It had lost its contracts, its wage scales, its membership. Its once
great treasury, the pride of America's unions, was thin and insecure. It had
no strength to resist the operators, who could even count on the support of
Lewis himself when they needed it.[111]

The decline in membership and the attempts to form breakaway
unions apparently persuaded Lewis to change course dramatically.
Almost overnight he changed from being one of the most conservative to become one of the most militant union leaders. 'The strick-
en union arose. It revived. The feat was accomplished in a few
hectic months, as in blitz times when wars are won.'[112] In 1933 the
leaders of the union initiated and supported a successful series of
strikes for wage increases. The contract negotiated as a settlement
following strikes in the Appalachian coalfield covered a wide range
of issues from the check-off to the eight hour day and has been
called '"the greatest in magnitude and scope" ever negotiated in
the United States'.[113] The members came flocking back to the
union. 'Enthusiasm was so high that miners were sworn into membership by mass inductions . . . Organisers who had not signed a
new member in years were deluged with requests to join the new

army. They told each other in amazement, "By God, the old union is coming back." '[114]

The case of Lewis was cited by Lipset[115] when he accepted the notion that union leaders in a general sense must be responsive to the demands of their members. Thus Lipset *et al.* said:

A union oligarchy which does not defend the economic interests of the rank and file may find its membership disappearing either into another union or into nonmembership in any union, as John L. Lewis did in the twenties and early thirties. Lewis, then a trade union as well as a political conservative, almost lost the United Mine Workers. Only after adopting the militant tactics for which he is now famous was he able to rebuild the union. A trade union which is not an economic defense organisation has no function and will not long remain on the scene.[116]

Lipset makes it clear that he feels that this does not negate his or Michels' thesis. Thus he states that to recognise that a union must be responsive to demands made by members or signs of dissatisfaction 'does not involve declaring that a trade union is necessarily representative of its members' interests, or must be considered a democratic organisation'.[117] Often members will simply not express an opinion openly or forcefully or not be able to do so. Nevertheless, Lipset makes it clear that if members do express an opinion forcefully then the leadership cannot ignore it.

This general point seems to be accepted by Warner.[118] He argues that even in a large union, where the closed shop is in operation the 'membership must be kept minimally happy, and never taken for granted'. If there is widespread dissatisfaction the union rank and file must be satisfied. 'Otherwise membership will drop and the power of the union and of its leaders will drop with it.'[119]

Again, Fox argues, that there 'is still the minimum of service which leaders must render to members' goals if they are to retain their authority. Cases are numerous', he says, 'where in the absence of the minimum, members have withdrawn legitimacy and vested it in the unofficial leaders of lower level collectivities. Grass roots power born of labour scarcity has greatly enhanced their power to do so, younger and more militant aspirants to office will not be slow to make use of the fact.'[120]

Wright-Mills[121] makes a similar point in general terms. He clearly believes that union leaders have a great deal of power over their members and members are often in no position to judge the actions of the leaders; much of the activity of the leadership is hidden from view. However leaders have to react to changing economic conditions and the demands of the membership. If they do not then they are likely to be overthrown. Thus he states: 'During slumps, especially when the rank and file are militant, leaders of labor must shift to more militant ways or gamble on losing their leadership.'[122]

Many union leaders themselves have echoed the claim of academics that to a certain extent they must be seen by their members to be 'delivering the goods'. Possibly the most flamboyant statement of this kind has come from Hoffa, the President of the American Teamsters Union. 'Most people do not want to participate in the day-to-day operations of their union – this is the business agent's job. But when people are really dissatisfied or hurt, watch out for the fireworks. A leader must deliver what the people really want.'[123]

Moran,[124] after his study of the Union of Post Office Workers, argued that one should not be misled because of the apathy of union members on some issues (such as socialist aspirations) into believing that union members are likely to be apathetic on all issues. There are certain issues, mainly concerning the terms and conditions of employment, about which the union member is keenly concerned. If the union leaders adopt a policy on these issues contrary to the wishes of the membership then there is likely to be a backlash. Moran gave one instance of an attempt by the leaders of the post office workers' union in the 1920s to impose a policy to which the majority of members seemed to object. The policy involved the setting up of a strike fund and a levy to support that fund. The bulk of the membership, Moran argues, opposed these moves, and were particularly incensed by the levy. As a result the union lost over half its membership.

The revised Allen thesis almost ironically also seems to be compatible with Michels' iron law of oligarchy. One of the central themes of Michels' argument is that union leaders are concerned to protect their own position. This normally means that they act in a conservative fashion. However, if they were faced with a challenge to their position, on the basis of the Michels thesis, one would not expect them to stand by some policy on principle. If the challenge was genuine then the likely outcome, following the Michels thesis, surely would be for them to change their policy to protect this position. Michels did not pay a great deal of attention to such developments because he believed that expressions of membership discontent were unlikely; however, as has been noted, subsequent writers have argued that although expressions of membership discontent are unlikely they are nevertheless perfectly possible and on occasions do occur.

A NOTE OF CAUTION

It would be unwise to suggest as a result of this discussion that there is agreement between all of the writers reviewed on what has been termed a 'revised Allen thesis'. Important differences of approach remain, and the marrying of the different approaches has only been possible because a very restricted issue has been considered. Further, so far the proposition has been expressed in very general terms: if a more detailed proposition were expounded then the common ground would very quickly disappear. Nevertheless, it is interesting that many authors, from different positions, and with different explanations, seem to accept that union leaders will not pursue a course of action which is seriously attacked by a large proportion of the membership, especially if this attack leads to a major loss of membership.

However, despite this broad acceptance even this position is not immune from criticism. Examples can be quoted of where union leaders and union executives have pursued policies which clearly and in some cases quite seriously have been opposed by their membership and they have not been forced to change them. For example, the Transport and General Workers Union, from its formation to the end of the 1960s, pursued a policy in relation to the de-casualisation of dock labour in Britain which at times was opposed by a substantial proportion (it is impossible to say whether a majority or not) of its membership in the industry. Crucially, at times this policy led members to leave the union and even to set up rival organisations. Yet the Transport and General Workers Union did not respond to such opposition by changing its policy. On the contrary; it pursued a fairly consistent line throughout, virtually unmoved by the opposition.[125]

There are many factors that help to explain the policy of the Transport and General Workers Union on this issue. One of the most important is the effect of the views and personality of its first leader, Bevin.[126] There is little doubt that Bevin believed that the opposition to his and the union's policy was misplaced, and that to give in to pressure would be against the dock workers' interest, even against the interest of those who opposed him. After Bevin gave up the leadership of the union, the policy remained the same partly because it had become almost an unchallengeable article of faith within the union, but also partly because it was supported by subsequent leaders.

Looked at from the pessimistic tradition on union democracy such behaviour would be difficult to explain. This point of view suggests that union leaders try to protect their own position in the organisation, and if necessary that they will be willing to compromise to do so. Bevin could have changed his attitude and persuaded the union to change its policy to deflect the attacks on him but did not do so, primarily because of his personal commitment over a long period of time to the principles inherent in the policy. Essentially, the pessimistic tradition assumes that union leaders are organisation men who have lost all personal and political commitment and are simply interested in power. While few would argue that Bevin was not interested in power, in this case there is no evidence that he lost his original personal commitment. The documentation on later union leaders is not as full yet it is clear that some retained a belief in the social desirability of decasualisation and consequently refused to change union policy. Looked at from the optimistic tradition, the Transport and General Workers Union's policy on decasualisation is also difficult to explain. Why did the pressure of the membership not force the union leadership to change its policy? It might be argued that the pressure was not sufficiently strong. Yet it is difficult to believe that this is a satisfactory explanation, given the fact that members left in substantial numbers in some ports and joined or set up rival organisations. The answer may be that in a union of a type like the Transport and General Workers, considerable pressure can be resisted even if it encompasses the majority of the membership in any industry, because the union has membership from a variety of industries. A 'general union', then, may be able to resist pressure more than most because of the breadth of its membership.

To some extent the factors isolated to explain the case of the Transport and General Workers Union's policy on decasualisation might be seen as particular and therefore might lead one to question their relevance to a more general argument. However, while the factors related may not apply to all unions in all situations or even to most unions in most situations, they are not merely of relevance to the case cited. For example, a number of unions have a membership which extends beyond one trade or industry. The question of the personal commitment (or the extent of such commitment) of union leaders would have to be established by more detailed enquiry. The point being made here is that such enquiry should take place and lack of commitment should not be assumed, as it is in some writing on the subject.

CONCLUSIONS

It has already been emphasised on a number of occasions that unions vary considerably. In this instance it is important to stress that unions vary in their internal structure and such variations can affect internal democracy. Some internal devices may inhibit the ability of the general membership to control the leadership, others may have the reverse effect.

A number of authors (such as Banks, and Child, Loveridge and Warner) have noted, however, that when discussing internal democracy it is not sufficient simply to look at variations in the structure of trade unions. It is also important to look at the way in which the members react to the opportunities or limitations imposed by that structure. In other words the same internal device may inhibit some members from controlling their leaders, but may be used in a different way by members of another union.

A further dimension is also important. Not only do union members vary in the way in which they use the facilities available to them, so also do union leaders. Some union leaders retain a sense of commitment to social or political ideas throughout their careers; others may never have held such commitments or may have lost them in the process of struggling for power.

A study of internal union democracy, then, cannot provide general rules to cover all unions on all occasions. There are an almost infinite variety of different combinations of internal structure, membership reaction and leader reaction. An understanding of union democracy needs to be aware of such possible combinations and to avoid over-hasty generalisation.

NOTES

1. Their books *A History of Trade Unionism* (Longman, London, 1896) and *Industrial Democracy*, (Longmans, Green & Co, London, 1920) have been given the status of industrial relations 'classics'. V.L. Allen in *The Sociology of Industrial Relations* (Longmans, London, 1971) says 'There was in a sense, no trade union history until they [the Webbs] wrote it' (p. 28) while G.S. Bain and H.A. Clegg in 'A strategy for industrial relations research in Great Britain' (*British Journal of Industrial Relations*, vol. VII (1974), no. 1,) refer to *Industrial Democracy* as industrial relations, 'major and perhaps only classic' (p. 98).

2. S. and B. Webb, 1920, *op. cit.*, pp. 3–4.
3. *Ibid.*, p. 8.
4. The vast majority of trade unions in Britain were still fairly small when compared to current standards. No union approached the two million members currently claimed by Britain's largest union, the Transport and General Workers Union. A number of writers have argued that the problems of democracy in trade unions are linked to size; see, for example, M. Warner, L. Donaldson, 'Dimensions of organisation in occupational interest associations: some preliminary findings', Third Joint Conference on Behavioural Science and Operational Research, London, 1971, who looked, in particular, at the ability of members to control officers in unions of differing size.
5. S. and B. Webb, 1920, *op. cit.*, p. 8.
6. *Ibid.*, pp. 36–7.
7. *Ibid.*, p. 41.
8. It is worthwhile noting that very few British unions have, in fact, adopted the Webbs' model of representative democracy machinery.
9. J.E.T. Eldridge in *Sociology and Industrial Life* (Nelson, London, 1973) implies that the Webbs' conclusion was pessimistic (pp. 177–78) and states that they came to the same conclusion as Michels. While it is correct to state that the Webbs and Michels looked at the same phenomena and highlighted similar tendencies it is difficult to view the Webbs' account in such a pessimistic light because they saw a way of overcoming the problems observed, whereas Michels did not.
10. R. Michels, *Political Parties*, Free Press, New York, 1962.
11. *Ibid.*, p. 16.
12. *Ibid.*, p. 17.
13. *Ibid.*, p. 365.
14. *Ibid.*, p. 353.
15. *Ibid.*, p. 353.
16. *Ibid.*, p. 154.
17. N. Bukharin in *Historical Materialism: A system of Sociology* (International Publishers, New York, 1925) recognised that the transition from capitalism to socialism, the period of the 'proletarian dictatorship' might present problems and might lead to the emergence of a new leading stratum. See, also, P. Selznick, *The Organisational Weapon: A Study of Bolshevik Strategy and Tactics*, McGraw-Hill, New York, 1952.

18. Quoted by S.M. Lipset, in his introduction to R. Michels, *op. cit.*, p. 26.
19. T. Lane, *The Union Makes Us Strong*, Arrow Books, London, 1974, p. 30.
20. Michels, *op. cit.*, p. 367.
21. *Ibid.*
22. S.M. Lipset, M.A. Trow, J.S. Coleman, *Union Democracy*, Free Press, New York, 1956.
23. *Ibid.*, p. 13.
24. *Ibid.*, p. 413.
25. J. Goldstein, *The Government of a British Trade Union*, Free Press, Glencoe, 1952.
26. *Ibid.*, p. 70.
27. *Ibid.*, p. 73.
28. *Ibid.*, p. 113.
29. *Ibid.*, p. 132.
30. *Ibid.*, p. 269.
31. B.C. Roberts, *Trade Union Government and Administration in Great Britain*, Harvard U.P., Cambridge (Mass), 1956.
32. *Political and Economic Planning*, PEP, London, 1948.
33. J.H. Goldthorpe, D. Lockwood, F. Bechhofer, J. Platt, *The Affluent Worker: Industrial Attitudes and Behaviour*, Cambridge U.P., London, 1968.
34. See, J. Seidman, B. Karsh, D. Tagliacozzo, 'A typology of rank-and-file union members', *American Journal of Sociology*, vol. 4 (1956), pp. 546–53; J. Seidman, J. London, B. Karsh, D. Tagliacozzo, *The Worker Views His Union*, University of Chicago Press, Chicago, 1958.
35. R. Lumley, *White Collar Unionism in Britain*, Methuen, London, 1973.
36. G.D.H. Cole, *An Introduction to Trade Unionism*, Allen & Unwin, London, 1953.
37. G. Cyriax, R. Oakeshott, *The Bargainers*, Faber, London, 1960, pp. 74–5.
38. International Labour Office, *The Trade Union Situation in the United Kingdom*, ILO, Geneva, 1961.
39. For details of ballots, see M.P. Jackson, *The Price of Coal*, Croom Helm, London, 1974.
40. L. Sayles, G. Strauss, *The Local Union*, Harcourt Brace, New York, 1953.
41. A.S. Tannenbaum, R.L. Kahn, *Participation in Union Locals*, Row & Peterson, Evanston (Illinois) 1958.

42. C. Wright-Mills, *The New Men of Power*, Harcourt Brace, New York, 1948 (1971 reprint by Augustus M. Keeley).
43. C. Wright-Mills, *The Power Elite*, Oxford U.P., New York, 1959.
44. See also, R.A. Dahl, 'A critique of the ruling elite model', *American Political Science Review*, vol. 52 (1958), pp. 463–69 for criticism of Wright-Mills' thesis.
45. J.R. Coleman, 'The compulsive pressures of union democracy', *American Journal of Sociology*, vol. 61 (1955), no. 6, pp. 519–26.
46. B. Hall (ed.), *Autocracy and Insurgency in Organised Labor*, Transaction Books, New Brunswick, 1972.
47. B.C. Roberts, *Trade Unions in a Free Society*, Hutchinson, London, 1962, p. 125.
48. *Ibid.*, p. 35.
49. C. Kerr, *Unions and Union Leaders of Their Own Choosing*, The Fund for the Republic, New York, 1957.
50. C. Summers, 'Union democracy and union discipline', *Proceedings of New York Universities' Fifth Annual Conference on Labor*, Matthew Bender, New York, 1952.
51. W.M. Leiserson, *American Trade Union Democracy*, Columbia, U.P., New York, 1959.
52. L. Broomwich, *Union Constitutions*, The Fund for the Republic, New York, 1959.
53. S.M. Lipset, M.A. Trow, J.S. Coleman, *op. cit.*, p. 412.
54. J. Goldstein, *op. cit.*, p. 271.
55. *Ibid.*, p. 270.
56. *Ibid.*, p. 271.
57. *Ibid.*, pp. 271–2.
58. H.A. Turner, *Trade Union Growth, Structure and Policy*, Allen & Unwin, London, 1962.
59. See, for example, J.D. Edelstein, 'An organisational theory of union democracy', *American Sociological Review*, vol. 32 (1967), pp. 19–31.
60. J.D. Edelstein, M. Warner, *Comparative Union Democracy*, Transaction Books, New Brunswick, 1979, p. 112.
61. J. Barbash, *American Unions*, Random House, New York, 1967.
62. A. Flanders, *Trade Unions*, Hutchinson, London, 1968, p. 49.
63. H.A. Clegg, *General Union*, Blackwell, Oxford, 1954, p. 344.
64. *Ibid.*, p. 344.

65. R. Martin, 'Union democracy: an explanatory framework', *Sociology*, vol. 2 (1968), pp. 205–20.
66. A.W. Nicholas, 'Factions: a comparative analysis', ASA Monograph no. 2, *Political Systems and the Distribution of Power*, Tavistock, London, 1965.
67. W.E.J. McCarthy, S.R. Parker, *Shop Stewards and Workshop Relations*, Royal Commission on Trade Unions and Employers' Associations, 1965–68, Research Paper 10, HMSO, London, 1968.
68. *Ibid.*
69. G. Cyriax, R. Oakeshott, *op. cit.*
70. See, for example, J.F.B. Goodman, T.G. Whittingham, *Shop Stewards in British Industry*, McGraw-Hill, London, 1969. For a more recent study of workshop relations, see M.G. Wilders, S.R. Parker, 'Changes in Workplace Industrial Relations, 1966–72', *British Journal of Industrial Relations*, vol. xiii (1975), no. 1, pp. 14–22.
71. J.A. Banks, *Trade Unionism*, Collier MacMillan, London, 1974.
72. *Ibid.*, p. 90.
    R. Hyman, *Industrial Relations : A Marxist Introduction*, Macmillan, London, 1975, argues that it is still inappropriate to state that unions are run democratically; there is a difference between a polyarchy and a democracy.
73. *Ibid.*, p. 93.
74. J. Child, R. Loveridge, M. Warner, 'Towards an organisational study of trade unions', *Sociology*, vol. 7 (1973), pp. 71–91.
75. See W. Spinard, 'Correlates of trade union participation : a summary of the literature', *American Sociological Review*, vol. 25 (1960), pp. 237–44. Spinard reviews a number of other studies of trade union participation and shows how factors such as personal association, the conditions of the job and the extent to which work is a central life interest, have been seen as indicators.
76. D. Silverman, *The Theory of Organisations*, Heinemann, London, 1970.
77. V.L. Allen, *Power in Trade Unions*, Longmans, Green & Co, London, 1954.
78. Subsequently such a definition was used by S.M. Lipset, M.A. Trow, J.S. Coleman, *op. cit.* See, also, J. Steiber, *Governing the UAW*, Wiley, New York, 1967. He argues that

democracy is a general phenomenon and there cannot be a special type for trade unions.

79. V.L. Allen, 1954, *op. cit.*, p. 10.
80. He also notes that trade unions compare favourably with other voluntary associations in terms of internal democratic procedures.
81. V.L. Allen, 1954, *op. cit.*, p. 11.
82. *Ibid.*, p. 15.
83. Allen seems to accept a point stressed by many other writers that there may be some conflict between efficiency and internal democratic procedures. He does not see the conflict as inevitable but, when such conflict occurs, seems to believe that efficiency is of prime importance.
84. V.L. Allen, 1954, *op. cit.*, p. 21.
85. *Ibid.*, p. 26.
86. *Ibid.*, pp. 26–7.
87. *Ibid.*, p. 28.
88. *Ibid.*, p. 28.
89. *Ibid.*, p. 59.
90. J. Hughes, *Trade Union Structure and Government*, Research Paper 5, Part 2, Royal Commission on Trade Unions and Employers' Association, 1965–68, HMSO, London, 1968.
91. C.P. Magrath, 'Democracy in overalls : the futile quest for union democracy', *Industrial and Labor Relations Review*, vol. 12 (1958–9), pp. 503–25.
92. S.M. Lipset, M.A. Trow, J.S. Coleman, *op. cit.*, p. 410.
93. B. Hall (ed.), *op. cit.*
94. This point of view is challenged by P. Taft, 'Internal affairs of unions and the Taft-Hartley Act', *Industrial and Labor Relations Review*, vol II (1958), no. 3, pp. 354–5.
95. A. Flanders, *op. cit.*, p. 44.
96. W.E.J. McCarthy, *The Closed Shop in Britain*, Blackwell, Oxford, 1964.
97. A. Flanders, *op. ci.t*, p. 44.
98. S.H. Slichter, *Challenge of Industrial Relations*, Cornell, U.P., Ithaca, 1947.
99. G. Cyriax, R. Oakeshott, *op. cit.*, p. 75.
100. M. Moran, *The Union of Post Office Workers: A Study of Political Sociology*, Macmillan, London, 1974.
101. J.H. Goldthorpe, D. Lockwood, F. Bechhofer, J. Platt, *op. cit.*
102. J. Goldstein, *op. cit.*

103. J. Hughes, *op. cit.*

104. J.E.T. Eldridge, *op. cit.*, p. 180.

105. W. Kendall, *The Labour Movement in Europe*, Allen Lane, London, 1975.

106. H.A. Clegg, A.J. Killick, R. Adams, *Trade Union Officers*, Blackwell, Oxford, 1961.

107. J.M. Howells, A.E. Woodfield, 'The ability of managers and trade union officers to predict workers' preferences', *British Journal of Industrial Relations*, vol. VIII (1970), pp. 237–51.

108. J.E. Finley, *The Corrupt Kingdom*, Simon & Shuster, New York, 1972, p. 48.

109. *Ibid.*, p. 74.

110. *Ibid.*, p. 61.

111. *Ibid.*, p. 73.

112. *Ibid.*, p. 77.

113. *Ibid.*, p. 83.

114. *Ibid.*, p. 79.

115. In both S.M. Lipset, M.A. Trow, J.S. Coleman, *op. cit.*, and Lipset's introduction to R. Michels, *op. cit.*

116. S.M. Lipset, M.A. Trow, J.S. Coleman, *op. cit.*, p. 409.

117. *Ibid.*, p. 409.

118. M. Warner, 'Industrial conflict revisited', in M. Warner (ed.) *The Sociology of the Workplace*, Allen & Unwin, London, 1973, pp. 256–73.

119. *Ibid.*, p. 369. See, also, J.E.T. Eldridge, *op. cit.* Eldridge reviews Allen's work and comments that there is a clear distinction between Allen's assertion that members will leave a union if they disagree with policy and Lipset's acceptance that union leaders will have to take note of expressions of rank and file discontent. However, Eldridge does not challenge Lipset's assertion as such and thus implicitly might be seen as giving some support to the revised Allen thesis.

120. A. Fox, *A Sociology of Work in Industry*, Collier-Macmillan, London, 1972, p. 123.

121. C. Wright-Mills, 1948, *op. cit.*

122. *Ibid.*, p. 106.

123. Quoted by S. Romer, *The International Brotherhood of Teamsters*, Wiley, New York, 1967, p. 142. For a more extensive discussion of Hoffa's leadership see R.C. James, E.D. James, *Hoffa and the Teamsters*, D. Van Nostrand, Princeton, 1965.

124. M. Moran, *op. cit.*

125. For a review of the attempts to decasualise dock labour in Britain see M.P. Jackson, *Labour Relations on the Docks*, Saxon House, Farnborough, 1973.
126. See A. Bullock, *The Life and Times of Ernest Bevin*, vol. 1, Heinemann, London, 1960.

Chapter five

THE CHALLENGE FROM THE SHOP FLOOR

Workplace organisation and bargaining are by no means unique to the post Second World War period. Hinton[1] records that they were a feature of the British engineering industry as long ago as the mid Victorian era. Similar comments have been made by Cole[2] and Clegg[3] about the early part of the twentieth century. The activities of the shop stewards' movement in Britain during the First World War are well documented. However, attention tended to be diverted from such issues during the inter-war years and it was not until the mid 1960s that they regained prominence.

In Britain the discussion of workplace organisation and bargaining in the 1960s owes much to the writing of Alan Flanders.[4] He pointed out that descriptions of collective bargaining which looked simply or mainly at national machinery were missing a great deal. Workplace bargaining was just as, if not more, important than its national counterpart. He suggested that evidence to support this contention could be gained by looking at wage drift, which despite its uneven incidence was a universal phenomenon.

Flander's work had a great deal of influence on the deliberations and report of the Donovan Commission.[5] They too cited the evidence of wage drift to support their assertion about the importance of local bargaining. They pointed out, for example, that between October 1962 and October 1967, average weekly wage rates increased by 17.9 per cent in the textile industry, by 18.4 per cent in the timber and furniture industry and by 21.7 per cent in the construction industry. However, over the same period average earnings increased by 37.7 per cent in textiles, 35.8 per cent in timber and furniture and by 35.9 per cent in construction. This meant that there had been 'earnings drift' of 19.8 per cent in textiles, 17.4 per cent in timber and furniture and 14.2 per cent in construction.[6]

However, the Donovan Commission's evidence was not restricted to statistics on wage drift. They were also able to point to the extent of unofficial strikes. There was broad agreement amongst most authorities at the time that Britain's 'strike problem' centred on the number of short, local and usually unofficial strikes (between 1964 and 1966, 95 per cent of all stoppages of work had been due to unofficial strikes and on average each strike involved about 300 workers and lasted for 2½ days).[7]

Crucially, though, the Donovan Commission was also able to present evidence collected by its research team on the extent and importance of the activity of shop stewards in British industry.[8] Although, according to most union rule books, shop stewards have a very limited role (essentially, one restricted to collecting union dues and distributing union literature), in practice most shop stewards exercise considerable influence. A national survey of shop stewards showed that, despite considerable variations, a majority bargained over wages, working conditions, discipline and other employment matters. Shop stewards had gained their power and influence, it was argued, largely at the expense of the full-time trade union official.

The Donovan Commission concluded that there were two systems of industrial relations, the formal and the informal. The formal system was based on industry-wide agreements negotiated by national union officials and employers' leaders. The informal system was based on local negotiations between shop stewards and plant management. Bargaining at the local level often was not controlled by set procedures: to the contrary, it existed despite the official procedures and circumvented them. The agreements reached were frequently not formally recorded but simply became part of custom and practice. The Donovan Commission argued that the informal undermined the formal system and weakened the position of the main actors, including the official union leaders.

The Donovan Commission's analysis of British industrial relations was extremely influential and became part of the 'accepted wisdom'. Its general solution, the establishment of formal procedures to cover local bargaining (its aim, essentially, was not to eliminate local bargaining but to control and regulate it), if not its particular remedial measures (some of which, and certainly the spirit of voluntarism and the absence of legal enforcement, were overtaken by 'In Place of Strife' and the Industrial Relations Act of 1971) was also influential.

A number of changes have taken place in British workplace relations since the publication of the Donovan report. For example, it appears that the number of shop stewards operating in British industry may have increased significantly. A study of the manufacturing industry concluded that the number of shop stewards operating in that industry may have quadrupled between 1966 and 1976.[9] Other studies have suggested that shop stewards may now be better trained than they used to be, that their role may be formally recognised and that they may have been given better facilities at the workplace.[10]

More generally, however, the evidence on the formalisation of workplace bargaining is patchy and in parts contradictory. A national survey completed in the early 1970s concluded that some attempts had been made to formalise local bargaining since the publication of the Donovan report, but that such bargaining was still largely informal.[11] A more restricted survey of four industries (brewing, man-made fibres, mechanical engineering and bus transport) in the North-West of England conducted between 1970 and 1972 suggested that rather than decreasing, the scope of workplace bargaining had increased over the previous five years.[12] Of 141 stewards surveyed, 70 said that there had been an increase in the scope of local bargaining: only one said that there had been a decrease. Further, there was little evidence that this bargaining was constrained by formal regulations or full-time union officials.

One of the reasons why the ambitions of the Donovan Commission in this area do not seem to have been fully met may be that reliance was placed on voluntary effort for bringing about the desired changes (in this the Commission was supported by the analysis of Fox and Flanders[13] who argued that the problems over local bargaining were the result of the breakdown of normative order or anomie and that the situation could only be remedied by a re-establishment of normative order which might be encouraged by the state but which could not be brought about by the use of legal sanctions). Another, related factor is that suggested by Terry.[14] He argues that informality was itself valued by the industrial participants: he goes so far as to talk about the 'inevitability of informality'.

Terry's observation may be important because, as he notes, the Donovan Commission assumed that you could solve the 'problem' of informal bargaining by simply making informal local bargaining formal. This ignored the fact that different parties are involved in negotiating and enforcing more formal than informal agreements. An informal agreement may be valued not simply because of its substantive nature but also because it gives power to certain parties in the workplace. Terry quotes an example of a factory where, post Donovan, an informal custom and practice agreement restricting the right of management to move a worker from one job to another was made part of a formal agreement. In the succeeding six months a spate of complaints arose about the operation of the agreement and eventually the workforce began to demand not simply the right to veto, but also the right to initiate job changes. As far as could be seen this demand had never been made before and represented a significant extension of past custom and practice. The dispute was eventually resolved by an agreement that all internal vacancies would be notified on a blackboard and workers would have the right to initiate the move to another job by applying for it. Terry claims that this example illustrates that the previous custom and practice in the factory was not only valued because of the substantive nature of the agreement but also because it was initiated and maintained by shop-floor leaders. The formalisation of the agreement meant that it was put in the hands of new custodians, official leaders, and as a result was not as highly valued.

The development of unofficial workplace activity has not been restricted to Britain but has been a feature of most Western industrialised nations. Evidence of its importance can be gained by reference to factors similar to those highlighted during the discussion of the British experience. For example, widespread local and unofficial strikes were a feature of most Western European countries in the late 1960s and early 1970s.

Perhaps the most spectacular strikes of this kind occurred in Italy. There had been signs of a challenge to the central union control of industrial relations in Italy since the late 1950s but attempts had been made to regulate such developments through articulated bargaining which gave a role, if only a restricted one, to local bargaining. However, in the autumn and winter of 1968/69 a series of strikes, which started in the metal industries, led to a period of 'industrial ferment' and 'continuous bargaining'. The strikes were largely a spontaneous development originating from rank and file workers: they were not the traditional officially orchestrated set-piece confrontations. In the 1970s the control of strikes was largely left in the hands of local plant committees who used short but frequent stoppages of work to press home their demands.[15]

A similar pattern can be seen in Belgium. The major cycle of strikes in the early 1970s in Belgium was sparked off by the action of the Limbourg miners. The coal mining industry in Belgium, as elsewhere in Western Europe, had suffered from the decline in coal consumption during the 1960s. The consequences of the decline had not been fully felt by the Belgian miners because of Government subsidies, but the threat and implementation of mine closures clearly had made an impact and set the tone. The miners struck for eight weeks and this heralded a rash of strikes throughout Belgian industry in 1970. The strikes broke with the traditional orderly conduct of industrial relations in Belgium and have been viewed by many commentators as a spontaneous expression of frustration at developments during the 1960s. Although strike activity subsided at the end of 1970 a further wave of strikes occurred in 1973 over cost-of-living bonuses and the escalator clauses in contracts.

However, in some ways the most interesting examples of the development of strike action come from two of the most commercially successful Western industrial nations in recent years, Sweden and West Germany. Sweden had been relatively strike-free for the twenty years following the end of the Second World War. Towards the end of the 1960s, however, the number of strikes increased significantly and, in particular, unofficial strikes dominated. In 1970, 216 unofficial strikes were recorded, at that time a highpoint for the post-war years, and the proportion of strikes which were illegal increased from 60 per cent of all strikes in 1969 to 100 per cent in 1970, 93 per cent in 1971 and 77 per cent in 1972. Otter also notes that changes occurred in the manner in which unofficial strikes were conducted. 'They were better organised. New strikes adopted tactics displayed by prior ones. Meetings were arranged with the workers, with the press and TV in attendance.'[16] The strike of dock-workers in Gothenburg in 1969 was also the first where strikers obtained substantial funds from the general public to carry on the fight without union support.

In West Germany the position was somewhat similar. The post Second World War years were relatively strike-free and both official and unofficial action was rare. However, the picture began to change in 1967 when a wage restraint policy was successfully introduced. Rainer Kalbitz in a study of post-war strikes in West Germany[17] has shown that the number of unofficial strikes increased from 21 in 1965 to 61 in 1967. In the following two years discontent increased and in 1969 there was a wave of spontaneous wildcat strikes. The events were 'quite unprecedented for the German trade union movement' and 'strongly affected the unions' wage policy and organisational structure'. They brought about a reversal of the state incomes policy and also endangered the established institutionalized co-operative representational system.[18] Bergmann and Muller-Jentsch warn us not to write off the strikes of 1969 as an isolated phenomenon: similar events occurred at the end of 1972 and in 1973. 'Internal organisational disputes unfolded in the wage negotiations in the metal industries, and another wave of wildcat strikes involved even more workers, forcing significant additional concessions by management and showing up the inadequacies of the existing industrial relations and representational structures.'[19]

Strikes are not the only evidence of workplace activity. There is also evidence of the growth in importance of workplace organisations and in some cases of the growth in importance of the role of shop stewards or similar officials. Giugni records the development of 'a new powerful form of organisation generally known as the factory council or "consiglio di fabrica"' in Italy.[20] The councils have been established almost spontaneously throughout Italian industry (in the metal industries alone there are more than 1,400) and appear to be unrestrained by official procedures or official industrial relations bodies. Brandini[21] disucsses the emergence of the shop delegate as a critical force in the union structure in Italy. He argues that before the strikes of the late 1960s shop-floor level union representatives simply served as a way of communicating orders from national union leaders and collecting dues and servicing the members. The plant level was dominated by members of the Internal Commission, elected by all blue and white collar employees. Since 1968, though, shop delegates have gained power and displaced the Internal Commission members in importance. The delegate is now involved in negotiations, representing the rank and file in deciding and then implementing policy and strategy.

In West Germany the shop steward has gained considerably more power in recent years in some sections of industry. Historically there has been a gap in union organisation at the plant level, partly as a result of the existence of works councils. Shop stewards, if they were active, played a restricted role. They were expected to represent union policy to members in the workplace but often had no place on official union policy-making bodies. However, as often the most active and politically articulate union members in the workplace, they were in a strong position to act as a focus for the discontent which had been manifest in many sections of West German industry since the late 1960s. The result has been a considerable expansion of their *de facto* role over the last decade.

Korpi argues that the Swedish system of industrial relations has never been so tightly under the control of the central union and employers' organisations as has been imagined. In theory, workplace bargaining simply has been the third tier of a highly integrated and centralised system (the other two tiers have been the negotiations at the national level between the Swedish Confederation of Trade Unions and the Swedish Confederation of Employers Organisations, and those between the national union and the corresponding employers' organisation in the branch of industry where the union operates). In practice, the main workplace bargaining organisation, the works club, always has operated with considerable independence: according to Korpi, workplace bargaining in Sweden has been no more under the control of the union hierarchy than it has been in Britain. Further, Korpi argues that 'Swedish workplace bargaining largely relies on informal agreements and tacit understandings'.[22]

There is evidence that in the 1970s the *de facto* freedom enjoyed by local bargainers in Sweden may have increased. In a number of instances strikes were called by unofficial strike committees against the instructions of the official union leadership, and in some cases after the strike finished the strike committee continued to operate as the focus for independent unofficial workplace activity.

Similar comments can be made about most other Western nations. A study in Denmark[23] has noted that a high proportion of earnings can be negotiated at the workplace level, a Belgian commentator[24] has referred to the growth of informal bargaining in that country and the appointment of shop stewards in sections of Dutch industry (until recently shop stewards were more or less unknown in Holland) has been recognised as an important development.[25] Local bargaining is more firmly established as part of the official structure in the USA than elsewhere. However, there is evidence of a growth of unofficial activity at the local level in the USA as well.

THE NATURE OF WORKPLACE ACTIVITY

Few authors would now deny the importance of workplace organisation and activity in most Western industrialised countries. Some would question whether it has expanded to the extent that is often assumed: it could be that because of changed management practices it has simply become more visible.[26] Further, workplace bargaining and organisations clearly has not developed uniformly in Western nations. However, this is not the same as questioning its current importance. There is debate, though, over the quality of the discussion of the phenomena. Hill argues that discussion of workplace organisation has been hampered by imprecise definition: 'Definitions and descriptions (of work groups) have lacked precision and documentation: composition, size and purpose are all left ambiguous, so that it is scarcely a caricature of present research to say that anything short of a trade union which displays some industrial relations behaviour appears as a work group.'[27] He goes on to suggest a framework for analysing work groups which presents a useful way of ordering the material available and making some headway in obtaining better definitions and more precise discussion.

Hill suggests that there are four major variables relevant to the empirical analysis of work groups. They are the structural conditions which affect group formation; the extent to which group consciousness exists; the nature of such consciousness; and the power of the group to pursue its objectives. Hill outlines certain empirical factors within these major variables which give substantive content to the framework.

According to Hill, the structural factors which encourage or impede work group formation have been fairly well elaborated. For example, a number of authors have outlined aspects of the technological system which might aid or retard group formation. These include the extent to which the work-process allows freedom of movement, the extent to which it requires workers to co-operate in production and the extent of occupational differentiation. 'What emerges is a range of conditions which are more or less favourable to work group formation, a continuum from encouraging conditions (Kuhn's tyre case), through facilitating conditions (the Affluent Worker toolmakers and machinists) to impeding conditions (some motor assembly lines).'[28]

It is also worth noting that group formation can be encouraged or impeded by deliberate management action. Ever since the results of the Hawthorne studies[29] became known management theorists have recognised the potential and dangers of work groups. Certain managements have attempted to foster group formation, for example, by substituting group incentive for individual incentive schemes, sometimes in the belief that groups offer an important source of satisfaction to employees. Others have been concerned to limit the formation of work groups in order to restrict the potential challenge to managerial prerogatives.

Hill suggests that much less is known about the extent of group consciousness than about the structural conditions that promote or impede group formation. Lockwood's distinction between three types of workers provides a useful typology of the nature and sources of orientations to work which can be linked to group consciousness.[30] The 'traditional proletarian' worker might be expected to value and seek strong attachments with fellow workers; 'traditional deferentials' might be expected to value work groups, but only to use them in so far as they do not conflict with management demands; while 'privatised workers' would be expected to place a low value on work groups, emphasising instead instrumental rewards. Lockwood's typology helps to show how non-work factors affect orientations to work, but like the Affluent Worker studies,[31] can be criticised for paying insufficient attention to work experience or the interaction between work and non-work factors. Experience of successful group organisation (for example, through an unofficial strike) might raise the consciousness of group activity and change an orientation held at the beginning of employment in the particular workplace.

Other writers have suggested that group consciousness may be affected by items like the size of the enterprise. Banks[32] argues that the growth in the size of the enterprise means that the centre of decision-making is taken further away from the immediate working environment. Recognition of the desirability of group formation can be seen to be stimulated by an appreciation of the need to combat this development. Coates and Topham[33] argue that the recent developments in work groups are an indication of an increase in group consciousness: they are a reflection of a desire by workers to gain control over their working conditions. The evidence on this issue is as yet fairly scanty. Economic conditions in the 1960s clearly gave workers greater opportunity to obtain economic rewards through group activity. Whether workers viewed their action as anything more than this is debatable. Of course, in the early 1970s economic conditions changed and in some ways inhibited group activity. Yet the evidence is that many workers felt the need to retain group activity, because they believed that the official union leadership was not looking after their interests.

While the degree of group consciousness is important, so is its nature. For example, work groups may exist or may be formed but they may or may not be used to oppose management or another group of workers. 'That is to say, the existence of a group consciousness is not necessarily evidence of the likelihood of a specific form of industrial relations behaviour such as fractional bargaining. The important issues here concern how group solidarity is defined, whether it is purely internal to the group or whether it is defined by reference to outsiders.'[34]

Sykes[35] in a study of a printing chapel showed how those workers used conflict with management to maintain their own internal group solidarity. On the other hand, Sayles' study of multi-occupational plants showed that groups based on clear-cut status hierarchies evaluated their position by relation to each other.[36]

The ability of the work group to press home their demands is centrally affected by the fourth of Hill's variables, their power position. A number of studies have pointed to the importance of the production system in this context. A system of production which is highly interdependent gives individual groups of workers considerable power: effectively they may be able to bring the whole production system to a halt themselves. This has been noted, for example, in discussions of assembly line technology, such as the motor car industry.

Lupton[37] suggests that the power position of the work group is also affected by the nature of the product market. He noted that management resistance to work group demands was positively related to the extent of competition for the product: the fiercer the competition the more concerned management is likely to be about any, even marginal, increase in costs, say as a result of a wage increase. Management resistance to work group demands may also be affected by the proportion of labour costs to total costs: the higher this proportion the greater their resistance is likely to be.

Terry[38] has argued that one of the reasons for the growth of informality in industrial relations and the growth in the power of the informal work group is management acceptance, and sometimes even encouragement of this development. Foremen, he argued, often had a major role in devising informal agreements. They provided one way of dealing with the foreman's often ambiguous position, and they made it tenable. Production management also welcomed informal agreements because their central concern was to maintain production. If negotiating with informal work groups helped to do this (as is often the case) then they were quite pleased to do so. One of the few groups to dislike informal bargaining and who may have been concerned to restrict the activities of work groups were personnel managers, but in many firms their own power was limited.

WORKPLACE GROUPS AND TRADE UNIONS

In this discussion considerable emphasis has been placed on the differences between work groups. Differences exist in terms of composition, direction, solidarity and the like. Consequently, in any comment about the implications of work groups for official trade unions one needs to exercise caution about attempts to generalise. Some work groups may have been developed with the support and encouragement of official trade unions: others may have been developed in spite of official trade union opposition. Further, the orientation of work groups may change: groups which initially were set up with the encouragement of official union leaders may now oppose these leaders and vice versa.

Without doubt one of the attractions of work groups for their members has been that they have afforded the opportunity for rank and file workers not only to challenge management prerogatives but also to take a more active part in formulating employee demands than that afforded by the official union structure. Also without doubt one of the reasons why many work groups came to prominence and became more active in the 1960s and 1970s was because of dissatisfaction with official union policy. This was particularly the case in many Western European countries where the official union movement had supported wage control policies initiated by the government.

Of course, it is as wrong to see this as the only reason for the formation and growing prominence of work groups as it is for one to argue that all unofficial strikes are strikes against the official union leaders (Cameron and Eldridge[39] point out that there are a number of different types of unofficial strike, some of which may be encouraged if not formally supported by the official union hierarchy). However, the development of work groups is important for trade unions and therefore it is important to see how trade unions have reacted.

In the Netherlands the trade unions have made a number of moves to try to deal with recent developments at the workplace. Traditionally, Dutch unions have been organised on a geographical basis at the local level. As early as the 1950s moves were started to supplement this with a plant organisation. However, such moves had no legal standing and made relatively little impact. Since the 1960s and the growth of workplace activity, these moves have gained new impetus and many unions have now established a dual structure, keeping geographical units but also integrating plant units into their hierarchy. 'For example, the Industriebond NVV introduced an "A-line", based on geographical groups, and a "B line" based on plant groupings. These two lines together elect the members of "district councils" (giving each member two forms of representation). The 14 district councils elect the union council (78 members).'[40] Albeda comments that now the plant group is 'simultaneously the organisational unit of the union and the unit of operation within the plant'. In this sense he claims the organisational structure reflects, 'the shifting focus of trade union activity – from the local, regional and national interest to the plant.'[41]

Another important and complementary development in the Netherlands has been the recognition of union plant representatives. The move to establish a network of plant representatives began inside the NVV metal union, and despite resistance from sections of the union (particularly full-time staff and administration) as well as employers, the scheme is gradually being implemented throughout the metal industry. Progress in other industries has been slow, but in 1973 an in principle agreement for the introduction of plant union representation was reached in the building industry. Other moves in a similar direction include decentralisation of wage bargaining.

In Sweden attempts have also been made to meet the aspirations of work groups. One important move in this direction is the recent decision to allow local unions a greater say in employment practices. Another is the expansion of the rights of safety stewards. Although such stewards have been in existence since 1942, recent legislation has considerably expanded their role and given them greater powers, including the right to order the stoppage of work if there is a safety hazard.

The reaction of British trade unions to the development of work groups has varied. They were exhorted by the Donovan Commission to pay more attention to their local organisation, and a number of official reports of unofficial activity in particular industries have argued that union neglect of local organisation was not an unimportant factor in encouraging unofficial activity.

Undy's review of the devolution of bargaining levels and responsibilities in the British Transport and General Workers Union is an interesting case study of one union's reaction to the pressure from the shop floor.[42] According to Undy the Transport and General Workers Union experienced major changes in bargaining levels and scope in the 1960s. For example, the growth in the popularity of productivity bargaining shifted the centre of bargaining attention.

However, it was not until the mid 1960s that the union responded to such developments by formally devolving bargaining responsibilities within the union. In fact, prior to 1965 lay attempts to devolve bargaining within the union were consistently rejected by the Union Conference on the advice of the National Executive. Undy notes, for example, a National Executive Policy Statement passed in 1963 which referred to 'the impracticability' of consulting members during the various stages of negotiation.

In the mid 1960s the union responded to the change in external conditions in a number of ways. First, marginal movements were made downwards in the bargaining levels. Second, the scope and relevance of lower level bargaining were quite radically changed. Third, the union attempted to increase lay participation in bargaining by directly involving shop stewards in negotiations. Fourth, the use of reference back procedures were encouraged.

According to Undy, while external developments played their part, the crucial factor in bringing about the changes noted in the Transport and General Workers Union was the attitude of senior officials, especially the recently elected General Secretary, Jack Jones. Clearly some officials resisted such moves, for Undy says:

... the use by J. Jones of the 'unique authority' vested in the position of General Secretary to reverse the past pattern of responsibilities in the bargaining field appeared to some of the Union's more long serving full-time officials to be a near revolutionary act. For this group of officials it was somewhat contradictory to say the least, that the centralised power of the General Secretary should be used in the late 1960s and early 1970s to devolve bargaining responsibilities which were traditionally their prerogative.[43] However, such resistance was overcome and the shift in bargaining responsibilities achieved.

As a caveat Undy notes that it is ironic that the defeat of Jack Jones at the Union delegate conference in 1977 on the question of wage restraint was closely connected with the developments referred to above which he had sponsored. Between 1945 and 1977 the Exective position had been overturned only twice by Conference, and then on fairly minor issues. 'No doubt the lay delegates in 1977, in rejecting the platform's proposals, felt disinclined to accept further nationally imposed restrictions over their relatively new found freedom to bargain locally. Hence, paradoxically, it can be argued that defeat for the General Secretary in 1977 was the final, if ironic tribute to the success of his previous policy of devolving bargaining responsibilities.'[44]

Undy's comment about the role of Jack Jones in bringing about a devolution of bargaining responsibilities within the Transport and General Workers Union is important, for it illustrates that while external conditions were important, in that they provided the correct environment for such a development, they were not sufficient on their own. This helps to explain why not all British unions have followed the Transport and General Workers Union's lead. In many instances central control has remained considerable and the pulls of local autonomy have been resisted by leaders who did not share Jack Jones' ideology.

In this context it is worthwhile referring to experience in another country in which the demands for greater local autonomy have been partly resisted by the unions. In West Germany some attempt has been made to decentralise wage negotiations. In the metal industry, for example, trade unions have granted their districts more autonomy in their wage policies. However, the moves made in this direction have been limited. Miller,[45] in a review of the metal workers union's response to the discontent of the late 1960s and early 1970s, concludes that although the union took definite steps to increase the scope of collective agreements to include terms and conditions traditionally bargained at the workplace, 'it did not change its policy with regard to the level of bargaining and consequently did not conclude procedural agreements to permit greater rank and file participation in the bargaining process'.[46] Further, generally unions in West Germany have been less tolerant of internal dissidents than have their counterparts elsewhere and they have been particularly harsh with initiators of rank and file unofficial movements. 'Procedures are being introduced and on occasion employed to exclude such people, dismiss troublesome local men, activists and officials, and dissolve troublesome elected local bodies.'[47] Thus it has been argued that while 'the trade union movement has made modest modifications both in procedure and demands in response to the rising unrest among the rank and file, it has not brooked insurgent movements which would challenge and change the cooperative wage policy and the prevailing superior position of the works council in the plant as compared with a rank and file shop steward structure'.[48]

CONCLUSION

Workplace organisation and activity is by now a well documented feature (even if, according to Hill, not a very well defined or clearly discussed one) of industrial activity in most Western nations. It is also one with considerable significance for trade unions. Depending on the way it develops it can be seen as, or could become, a challenge to the official union structure or a way of strengthening it.

The development of workplace activity has been, and undoubtedly will continue to be, influenced by a variety of factors largely out of the control of the official union leadership. Economic conditions can encourage or discourage local bargaining, as can the size of the enterprise, the nature of the task group, and the kind of technology employed. Some of these factors may affect workplace activity throughout a nation, or even throughout the Western world. For example, depressed economic conditions may reduce the likelihood of local bargaining in any industry or country. Other factors, like the kind of technology employed, are more specific.

However, while the direction of workplace activity undoubtedly will be influenced by such conditions, it will not be determined by them. Action by individuals at the local level might raise the consciousness of new forms of activity on a wide front. For example, the 'work-in' at Upper Clyde Shipbuilders in the early 1970s led to a spate of similar activity throughout British industry, and a recognition that local action could be taken to challenge national decisions. Similarly, trade unions themselves can have a major and probably even greater impact on workplace activity. If they react to evidence of local action by devolving bargaining power or setting up new workplace organisations, then they may be able to harness such activity to increase internal democracy and strengthen the union. On the other hand, if they react to evidence of local action through exceptionally coercive measures then they may inhibit internal democracy or, in particular circumstances, run the risk of losing control over the workplace and seeing organisations which challenge their authority flourish. It is impossible to offer general rules about what reaction particular forms of official union response will bring, but this should not lead to the importance of such action being underestimated.

The future of workplace activity and the future relations between workplace groups and the official union hierarchy, then, will depend partly on the conditions in which such activity develops, and partly on the reaction of individuals and the union to such activity. The conditions will limit the influence of individuals and the unions, but they will not erode the importance of them altogether.

NOTES

1. J. Hinton, *The First Shop Stewards' Movement*, Allen & Unwin, London, 1973.
2. G.O.H. Cole, *Workshop Organisation*, Oxford U.P., Oxford, 1923.
3. H.A. Clegg, *The System of Industrial Relations in Great Britain*, Blackwells, Oxford, 1979.
4. See, for example, A. Flanders, *Collective Bargaining*, Faber & Faber, London, 1967.
5. Royal Commission on Trade Unions and Employers Associations, *Report*, 1965–68, HMSO, London, 1968, Cmnd. 3623.
6. *Ibid.*, p. 16.
7. *Ibid.*, p. 97.
8. W.E.J. McCarthy, *The Role of Shop Stewards in British Industrial Relations*, Royal Commission on Trade Union and Employers Associations, Research Paper 1, HMSO London, 1966; W.E.J. McCarthy, S.R. Parker, *Shop Stewards and Workshop Relations*, Royal Commission on Trade Unions and Employers Associations, Research Paper 10, HMSO London, 1968.
9. W. Brown, R. Ebsworth, M. Terry, 'Factors shaping shop steward organisation in Britain', *British Journal of Industrial Relations*, vol. XVI (1978), no. 2. pp. 139–58.
10. W.E.J. McCarthy, P.A.L. Parker, W.R. Hawes, A.L. Lumb, *The Reform of Collective Bargaining at Plant and Company Level*, Department of Employment Manpower Papers, No. 5, HMSO London, 1971.
11. M.G. Wilders, S.R. Parker, 'Changes in workplace industrial relations', *British Journal of Industrial Relations*, vol. XIII (1975), no. 1, pp. 14–22.
12. J. Storey, 'Workplace collective bargaining and managerial prerogatives', *Industrial Relations Journal*, vol. 7 (1976/77), no. 3, pp. 40–55.
13. A. Fox, A. Flanders, 'The reform of collective bargaining : from Donovan to Durkheim' *British Journal of Industrial Relations*, vol. VII (1969), no. 2. pp. 151–80.
14. M. Terry, 'The inevitable growth of informality', *British Journal of Industrial Relations*, vol. XV (1977), no. 1, pp. 76–90.
15. See G. Giugni, 'Recent trends in collective bargaining in Italy' *International Labour Review*, vol. 104 (1971), pp. 307–28.
16. C.V. Otter, 'Sweden : labour reformism shapes the system', in

S. Barkin (ed.), *Worker Militancy and its Consequences, 1965–75* Praeger, New York, 1975, p. 214.

17. Quoted by D. Miller, 'Trade union workplace representation in the Federal Republic of Germany : an analysis of the post war Vertrauensleute policy of the German Metalworkers' Union (1952–77)', *British Journal of Industrial Relations*, vol. XVI (1978), no. 3, pp. 335–54.

18. J. Bergmann, W. Muller-Jentsch, 'The Federal Republic of Germany: co-operative unionism and dual bargaining system challenged', in Barkin (ed.), *op. cit.*, p. 259.

19. *Ibid.*, p. 236.

20. G. Giugni, *op. cit.*

21. P.M. Brandini, 'Italy : creating a new system of industrial relations from the bottom', in S. Barkin (ed.), *Worker Militancy and its Consequences 1965–75*, Praeger, New York, 1975, pp. 82–117.

22. W. Korpi, 'Workplace bargaining, the law and unofficial strikes: the case of Sweden', *British Journal of Industrial Relations*, vol. XVI (1978), no. 3, pp. 355–68.

23. Commission on Industrial Relations, *Workplace Participation and Collective Bargaining in Europe*, HMSO London, 1974.

24. R. Blanpain, 'Recent trends in collective bargaining in Belgium', *International Labour Review*, vol. 104 (1971), pp. 111–30.

25. W. Albeda, 'Recent trends in collective bargaining in the Netherlands', *International Labour Review*, vol. 103 (1971), pp. 247–68.

26. For a discussion of the impact of workplace bargaining on managerial prerogatives, see J. Storey, *op. cit.*

27. S. Hill, 'Norms, groups and power : the sociology of workplace industrial relations', *British Journal of Industrial Relations*, vol. XII (1974), no. 2. pp. 214–15. The discussion in this section is based on the framework he put forward. Many of his examples are referred to, though others are also noted.

28. *Ibid.*, p. 218.

29. See E. Mayo, *The Human Problems of an Industrial Civilisation*, Harvard U.P., Cambridge, (Mass), 1946.

30. D. Lockwood, 'Sources of variation in working class images of society', *Sociological Review*, vol. 14 (1966), no. 3. pp. 249–67.

31. J.H. Goldthorpe, D. Lockwood, F. Bechhofer, J. Platt, *The Affluent Worker*, Cambridge U.P., London, 1968.

32. J.A. Banks, *Trade Unionism*, Collier-MacMillan, London, 1974.
33. K. Coates, T. Topham, *Workers Control*, Panther, London, 1970.
34. S. Hill, *op. cit.*, p. 221.
35. A.J.M. Sykes, 'The cohesion of a trade union workshop organisation', *Sociology*, vol. 1 (1967), no. 2, pp. 141–63.
36. L.R. Sayles, *Behaviour of Industrial Work Groups : Prediction and Control*, Wiley, New York, 1958.
37. T. Lupton, *On The Shop Floor*, Pergamon, Oxford, 1963.
38. M. Terry, *op. cit.*
39. G.C. Cameron, J.E.T. Eldridge, 'Unofficial strikes' in J.E.T. Eldridge, *Industrial Disputes*, Routledge & Kegan Paul, London, 1968, pp. 68–90.
40. W. Albeda, 'Changing industrial relations in the Netherlands', *Industrial Relations*, vol. 16 (1977), no. 2, p. 137.
41. *Ibid.*, p. 137.
42. R. Undy, 'The devolution of bargaining levels and responsibilities in the Transport and General Workers Union, 1965–75', *Industrial Relations Journal*, vol. 9 (1978), no. 3. pp. 43–56.
43. *Ibid.*, p. 150.
44. *Ibid.*, p. 156.
45. D. Miller, *op. cit.*
46. *Ibid.*, p. 345.
47. J. Bergmann, W. Muller-Jentsch, *op. cit.*, pp. 273–4.
48. *Ibid.*, p. 274.

Chapter six

COLLECTIVE BARGAINING AND ECONOMIC
OBJECTIVES

The growth and establishment of collective bargaining machinery is one of the most important developments of the twentieth century in industrial relations. This is not to suggest that collective bargaining is a phenomenon unique to this century: collective bargaining was undertaken in many Western industrialised nations a good deal earlier. For example, in Britain there is evidence of collective bargaining in the eighteenth century (particularly in the silk weaving and ship-building industries) and by the latter part of the nineteenth century it had been firmly established in skilled trades (such as shipbuilding, engineering, building, furniture making and printing) and piece-work occupations (such as coal-mining, iron and steel and textile industries). However, in most countries it was not until the twentieth century that collective bargaining became firmly established through a wide range of industries.

Today collective bargaining is the most important mechanism for setting wages and terms and conditions of employment in most Western democracies. It is difficult to offer precise comparative figures for the extent of collective bargaining. However, the coverage is probably greatest in countries like Sweden where virtually all manual and the majority of non-manual workers are subject to collective agreements. It is also substantial in Australia, providing one is willing to accept that compulsory arbitration is not incompatible with collective bargaining. In Britain, France, West Germany, Italy and most other Western European countries the majority of the workforce come within the scope of collective bargaining agreements (again, the coverage is greatest amongst manual and public sector workers, and in Britain, for example, one has to decide whether the wages council machinery counts as collective bargaining). Collective bargaining is probably less extensive in North America than anywhere else in the Western world. However,

Chamberlain *et al.*[1] report that in 1974 approximately 25 million workers were covered by collective bargaining agreements in the USA (almost a quarter of the labour force) and the proportion is probably higher in Canada.

It is important, though, to note that although collective bargaining is widespread in all Western democracies, the form this bargaining takes differs considerably from country to country. For example, in Britain the formal bargaining machinery is concentrated at the industry and national level although, as has been noted earlier, in practice a great deal of bargaining also takes place (on an informal basis) at the local level. Bargaining in the USA offers a contrast, where much more formal emphasis is placed on the local level. In other countries, like France and West Germany, regional level bargaining is also important. If one were to look beyond the level at which bargaining takes place then other important differences would be apparent. The kind of issues over which bargaining occurs differ (in Britain, for example, bargaining over 'fringe benefits' and non-wage areas has been traditionally far less common than in most other Western nations) as does the role of the state in the bargaining process (again Britain provides an example of one extreme where traditionally the state has interfered very little, the USA an example of the opposite position where traditionally the state has taken a major interest in collective bargaining: this particular issue will be discussed more fully later).

It is also worthwhile noting that the way in which bargaining machinery has become established, and in particular the roles of the different parties in this process, have varied in different countries. In many countries employers have sought to restrict the spread of collective bargaining at certain times. They have refused to recognise unions and on occasions sought to withdraw recognition from unions previously recognised. This was particularly the case during the inter-war years when some employers sought to prevent workers joining unions by the use of what became known as the 'yellow-dog contracts' and by setting up their own 'company unions'. In the USA the National Association of Manufacturers led the fight against unionism during this period when under the banner of the 'American Plan' they fought for the 'open shop', 'as the natural habitat for the free and independent American workingmen'.[2] Taft and Ross[3] have also recorded the extent of violence in the USA associated with the struggles over union recognition and the extension of collective bargaining prior to the Second World War. However, by no means all employers have fought against the extension of collective bargaining. Clegg[4] records that in Britain employers' associations, even in the nineteenth century 'were always ready to deal with the unions when it suited them'.[5] He notes, for example, that even the fiercely anti-union General Builders' Association arranged with the Birmingham building unions for 'a public meeting of masters and operatives connected with the building trades for the purpose of appointing delegates on both sides to draw up rules',[6] and that some employers' association (like the North of England Ironmasters) took the lead in establishing collective bargaining because some agreement on the regulation of wages appeared to be in their own interest. More recently employers in many countries have come to recognise some potential benefits from union recognition and the extension of collective bargaining. While the majority may not have taken the initiative in granting recognition to unions or introducing collective bargaining machinery, many have accepted such developments when they have been pressed. This apparent change of heart has a number of sources. One was the decision that, on balance, fighting union recognition and collective bargaining was not 'worth the effort'. Another more positive reason was the appreciation that union recognition and the extension of collective bargaining can bring benefits for employers as well as unions. Potentially it has the advantage of regulating relationships and making them more predictable. Of course, there are still some employers who do not accept this point of view and there have been a number of occasions when employers have opposed union recognition. The violent confrontation in Britain at Grunwicks[7] in 1977 over union recognition is an example of the potential for disagreement that still exists. However, the balance of employer opinion has clearly changed.

There have also been important differences in the role that the state has played in the development of collective bargaining and the recognition of unions in different countries: arguably the differences in the attitude of the state have been greater than the differences in the attitude of employers. For example, in some countries the state has played a major role in extending union recognition and encouraging the development of collective bargaining machinery. In the USA, where unionisation was relatively low well into the twentieth century, the legislation of the 1930s, particularly the Wagner Act, was of major importance in the establishment of bargaining machinery and the recognition of trade unions. Similarly it has already been noted that in France the Matignon Agreement provided a major boost to union recognition, and the extension of bargaining rights and legislation in Sweden in the 1930s encouraged union recognition particularly amongst white collar workers. Unions had already gained recognition in certain areas in Australia before the government intervened to introduce compulsory arbitration but this intervention clearly helped extend wage regulation to some areas and centrally affected the way that collective bargaining developed. However, the position was rather different in Britain. The state here has always had a more passive role in industrial relations than in most other Western democracies and in line with this has not intervened as firmly to ensure union recognition or the extension of collective bargaining. Nevertheless, the government has not been entirely absent from the area. At various times it has stimulated even if it has not enforced development. For example, during the First World War the British government established the Whitley Committee,[8] and its reports, recommending amongst other things the setting up of Joint Industrial Councils, were a major factor in the development of national industry-based collective bargaining machinery after the First World War.

Both employers (and employers' associations) and governments, then, have had an impact on the speed and direction of the development of collective bargaining. So too, though, has the other major interest group involved in industrial relations, the trade unions. It would be a mistake to equate union growth with union recognition and the extension of collective bargaining. On occasions union growth has been encouraged by recognition, and sometimes recognition has been granted before a major union organisation in a plant or industry. Similarly, as has been noted, collective bargaining machinery sometimes has been established before a union has been strong enough to force such a development. As a result figures showing, for example, the increase in unionisation will not necessarily be the same as those showing the extension of collective bargaining. Nevertheless, it is clear that in the past, and at present where necessary, unions have continued to press for recognition from employers and the extension of bargaining rights. While they have not necessarily always been successful and such pressure has not always been a necessary prerequisite for the establishment of collective bargaining machinery, it has been an important factor in the equation. Where unions have not initiated the first moves towards the establishment of collective bargaining machinery, union growth and union interest in such areas undoubtedly has been a background factor in persuading others to make moves in this direction. Certainly the reverse has been true: when union membership has declined and unions have been seen as relatively weak, as during much of the inter-war period, employers have tried to take advantage of the situation and change if not eliminate the collective bargaining machinery. For example, in Britain, many of the Joint Industrial Councils set up after the reports of the Whitley Committee fell into disuse during the later 1920s and the 1930s and in the coal-mining industry employers used the weakness of the unions after the General Strike to press for moves from national to local bargaining.

The impact of trade unions on the development of collective bargaining, then, should not be underestimated. However, an interesting twist is given to this line of thought by Clegg[9] when he argues that when collective bargaining is the main way in which trade unions try to influence the terms and conditions of employment, not only will unions affect the development of collective bargaining but the development of bargaining will affect them. For example, he suggests that the level at which bargaining takes place (at the workshop level, regional, industry or national level) will affect several aspects of union behaviour: if bargaining is conducted on an industry or country-wide basis then union government will be relatively centralised, whereas if bargaining is conducted on a regional or plant basis it will be decentralised, and if bargaining is conducted at a high level unions are more likely to have developed schemes of industrial democracy than is the case if bargaining is conducted at a low level. Similarly, the degree of control exercised over collective agreements will affect other aspects of union behaviour: a high degree of control (that is where an agreement sets out to establish obligatory standards and erects effective machinery to see that standards are observed)[10] limits the power of workplace organisations compared to the central union organisation. Clegg also argues that although the structure of trade unionism (that is, the coverage by industry and grades) cannot be said to have been determined by the structure of collective bargaining (history alone can do that)[11], given that there is a historical explanation for the structure of trade unionism, the survival of particular patterns can be related to the structure of collective bargaining.

Clegg's ideas serve to illustrate the complexity of the relationship between the parties involved in industrial relations (he looked at trade unions; employers' associations could also have been examined) and the bargaining machinery, and as such point to an important lesson. Nonetheless, as far as trade unions are concerned their central interest in, and the reason for their support of, collective bargaining is because they believe (or in certain cases hope) that it will enable them to pursue the representation of their members' interests better; crucially, that it will allow them to negotiate better terms and conditions of employment.

THE IMPACT OF TRADE UNION ACTION THROUGH COLLECTIVE BARGAINING ON EARNINGS

If collective bargaining is, as has been argued, used and valued by trade unions in Western democracies primarily because they believe that through it they will be able to improve the terms and conditions of work of their members, then it is worthwhile looking at whether their expectations have been realised. Much of the evidence on the effectiveness of trade union action through collective bargaining in fact centres on the area of wages and earnings, though it is important to recognise at the outset that even this evidence is patchy and difficult to evaluate.

The best way to enter this debate is to look, first of all, at the changes that have taken place in this century in the distribution of the national income. Until fairly recently it was assumed that there had been very little change in the proportion of the national income accruing to labour. In 1939, Keynes wrote: 'the stability of the proportion of the national dividend accruing to labour is one of the most surprising and yet best established facts in the whole range of economic statistics'.[12] In fact, current evedence suggests that Keynes' statement needs to be modified.

Table 10 shows that although in the United Kingdom the proportion of the national income accruing to labour has remained constant for fairly lengthy periods, changes have occurred. Labour's share of the national income increased during both the First and the Second World Wars and between 1968 and 1975. As a result, if the whole of the period 1910 to 1976 is examined then labour's share of the national income increased from 55.3 per cent to 78.3 per cent. The picture is slightly more complicated than has been presented here because if the share of the national income accruing simply to wages were looked at then the same trend would not be discovered. Labour's share of the national income increased essentially because of increases in salaries, not wages, and because salary earners are now a much larger section of the workforce than they used to be. The details of the share of the national income accruing to labour vary in other Western democracies, but broadly similar patterns can be found. For example, in the USA labour's share of

Table 10:   The distribution of income between labour and property in the
United Kingdom 1910–76 (annual averages)

Year	Percentage of Gross National Product		Percentage of Gross Domestic Product	
	Labour	Property	Labour	Property
1910–14	55.3	44.7	60.2	39.8
1921–24	67.4	32.6	70.6	29.4
1925–29	66.4	33.6	70.5	29.5
1930–34	68.1	31.9	71.1	28.9
1935–38	67.1	32.9	70.0	30.0
1946–49	73.0	27.0	74.3	25.7
1950–54	72.1	27.9	73.7	26.3
1955–59	73.4	26.6	74.4	25.6
1960–63	73.6	26.4	74.5	25.5
1964–68	73.6	26.4	74.4	25.6
1969–73	75.6	24.4	76.6	23.4
1974	78.1	21.9	79.4	20.6
1975	80.2	19.8	81.0	19.0
1976	78.3	21.7	78.3	21.7

Source: B. Burkitt, D. Bowers, *Trade Unions and The Economy*, Macmillan, London, 1979.

the national income increased from 65.5 per cent in 1950 to 76.3 per cent in 1976.

This, however, is only the first stage of the debate. The next is to ask whether unions have been able to increase the wages of their members and, if they have done so, to ask whether their success has been at the expense of property owners or other (non-unionised) wage earners. Only if one can show that any gains unions might have made have been at the expense of property owners can one claim that unions through their wage bargaining have been responsible for at least some of the changes in the distribution of the national income.

There is some evidence that trade unions, in certain circumstances, have been able to increase the earnings of their members. Lewis,[13] in a study of the effect of unionisation on relative wages in the USA, estimated that unionisation had increased the wages of union members by about 15 per cent as compared to the wages of non-members: in a British study Pencavel[14] suggested that trade unions were able to increase the hourly earnings of their members above those of non-members by between nought to 10 per cent.

However, it is important to note that the estimates of the precise effect of unionisation on wages have differed. In part these differences may reflect the economic conditions that prevailed at the time of the estimates. They also point to the need for a better understanding of the way in which unions affect the wages of their members.

Phelps Brown's study[15] of the effect of unionisation and union activity presents one description on the way in which unions may be able to increase the earnings of members. He has suggested that there are two particular situations when union activity can be shown to have definite results. The first is when newly formed unions operate in a favourable environment (in terms of control of the supply of their labour and demand for the product) and can obtain a once and for all advantage which they may be able to retain afterwards; this is referred to as the 'impact effect'. The second is when unionised workers are able to resist wage cuts more satisfactorily than non-unionised workers; this is referred to as the 'ratchet effect'. The result, according to Phelps Brown, is that unionised workers can benefit when compared to non-unionised workers not because they get larger wage rises or smaller cuts in wage rates, but because the changes take place earlier or later and this means that unionised workers enjoy the high rate for a longer period of time.

In part, Phelps Brown's work in this area fits in with that of other writers: in particular, many have noted the ability of unionised workers to resist wage cuts longer than non-unionised workers. However, another dimension has been added by some who have referred to the possibility that in times of high demand unions, rather than gaining higher wage rises for their members, may actually prevent wages rising as fast as they would have done. The rationale behind this argument is that collective bargaining introduces certain rigidities into wage structures: collective agreements often run for a specified period, say a year or more, and while unions are able to use this to help them to resist wage cuts in periods of low demand, employers are able to use this to help them to resist demands for wage increases during periods of high demand. It might be imagined that this factor would be less important in Britain than, say in the USA because fixed term agreements are less common in Britain: however, Demery and McNabb[16] produce evidence to suggest that trade unions have had a 'wage-rigidity' effect in Britain as well.

The 'wage-rigidity' thesis is not accepted by all commentators. Reder,[17] using data from the USA, questions the basis of the 'wage-rigidity' thesis and argues that many writers have not paid sufficient attention to the complexity of the effect of political forces upon relative wages. Moore and Raisian[18] also argue for more detailed analysis of the 'wage-rigidity' thesis. They present data which uses industry as well as national based analysis, and show considerable variations in wage patterns and the effect of unionisation on them. They also argue that the effect of unionisation on wages may be different in recent years to what it was in the 1920s to 1960s period. The qualifications they introduce into the debate are important yet, as they recognise, currently 'the wage-rigidity hypothesis appears (to be) part of the "conventional wisdom" in the literature'.[19]

A further twist to this debate is introduced by the work of Johnson and Mieszkowski.[20] Reviewing the work of Lewis and others, they accept that unions increase the wages of their members relative to the wages of non-unionised workers. However, they argue that the benefits gained by unions for members are not gained at the expense of owners but at the expense of non-unionised workers. They stress that their conclusions (drawn from USA evidence) are for a partially unionised economy (in practice, as has been noted, unionisation is lower in the USA than in any other major Western nation). When they ask what the effect would be if the economy were more highly unionised, though, their answer is no less pessimistic for the impact of unionisation. They argue that if unionisation increases in a country 'the gains of "new" members will come in large measure at the expense of the workers who remain unorganised'. If unionisation should increase to such an extent that virtually all workers are covered, 'then, so long as there are no monopsonistic rents and unions are not able to "tax away" a share of monopoly profits, the distribution of income will be essentially the same as the distribution in an economy in which unions do not exist'.[21]

Other evidence challenges this view. Some commentators have argued that as unions recruit more members they are able to use their increased strength to raise wage levels and reduce profits. Phelps Brown[22] in some of his work has suggested that this may be a factor to take into account: however, he has argued that for unions to be able to raise the proportion of the national income accruing to labour they also need favourable economic conditions (the market environment needs to be such that owners cannot pass on wage increases in the form of higher prices but have to take a cut in profits).

The research evidence, then, raises a number of questions. Unions may affect the wages of their members and gain extra benefits for them, but are these benefits only gained when particular economic conditions prevail; are the benefits gained under one set of economic conditions lost when these conditions change; and do the benefits gained make any impact on the distribution of income between labour and property (or are the gains of unionised workers at the expense of other workers rather than property owners)? There is not a broad agreed view with which it is possible to conclude. The best one can say is that most of those who have looked at this question would accept that unions have had some effect on the earnings of their members and on the proportion of the national income gained by labour but, particularly in the latter case, the effect has been limited (for example, taxation may have had a greater effect).

It is also important to refer to a number of other issues before concluding this overview. For example, even some of the writers who accept that trade unions have been unable to increase the share of the national income accruing to labour through collective bargaining argue that the effect of trade unions on wages and earnings should not be ignored altogether. Some, taking their cue from the evidence which suggests that unions may have been able to resist wage cuts in times of low demand, have argued that although unions may not have been able to increase the share of the national income accruing to labour, they may have been able to prevent that share decreasing. Others have argued that unions, through collective bargaining, have been able to play a role in increasing economic growth, efficiency and real wages. Thus, although their intervention through collective bargaining has not resulted in labour increasing its share of the national income, it may have resulted in the size of the national income increasing faster than it would have done otherwise. It is also worthwhile noting that the effect unions have through bargaining on the wages of members, even if it is at the expense of non-members (as has been argued above), may still be considered important for those people who benefit. Many workers are as, if not more, interested in increasing their differentials over other workers as they are in increasing the proportion of the national income accruing to labour.

Further, one needs to be aware that the debate about the effect of trade union action through collective bargaining on wages and earnings by no means covers the whole of the area of the effect of collective bargaining on terms and conditions of employment. In recent years considerable emphasis has been placed on non-wage matters, particularly issues which previously have been viewed as managerial prerogatives: for example, discipline, supervision, hiring and firing. There is some evidence from British strike statistics of the increased union interest in this area: since the Second World War there has been a major increase in strikes said to have been started as a result of disputes over this range of issues (it is now the second most frequent recorded cause of strikes). Not all of this activity, nor all of the pressure on these issues has been the result of official union action; much has been initiated locally and often unofficially. Nevertheless, major restrictions on the rights of employers to discipline, hire and fire have been imposed in recent years. Some of these restrictions have been the result of government action but, of course, not all such government action has been independent of union action and pressure.

TRADE UNIONS, INFLATION AND THE LEVEL OF EMPLOYMENT

If the debate over the effect of trade union action on earnings and the distribution of wealth is complex, so too is the related debate over the effect that trade unions have on the rate of inflation and the level of employment. It is complicated not only because much of the empirical evidence is inconclusive but also because it involves different assumptions about the working of the economy and different economic schools of thought.

Inflation is by no means peculiar to the post Second World War period: the rapid inflation in Germany after the First World War is testimony to this. Nevertheless, the post Second World War years saw an increase in the general and persistent rate of inflation in Western democracies to about 3 to 4 per cent in the 1950s and 1960s and then to far higher ranges in the 1970s. Chamberlain, Cullen and Lewin[23] have produced figures that show a rate of inflation between 1970 and 1977 varying from 46 per cent in West Germany to 149 per cent in the United Kingdom (of the other countries covered, the USA and Canada returned figures at the lower end of the range, Australia, Japan and Italy at the higher end, while Sweden and France were between the two extremes).

It is hardly surprising, then, that in recent years considerable attention has been focused on explaining the causes of inflation. Essentially, two broad schools of thought exist, though within them there are differences of emphasis. One is normally referred to as the 'cost-push', the other as the 'demand-pull' school.

In outline the 'cost-push' school of thought argues that inflation is the result of increases in the costs of production which exert upward pressure on the price level. A variety of costs can be looked at under this heading, including the costs of raw materials and the costs of labour. Jackson, Turner and Wilkinson,[24] in their analysis of the causes of the increase in the rate of inflation in the early 1970s in Britain, argued that a variety of cost increases help to explain what happened. For example, the increase in food prices (partly a result of the Russian purchase of surplus grain from the USA), the increase in oil prices (following the 1973 Arab-Israeli War) and the increase in labour unrest (which Jackson *et al.* argue was largely brought about by the increase in direct taxation on wage earners in the late 1960s) are viewed as important factors. Together, and against a background of devaluations of the pound, they were sufficient to bring an end to the fragile stability of the 1950s and 1960s. According to Jackson *et al.*: 'The system could survive occasional shocks but was vulnerable to a combination of them.'[25]

From this point of view, then, trade union action may be one of the causes of the increase in costs that led in turn to the increase in the rate of inflation in the 1970s. However, while Jackson *et al.* recognise that 'unions do contribute to inflationary processes' they argue that not merely are 'unions far from being the only significant factor in the inflationary process', they are not even normally 'an independent factor in it'.[26] Union action, in pressing for higher wages, is usually a response to other factors (in the case of the early 1970s inflation, the increase in direct taxation).

One of the most widely discussed attempts to look in detail at the extent to which trade unions cause inflation is Hine's[27] examination of the effect of trade union recruitment policies on inflation. He looked at the rate of change in money wages between 1893 and 1961 (in a subsequent study also at the 1948–62 period)[28] and related it to changes in union density. The basis of his argument was that when unions attempt to recruit new members they try to make themselves appear more attractive by adopting more militant tactics in their relationship with employers and these militant tactics lead to higher wage claims. He concluded: 'It has been shown that an index of trade union pushfulness, namely the rate of change of unionisation, is closely associated with the rate of change of money wage rates and that this index cannot be explained by the level and/or rate of change in the demand for labour.'[29] However,

Hines' findings have not gone unchallenged. Purdy and Zis[30] questioned the link that he assumed between union density and militancy, Thomas and Stoney[31] argued that the model he produced was 'dynamically unstable' while Wilkinson and Burkitt[32] suggested that when his variables were respecified so as to align them to the mid-point of the year the relationship between wages and unionisation was far weaker. A further study by Burkitt (this time with Bowers) suggested that there might be a strong correlation between money wages and unionisation in the inter-war years but that there was no relationship at all between 1949 and 1967. In part the differences outlined above are a reflection of the difficulty of obtaining adequate data and testing the relationships under investigation.

A 'cost-push' explanation, then, can encompass the view that trade union action can help to cause inflation even though the precise impact of this action is the subject of considerable debate and has not been detailed even to the satisfaction of members of the 'cost-push' school. The views of this school can also encompass the position that by negotiating significant increases in earnings trade unions might help to increase the level of unemployment. For example, if an employer is unable to recoup higher costs by charging a higher price for the goods he produces then he can either accept a reduction in the level of profit or attempt to reduce costs: if high wage costs are the main problem then he may reduce those costs by reducing the amount of labour he employs (this could mean a reduction in the level of production or a substitution of capital for labour). However, if this particular example is followed through it is clear that none of this is inevitable. The employer may be able to charge higher prices (particularly if others are doing so), he may be able to reduce non-labour costs (and trade union pressure may mean that he will try to do so first) and even if one employer reduces the amount of labour he employs the overall level of unemployment need not rise if others take on the surplus. In essence, then, a 'cost-push' explanation can encompass the view that trade union pressure for higher wages can increase the level of unemployment but whether this will be the case or not will be dependent on other factors as well, and the precise effect of trade union pressure for higher wages on the level of employment is a matter for detailed debate.

The 'demand-pull' school of thought offers a different kind of explanation and a different approach to most of the issues referred to so far. According to this point of view, inflation is the result of excess demand in the economy, the excess demand being created by government policy. Thus the inflation experienced by Western industrial nations in the post Second World War years can be explained by the commitment of governments to full employment; their attempts to deal with unemployment through fiscal or monetary policy led to the creation of excess demand. The role of trade unions, if one adopts this perspective, is limited. Trade unions may negotiate higher wage rates which will lead to higher costs: however, they will only be able to do so if government policy has created excess demand in the market.

The link between unemployment and inflation is taken further by the work of Phillips.[33] His study involved an examination of changes in wage rates and the level of unemployment in the United Kingdom between 1861 and 1957. He argued that there was a strong and definable relationship between the two variables: when unemployment was at about 2.5 per cent of the total workforce wage increases would be broadly in line with productivity, and prices would be stable: when unemployment was below this level the rate of wage increases would rise and presumably so would prices. Thus, according to this view there was a trade-off between the level of wage increases (and presumably price increases, thus also inflation) and the level of unemployment, and governments faced a clear choice. Although Phillips' findings were based on a study of the economy of the United Kingdom, his work has been replicated elsewhere and discussion of what has become known as the 'Phillips curve' has been widespread. For 'demand-pull' theorists the Phillips curve might be used to enable them to determine the level of inflation that a particular level of 'excess demand' for labour (or lower unemployment) would give. However, recently doubt has been thrown on the stability of the Phillips curve. In their study of USA data Samuelson and Solow[34] suggested that the relationship between unemployment, prices and wages seemed to change after the Second World War. Before the war, when the level of unemployment was about 3 per cent, the level of wage increases could be kept to about 3 per cent, about the same as the rise in the level of productivity. After the war an unemployment rate of 4 to 5 per cent would have been needed to keep the rate of wage increases to 3 per cent. This evidence that the Phillips curve could shift has since been reinforced and suggestions have been put forward as to why this might happen. These suggestions have included changes in the operation of the labour market and the possibility that trade union action might succeed in forcing higher wage rises at a particular level of unemployment.

Some 'demand-pull' theorists have linked discussion of the Phillips curve to what they term the 'natural rate of unemployment', which in essence is the rate at which inflation will be steady. From one point of view, in the long term the economy will always adjust to the natural rate of unemployment. Such a point of view gives trade unions only restricted scope to influence events. However, others from within the 'demand-pull' school accept that there are imperfections in the labour market. Despite tight monetary controls unions may push for higher wage rates: if they do so they will not cause inflation but their action will result in a reduction in the willingness of employers to hire labour and thus an increase in the rate of unemployment.

One result of having such different schools of thought on the causes of inflation is that there is widespread disagreement on how the evidence about the role of trade unions should be interpreted. This can be highlighted by reference to two recent reviews of this debate which were published at approximately the same time and looked at similar evidence. One said: 'The weight of evidence suggests that trade-union bargaining power can effect money wage movements and introduce an inflationary bias into the labour market. In seeking to maintain their members' real living standards unions escalate the reaction of wages to price changes, while their existence seems to facilitate the generalisation of key wage bargains.'[35] The other said that 'trade unions in Britain and the USA have had relatively insignificant effects on the rate of wage inflation. Market forces appear to have been the dominant cause of wage inflation, and expansionary government policies have probably been the source of the market forces which have caused the rapid wage inflation which has characterised the industrialised countries in most of the post-war period.'[36]

It should also be noted that even if one could show that union action had an appreciable affect on the rate of inflation or the level of unemployment this would not necessarily imply that unions could be expected to act in any other way. In part, at least, unions pursue higher wages because of pressure from their members, and this pressure may be generated by rising expectations, rising prices (which may or may not have been caused by wage rises: in the case of a price and wages spiral the origin is probably of little interest once the trends have been established), or changes in wage differentials. Of course, they may also pursue higher wages because they view this as a way of reducing inequalities in society and giving labour a greater share of the national wealth. Whatever the reason, because in most Western nations (with the possible exception of some Scandinavian countries, in particular Sweden) unions operate sectionally, few can afford not to press for the highest possible wage level. Thus in the absence of any fairly tight agreement on wage levels across industries (in most cases government enforced) unions would probably feel that not to press for the highest possible wage level would be sacrificing the interests of their members, either to those of workers in other industries or to employers. The suggestion that higher wage levels on their own might lead to greater unemployment probably will not be sufficient to lead to a general reduction in wage claims because not only is the evidence difficult to evaluate but also in many cases even if the effect exists it is not necessarily a direct one.

CONCLUSIONS

Most trade unions in Western industrial nations have as one of their primary aims the improvement of the terms and conditions of employment of their members. This is not their only aim but it is an important, probably the most important, one. Again, most Western unions pursue this aim primarily through collective bargaining.

The available evidence about the effectiveness of union action to improve their members' terms and conditions of employment, in particular their earnings, is inconclusive, though on balance there is little to suggest that they have been able to make anything more than limited steps forward. Other factors, like taxation, may have been as responsible for what progress has been made. Similarly, if one looks at possible negative consequences of union action in this area, the evidence is inconclusive but on balance suggests that at the most they have had only a limited impact on the level of inflation or the level of employment. Other cost rises and government policy seem to have been more important.

However, one line of thought that has not been explored so far is that union action over economic issues, while it may have had only limited effect in this restricted area, may have had more of an effect on and even may have inhibited the pursuit of other objectives; in particular, broad social and political objectives. This will be examined in the next chapter.

NOTES

1. N.W. Chamberlain, D.E. Cullen, D. Lewin, *The Labor Sector*, McGraw-Hill, New York, 1980.
2. E.V. Schneider, *Industrial Sociology*, McGraw-Hill, London, 1971.
3. P. Taft, P. Ross, 'American labor violence: its causes, character and outcome' in H.E. Graham, T.R. Gurr (eds), *Violence in America*, Bantam, New York, 1980.
4. H.A. Clegg, *The Changing System of Industrial Relations in Great Britain*, Blackwell, Oxford, 1979.
5. *Ibid.*, p. 64.
6. *Ibid.*, p. 65.
7. In this case a minority of employees striked and then joined a union. The employer dismissed all of the strikers.
8. *Committee on the Relations between Employers and Employed* Reports, HMSO, London, 1916–18 cd 8606, 9001, 9002, 9099, 9153.
9. H.A. Clegg, *Trade Unionism under Collective Bargaining*, Blackwells, Oxford, 1976.
10. *Ibid.*, p. 9.
11. *Ibid.*, p. 10.
12. J.E. Keynes, 'Relative movements of real wages and output', *Economic Journal*, 1934, quoted by B. Burkitt, D. Bowers, *Trade Unions and the Economy*, Macmillan, London, 1979.
13. H.G. Lewis, *Unionism and Relative Wages in the United States*, Chicago U.P., 1965.
14. J.H. Pencavel, 'The distribution and efficiency effect of trade unions in Britain', *British Journal of Industrial Relations*, vol. XV, (1977), no. 2, p. 137–56.
15. E.H. Phelps Brown, *The Economics of Labour*, Yale U.P., New Haven, 1962.
16. D. Demery, R. McNabb, 'The effects of demand on the union relative wage effect in the United Kingdom', *British Journal of Industrial Relations*, vol. XXI (1978), no. 3, pp. 303–308.
17. M.W. Reder, 'The Theory of union wage policy', *Review of Economics and Statistics*, vol. 34 (1952), pp. 34–45.
18. W.J. Moore, J. Raisian, 'Cyclical sensitivity of union/nonunion relative wage effects', *Journal of Labour Research*, vol. 1 (1980), no. 1, pp. 115–32.
19 *Ibid.*, p. 121.

20. H.G. Johnson, P. Mieszkowski 'The effects of unionisation on the distribution of income : a general equilibrium approach', *Quarterly Journal of Economics*, vol. XXXIV (1970), no. 4, pp. 537–61.
21. *Ibid.*, p. 561.
22. E.H. Phelps Brown, 'The long-term movement of real wages', in J.T. Dunlop (ed.), *The Theory of Wage Determination*, Macmillan, London, 1957.
23. *Op. cit.*
24. D. Jackson, H.A. Turner, F. Wilkinson, *Do Trade Unions Casuse Inflation?* Cambridge U.P., London, 1975.
25. *Ibid.*
26. *Ibid.*, p. 113.
27. A.G. Hines, 'Trade unions and wage inflation in the United Kingdom, 1893–1961', *Review of Economic Studies*, vol. XXI (1964), pp. 221–52.
28. A.G. Hines, 'Wage inflation in the United Kingdom 1948–1962: a disaggregated study', *Economic Journal*, vol. 79 (1969), pp. 66–89.
29. A.G. Hines, (1964), *op. cit.*, p. 242.
30. D.L. Purdy, G. Zis, 'On the concept and measurement of union militancy' in D. Candler, D.C. Purdy (eds) *Inflation and the Labour Markets*, Manchester U.P., 1974.
31. R.L. Thomas, P.J.M. Stoney, 'A note on the dynamic properties of the Hines inflation model', *Review of Economic Studies*, vol. 37 (1970), pp. 286–94.
32. R.K. Wilkinson, B. Burkitt, 'Wage determination and trade unions' *Scottish Journal of Political Economy*, vol. 20, pp. 107–21.
33. A.W. Phillips, 'The relation between unemployment and the rate of change of money wages in the United Kingdom, 1861–1957' *Economica*, vol. 25 (1958), pp. 238–99.
34. P.A. Samuelson, R.A. Solow, 'Analytical Aspects of Anti-Inflation Policy', *American Economic Review*, vol. 50 (1960), pp. 177–94.
35. D. Burkitt, D. Bowers, *op. cit.*
36. C. Mulvey, *The Economic Analysis of Trade Unions*, Martin Robertson, Oxford, 1978.

Chapter Seven

TRADE UNIONS: CONFLICT OR COMPROMISE

POLITICAL OBJECTIVES

The new model unions established in Britain in the middle of the nineteenth century were essentially fairly conservative bodies. Their aim was to fashion organisations capable of defending the narrow interests of craftsmen. The unskilled manual workers' unions that developed at the end of the nineteenth century followed a different course. They were much more radical bodies, in many instances supporting broad socialist movements. These early divisions have never completely disappeared: there have always been different political orientations within the British trade union movement, though they have not always followed an unskilled/craft worker divide. Today most British unions would like to see some change to the political/economic structure of society. Nearly all would want to see the change take the same direction but they differ over the extent of the change they would like to see. In some cases the demands they make indicate support for almost total social ownership of the means of production while in others the demands suggest that some reduction in the disparities of wealth really are all that is sought.

In many Western European nations and in Australia the picture is similar. There is general, though uneven, support for radical social change. The support is possibly strongest amongst sections of the French and Italian trade union movements and weakest in countries like West Germany.

Trade unions in the USA, on the other hand, are far less politically directed. In particular there is far less questioning of the basis of the current political/economic structure. Thus, it might be noted that an International Labour Organisation Commission, after a study of trade unionism in the USA, said that they were

... struck in their discussions with union leaders by the almost total absence of any questioning of the bases of the American economic and social system. Unlike many labour movements in Europe and elsewhere, the trade unions in the United States did not appear even to consider, still less to advocate, any major change in the system in which they operated, in spite of the many bitter battles that have occurred between unions and capital.[1]

Some commentators have used this to suggest that there are two types of trade unionism in Western nations, welfare unionism and business unionism.[2] The former implies that while trade unions are interested in industrial matters relating directly to their membership, this is not their sole concern: they are also a pressure group and a 'cause movement' with wider aims and aspirations. The latter implies that the objectives of the unions are much more restricted: they concentrate on industrial matters and show an interest in political matters only when they are of direct relevance to their members. Such distinctions may be a little oversimplified, if only because it is not easy to specify a union's aims and objectives: unions are often coalitions of a number of different interests and orientations rather than simply expressions of what is stated in, say, their rules or constitutions. Nevertheless, the distinction between welfare and business unionism does have some value, if only because it enables one to stress the variety of approaches taken by trade unions towards political matters.

TRADE UNIONS AND POLITICAL PARTIES

At the end of the nineteenth century many British trade unions were uncertain about how to pursue their political objectives. For a while some saw the Liberal Party as offering a better vehicle for the expression of their political objectives than any of the existing socialist organisations. As a result of the 1885 election the number of trade unionists in the House of Commons was increased from two to eleven but all of them sat as Liberals. The Miners Federation of Great Britain (later to become the National Union of Mineworkers (NUM)) maintained their support for the Liberal Party until 1911. However, by the end of the nineteenth century many unions were beginning to believe that separate socialist parliamentary representation was essential.

Many trade unionists, particularly leaders of unskilled workers' unions, were active in the Independent Labour Party and when the

Labour Representation Committee was set up in 1900 a number of
unions and trades councils affiliated (covering 353,070 members).
These early affiliations were soon joined by others (by 1903 unions
and councils representing 847,315 members were affiliated). Interestingly, in the light of the discussion about the distinction between welfare and business unionism, the main spur to affiliation
was the realisation that political representation was important if
unions were to achieve their industrial let alone their broader social
objectives. This realisation was the result of a series of adverse
court decisions, in particular in the *Quinn* v. *Leatham*[3] and *Taff
Vale*[4] cases, which severely restricted the ability of unions to engage in strike action, and which could only be reversed by parliamentary action. The Labour Representation Committee changed
its name to the Labour Party following the 1906 general election.

British trade unions have maintained these early strong links
with the Labour Party. Many trade unionists today pay a political
levy to their union to allow them to become affiliated members of
the Labour Party. In practice this means that the trade unions hold
a considerable proportion of the total membership of the Labour
Party, and currently at the Annual Conference the union block
votes account for approaching 90 per cent of all votes. It also means
that the trade unions provide a similar proportion of the Labour
Party's income from membership subscription. This is added to at
various points by special donations, particularly before important
elections.

As well as these membership links there are a number of other
important points of contact. For example, many trade unions spon-
sor Labour Party parliamentary candidates. This means that they
pay at least a proportion of the election expenses of the candidates.
While the extent of the overt control sponsoring unions can exert
over these MPs is a matter of debate[5] it is clear that such devices
help to cement the links between the Labour Party and the trade
unions. So too does the fact that many Labour MPs have been, and
some still are, active trade unionists. On a number of occasions
Labour governments have tried to maintain the support of the
trade unions by inviting their leaders to stand for Parliament and
join the Cabinet: for instance the Wilson government of the 1960s
invited Frank Cousins, the then leader of the Transport and General Workers Union, to join the Cabinet, and a parliamentary seat
was found for him. Such direct invitations to join the Cabinet may
be relatively rare but they serve to highlight the close links between
the trade unions and the Labour Party.

It is in Australia that the relationship between the trade unions and the Labour Party is closest to the British model. The Australian (like the British) Labour Party was set up, in this case in 1891, with the strong support of the trade unions. These early links were later built upon and, again like their British counterparts, today most major Australian trade unions are affiliated to the Australian Labour Party. Arguably in some instances the links between the Australian Labour Party and trade unions have been taken further than in Britain. As in Britain, the unions provide considerable financial support through affiliation fees and election expenses: however, the organisational links between unions and the Labour Party are closer than in Britain (in Western Australia prior to 1963 one organisation was the supreme body for both the Party and the union) and the unions exert greater influence over the voting patterns of union-supported politicians. One commentator has concluded that, to a greater extent than in any other country, Australian unions 'tend to regard the Labour Party as being the creation of the unions and therefore subject to their control'.[6]

The ties between the political parties and the trade unions in Italy have been almost equally as close as those in Britain and Australia but the basis of the relationship is rather different. The trade unions, re-established since the end of the Second World War, have been supported by the political parties rather than the other way around. Kendall has commented that each of the major trade union confederations 'is to some extent dependent on funds from outside sources', largely the political parties, and in the case of the CGIL and CISL (the Italian Confederation of Labour and the Italian Confederation of Workers Unions) 'key posts in the secretariat have become fiefs of the political parties with which they are associated'.[7] Another commentator argued that after the Second World War Italian trade unions were substantially financed by the political parties and that the 'CGIL leaders were often assigned to the trade union movement by the political parties, with individuals shifting from political to trade union operations or the reverse as the party decisions dictated'.[8]

In recent years there have been some attempts to weaken the hold of political parties over Italian trade unions. In part this has been a response to the moves towards workplace bargaining and greater rank and file influence in decision-making. For some time there has been evidence that the majority of the union membership did not share the views of their leaders about the desirability of strong links between the unions and the political parties. Important moves on this issue were made in 1969 when all of the major trade union confederations took up the issue of political control. The largest union, the CGIL, asked its General Secretary to resign his post with the Communist party and give up his seat in Parliament: instead he resigned his union job. The struggle in Italy on this matter is not yet over. The political parties have been reluctant to relinquish control over the trade unions and the financial ties have proved to be important. Nevertheless the strains created by the relationship are clear and may have an important effect on the future direction of Italian industrial relations.

In other Western European countries a variety of different links exist between trade unions and political parties. In Sweden trade unions affiliate to local branches of the Social Democratic Party, in West Germany the trade unions do not directly affiliate to any political party but there are strong links (overlapping membership and personal ties: in 1976, 63 per cent of those elected to the Bundestag were union members though only a small proportion were officials) between most unions and the Social Democratic Party, while in France the unions are notionally completely independent from the political parties though in practice there are close links between the main trade union federation, the Confédération Générale du Travail (CGT), and the Communist Party.

Trade unions in the USA probably have the loosest ties with political parties of any unions in Western nations. Historically neither of the two major union federations, the AFL and the CIO, has played a particularly active role in general political matters. It is often argued, with some reason, that the CIO was more politically aware than the AFL (Samuel Gompers, one of the foremost AFL leaders, argued against all forms of partisan activity by the Federation) before the Second World War but neither had an entirely consistent political line. The position changed a little after the end of the Second World War when the Republican government introduced the Taft-Hartley legislation. This alerted both the AFL and the CIO to the importance of political activity, even for narrow industrial purposes, and when the two federations merged in 1955 the new organisation took a stronger interest in political affairs.

In recent years USA unions have been far more active in political matters. They have been major financial contributors to political campaigns: a good deal of the money has been channelled to candidates through the AFL/CIO's Committee on Political Action, though in financial terms individual unions remain the major contributors.[9] Trade unions have also lent considerable organisational assistance to election campaigns, including registration drives, and seem to have had some success in endorsing particular candidates and persuading their members to vote for them. Wilson[10] recalls that the AFL/CIO's Committee on Political Action endorsed a Republican candidate, Richard Schweiker, in the 1972 Senate election. Support for Republicans was unusual and it presented a useful test as to whether the AFL/CIO could persuade its members to switch from their normal political allegiance. The evidence is that they did, for although 72.9 per cent voted for the Democratic candidate for Governor (elected at the same time) 73.9 per cent voted for the Republican, Schweiker: in fact the AFL/CIO had recommended their members to vote in a cross-party fashion for both of the successful candidates. More generally it is interesting to note that a report by an AFL/CIO executive in 1975 argued that it had achieved a 70 per cent success rate in getting candidates for the House of Representatives, Senate and state governorships elected, and trade union support played an important role in Carter's election victory of 1976 (63 per cent of union voters supported him as against 36 per cent of non-union voters).

It is crucial, though, to stress that while USA unions have been involved in politics they have chosen to influence political decisions through indirect means (financing and endorsing favoured candidates) rather than by direct affiliation to a political party. Further, though generally they have supported the Democrats they have been willing to switch their allegiance between political parties and, as has been illustrated, have done so on particular occasions.

TRADE UNIONS AND DIRECT POLITICAL ACTION

The links between trade unions and political parties in some Western nations have meant that frequently a trade union's industrial and political aspirations have been pursued separately. The industrial aspirations have been pursued through collective bargaining or by trying to persuade governments to introduce certain kinds of employment and industrial legislation. The political aspirations have been pursued through the political party. This has been the case not only where the union movement has been directly affiliated but also where the union movement has simply had close ties with one particular party.

Nevertheless, in some cases trade unions have felt that they themselves should engage in direct political action, or that their industrial activities should be designed to have important political consequences. Historically such views have been most systematically and importantly expressed through the doctrines of syndicalism.

There are clear links between syndicalism and Marxism, with the former drawing strongly on the latter for its analysis of the structure of capitalist society. However, syndicalism also has been strongly influenced by anarchism: one author has referred to syndicalism as 'the industrial manifestation of anarchism'.[11]

The centre of attention for syndicalists is the syndicat, an industrial, workplace-based trade union. They believe that the syndicats are the bodies that can initiate revolutionary social change and envisage that industrial activity in particular areas will culminate in a general strike. There is a difference of opinion over what else, if anything, is necessary to bring about revolutionary change. Some believe that the general strike in itself will be sufficient, while others, like Malatesta, have argued that the general strike is simply the prelude to armed insurrection. Thus Malatesta stated that while the general strike always seemed to him to be 'an excellent means for starting the social revolution', syndicalists must be on their guard 'against falling into the disastrous illusion that the general strike makes armed insurrection unnecessary'.[12]

However, the crucial feature of syndicalism in this context is that it sees no role for an independent political party. Political change, specifically revolutionary change, is initiated and carried through by the trade unions or syndicats. After the revolution the political party again has no role. The syndicat is seen as the basis for post-revolutionary government: although there may be some federal organisation to co-ordinate activities, such an organisation would have very limited powers and little, if anything, in the way of a bureaucratic administration.

Syndicalism had its strongest influence on the French trade union movement, particularly at the end of the nineteenth and beginning of the twentieth centuries. The main French trade union federation, the Confédération Générale du Travail (CGT), adopted syndicalism 'as its ideological guideline down to 1914'.[13] The influence of syndicalism waned somewhat subsequently, though Clegg has argued that while French trade unions have undergone considerable change since the early part of the twentieth century, syndicalism and the message it had for trade unions (that 'trade union action (was) capable of achieving all that workers could want, including the revolution')[14] has not entirely lost its appeal. It is, he claims, one of the reasons why French trade unions are still more committed to direct political action themselves than movements in other countries. French trade unions have not abandoned collective bargaining altogether, but they place a high value on political action.

Syndicalism was not only influential in France. It had some adherents in most Western nations. In Britain it reached its highest point of popularity at the beginning of the twentieth century, in particular just before the start of the First World War. The British version of syndicalism was strongly influenced by both the French and North American experience. The French influence could be seen through the wide circulation of the views of Sorel,[15] in particular his advocacy of the general strike: the North American influence could be seen through the popularity of the Industrial Workers of the World, an organisation founded in Chicago in 1905 with the aim of reorganising trade unionism on an industrial basis.

One of the leaders of the syndicalist movement in Britain was Tom Mann, a member of the engineers' union and one of the most influential figures in the development of trade unionism in the late nineteenth century. In 1910 he started a monthly journal, *The Industrial Syndicalist*, and the Industrial Syndicalist Education League. He also began to agitate for amalgamation between unions operating in the same industry and achieved some success with the formation of the National Transport Workers Federation (covering both dockers and seamen).

Mann also found support for his cause amongst the ranks of the South Wales miners. Partly as a reaction against the policies of the national union leadership, they established their own unofficial organisation, to become known as the Unofficial Reform Committee, to put forward a more radical programme. In 1911 they produced a pamphlet entitled *Miners, Wake Up*, in which they called for greater militancy, and the following year they published the pamphlet *The Miners' Next Step*. This argued that the miners ought to fight for more than merely the nationalisation of their industry; they ought to fight for workers' control. It said that the miners themselves should 'determine under what conditions and how the work should be done. This would mean real democracy in real life, making for real manhood and womanhood. Any other form of democracy (would be) a delusion and a snare.'[16] Subsequently the members of this unofficial committee took over many of the official posts of the South Wales Miners Federation.

Pelling,[17] however, warns us not to exaggerate the importance of syndicalism for the British trade union movement as a whole. He notes that the amalgamation movement launched by Tom Mann did not get very far. Apart from the formation of the National Transport Workers Federation the movement

> ... secured only one noteworthy success before 1914, and even that was an incomplete one. In 1913 the Amalgamated Society of Railway Servants united with the General Railway Workers Union, and a smaller body called the United Pointsmen and Signalmen's Society, to form the National Union of Railwaymen. But both the Associated Society of Locomotive Engineers and Firemen and the Railway Clerks Association retained their separate existence, so that it could not be said that an 'industrial' union of railwaymen had been achieved.[18]

The Triple Alliance, formed in 1914 between the miners, railwaymen and transport workers, because it was an agreement to undertake simultaneous industrial action and therefore seemed to be moving in the direction of a general strike, might have been seen as a more hopeful sign by syndicalists. However, the Triple Alliance was a long way from the syndicalists' ideal of a political strike: 'while its object was to bring pressure on the Government as well as on the employers, it did not have any ulterior purpose beyond the immediate improvement of the wages and conditions of the workers concerned'.[19]

A related doctrine, guild socialism, probably had as much impact on British trade unions in this period as syndicalism in its pure form. Guild socialism was a 'milder' version of syndicalism. It accepted the notion of workers' control of industry but it differed from the more straightforward version of syndicalism in two important ways. First, it placed less emphasis on the role of 'direct action' by workers as a way of bringing about the desired change. Second, it placed more constraints on the freedom of action of the workers when controlling their own industry. Thus Cole, one of its foremost exponents, said: 'workers ought to control the normal conduct of industry; but they ought not to regulate the price of commodities at will, to dictate to the consumer what he shall consume, or, in short, to exploit the community as the individual profiteer exploits it today'. The solution according to Cole was for 'a division of functions between the State as the representative of the organised consumers and the Trade Unions, or bodies arising out of them through industrial unionism (he called these the National Guilds), as the representatives of the organised producers'.[20]

Guild socialism, like syndicalism, found support amongst members of the miners' union. In their evidence to the Sankey Commission, established at the end of the First World War to investigate affairs in the coal-mining industry,[21] a number of leaders of the Miners Federation argued for the workers' control of the industry. Hodges, then secretary of the Federation, wrote explicitly of how he saw the nationalisation of the mines as the first step along the road to guild socialism. Guild socialism also found support amongst other branches of the union movement, particularly in the immediate post First World War years. In some industries unions started to try to encourage the move towards guild socialism by organising their own co-operatives: for example, trade unions formed a number of guilds in the building industry and initially they successfully contracted for work, particularly from local authorities.

The guild socialist movement, though, started to weaken in the early 1920s. The attempts to establish co-operatives faced greater difficulties because of the recession: in 1922 the National Building Guild had to go into liquidation. The appeal of workers' control also seemed to wane, especially for the official union movement: by the mid 1920s strong representations began to be made (which eventually found majority support) for the view that unions should not be involved in the management of publicly owned industry.

The General Strike of 1926 in effect marked the end of an era for the British trade union movement. Subsequently, membership declined and unions increasingly became concerned to preserve their organisations against external pressure. It is even debatable whether the General Strike itself should be seen as a significant 'political' act by the trade union movement. Although a general strike fits well into the syndicalist vision of trade union action designed to bring about political change, it is arguable that in this particular instance the union leaders, particularly the TUC, never intended to challenge the social and political order: for them the General Strike had industrial rather than political significance. Phillips, in his comment on the approach of the union movement at the time of the General Strike, argues that 'it was predominantly defensive in its objectives, disinclined to state its purpose in ideological terms, concerned primarily with the achievement of an effective organisation and internal discipline, not with any long term programme of social and political reconstruction'.[22]

In many ways the beginning of the twentieth century was the high point for political action by the trade union movements of most Western nations, although there has been evidence of political action since then. For example, the campaign and strikes organised by the British trade union movement against the 1971 Industrial Relations Act could be viewed as political action. The strikes were classified as political rather than industrial stoppages by the Department of Employment and as a result did not appear in their regular series of strike statistics. Clearly the aim of the campaign was to change government policy and as such was politically directed. However, at least for the official trade union movement, it was action designed to make an impact on the political sphere only in so far as it was necessary to do so to change the government's policy over industrial relations: there was no overt attempt by the official leadership to change the social and political structure of the country. Similarly, the strikes organised by the TUC against the government's economic policy in 1980 essentially had an industrial focus, even though it was recognised that action had to be directed against political bodies. In that case it is interesting to record that the TUC made strenuous efforts to deny that they were calling a 'general strike': they preferred the phrase 'Day of Action'.

Perhaps the best example of political action by trade unions in Western nations since the Second World War is to be found in France. The action of workers and students in 1968 clearly had a mixture of political and industrial motives. Their takeover of factories also had echoes of the syndicalist strategies dominant in earlier periods in the French trade union movement. One commentator, Guerin,[23] argued that the labour unrest of May 1968 showed that the spirit of syndicalism, for him in particular anarchosyndicalism, was not dead in France. Nevertheless, although subsequent strikes, particularly in the mid 1970s, reawakened memories of the 1968 unrest, these strikes had a primarily economic aim and the political aims of 1968 seem to have faded into the background as far as the unions are concerned, at least for the moment.

In most countries there are factions in the trade union movement which believe that unions should be used directly to pursue political objectives. Often these are the same people who believe that unions should strive to obtain 'workers' control' of industry. However, as far as the official trade union movement is concerned there are few Western nations where this view comes anywhere near holding the majority. Probably it comes nearest to doing so in France, though even the French trade union movement has not entirely forsaken economic action: as Clegg asserts, maybe 'the correct verdict is that French trade unions are ambivalent between collective bargaining and political action'.[24]

THE POLITICAL IMPLICATIONS OF TRADE UNIONS: THE MARXIST PERSPECTIVE

The discussion so far has centred on the way in which unions have tried to influence political events and decisions. However, many commentators have been concerned to discover not only what the political aims and methods of unions have been but also what effect trade union organisation and action could have and has had. In essence the question has been: are the activities of trade unions ever likely to result, whether intended or unintended, in a major and radical change in the nature of society, or do their actions inhibit such change?

Early Marxist writers clearly believed that trade unions held the potential to contribute to radical social change. Trade unions were seen as an expression of the common interest of the working class (recognition that workers had a common interest in fighting the ruling class, rather than fighting amongst themselves, was an important stage in the movement towards revolutionary social change). They were also seen by writers like Engels as an important way of raising class consciousness. Thus Engels argued that as 'schools of war, the unions are unexcelled': he described union-organised strikes as 'the military school of the working men in which they prepare themselves for the great struggle which cannot be avoided'.[25]

This does not mean that these early Marxist writers did not see any dangers in trade union action. For example, Marx argued that while trade unions 'work well as centres of resistance against the encroachments of capital' they would fail in their objectives if they indulged in the 'injudicious use of their power' or if they limited 'themselves to a guerrilla war against the effects of the existing system, instead of simultaneously trying to change it'.[26] Nevertheless, despite recognising such dangers, Marx and Engels viewed trade unions as organisations with considerable potential and as important vehicles for revolutionary change.

While these early Marxist writers (and others like syndicalists, with views which leant on Marxism for their understanding of industrial society) on balance were optimistic about the impact of trade unionism and trade union action, a number of later Marxist commentators showed rather more caution. For example, Lenin[27] argued that trade unions tended to concentrate on economic matters which often were only of sectional interest (such as the improvement of conditions in their own industry or factory). Such concentration was a mistake because it meant that workers often ignored non-economic issues (like the flogging of peasants, the corruption of officials) which might be of greater importance. As a result, Lenin argued that there was a need to go beyond purely 'trade union consciousness' (that is, the conviction that it is necessary to combine in unions to fight employers and to compel the government to pass necessary labour legislation) and approach 'class consciousness'. The development of class consciousness could not be achieved by trade union action alone: in order to develop class consciousness the working class would have to rely on explanations of socialism which grew out of 'the philosophical, historical and economic theories elaborated by elected representatives of the propertied class, by intellectuals'.[28]

Others writing around the same time expressed similar reservations about the impact of trade unions. For example, Trotsky argued that the effect of trade union activity might be limited because unions were being 'incorporated' into the state. Trade unions, in all kinds of societies, competed with capitalists to obtain the favour of the state. In order to prove their value trade union leaders tried to demonstrate how indispensable and reliable they were, and thus withdrew from radical action. Trotsky, like another writer from the same period, Rosa Luxemburg,[29] also argued that a gap had opened up between union leaders and rank and file members. In periods of class struggle the leaders were likely to oppose radical action and concentrate on the maintenance of their own organisations.

None of these writers dismissed trade unions altogether. For example, Trotsky argued that in the 'struggle for partial and transitional demands, the workers now more than ever before need mass organisations, principally trade unions'. Writing in 1938 he said that the 'powerful growth of trade unionism in France and the United States is the best refutation of the preachments of those ultra-left doctrinaires who have been teaching that trade unions have "outlived their usefulness"'.[30] However, they all believed that the impact of trade unions was likely to be limited and that on their own trade unions were unlikely to initiate revolutionary social change.

The role of trade unions in bringing about revolutionary social change, and in particular their relationship with other bodies interested in similar activity, was examined in some detail by another writer from the same period, Gramsci. One of his best known works contains an analysis of the operation of the workers' councils in Italy and their relationship to the trade union movement.[31] He argued that the trade union movement as it existed in Italy and throughout Western Europe in the early twentieth century was a type of 'proletarian organisation specific to the historical period dominated by capital'. Such trade unions had developed as a response to capitalist society: because workers were treated as a commodity they had banded together to sell their commodity. As a result trade unions were rather like monopolistic firms selling labour power. They were essentially competitive, not communist, bodies. Thus, the unions could not be 'the instrument for a radical renovation of society': they could 'provide the proletariat with efficient bureaucrats, technical experts on industrial questions of a general kind', but they could not 'be the basis for proletarian power'.[32]

According to Gramsci, the proletarian dictatorship could only be embodied in a type of organisation that was specific to the activity of producers rather than wage earners. The factory council was the 'nuclear cell' of this organisation. It was a body in which all branches of labour were represented in proportion to the contribution they made to production. 'Its raison d'être is in labour, in industrial production, i.e. in a permanent fact, and no longer in wages, in class divisions, i.e. in a transitory fact – precisely the one that we wish to supersede.'[33] The factory council, Gramsci suggested, realised the unity of the working class and was a model for the proletarian state.

Crucially, though, Gramsci saw both the trade union and the factory council as having an important role to play in bringing about revolutionary change. Further, the activities and stance of one body could have a beneficial effect on the other.

By its revolutionary spontaneity, the Factory Council tends to unleash the class war at any moment; by its bureaucratic form, the trade union tends to prevent the class war ever being unleashed. The relations between the two should be such that a capricious impulse on the part of the Councils should not cause a step backward by the working class, a working class defeat in other words; the Council should accept and assimilate the discipline of the union, while the revolutionary character of the Council exercises influence on the union as a reagent dissolving its bureaucratisation.[34]

This debate conducted by early Marxist writers over the impact and implications of trade unionism has continued to the present day. Some of the writing follows up on points made in the earlier periods. Allen, for example, looking at the role of trade unions in

Britain since the end of the Second World War, discusses the way in which trade unions have been integrated into the structure of capitalist society.

Trade unions are a generally accepted phenomenon in Britain. They have rights in law which can be regarded in some respects as privilege; they have established relations with the great majority of employers which are written into constitutional procedures for settling industrial disputes; they are accorded public and governmental recognition as political pressure groups so that they have access to government ministers and are asked their views on a range of economic and industrial matters; their opinions are heard or read on the media of mass communications and they are formally involved in the political decision-making process through their membership of government advisory committees.[35]

Allen goes on to comment that the political status of trade unions in Britain no longer depends on which political party is in power. They are accepted by all shades of political opinion because they 'carry no revolutionary significance' and 'are seen as institutions which perform politically necessary and industrially useful functions'.[36] It is worthwhile commenting that, like earlier writers, Allen does not dismiss trade unions as irrelevant. If changes were to be made then trade unions could become more radical bodies. One of the changes would be for unions to 'seek to free themselves of their legal dependence upon governments. So long as governments look upon much of their industrial legislation as concessions to unions they will demand equivalent concessions in terms of collaboration or a restriction on union activities in return. This price is too high for unions.'[37] However, Allen, is by no means certain that these changes will take place and as such echoes the doubts of writers from earlier periods.

Nevertheless, a number of other recent Marxist writers, while not denying the limitations of trade union action and the need for change if unions are to have a major impact on the nature of society, are rather more optimistic that such changes will take place. One of the reasons for their optimism is that traditionally capitalist society has been able to accommodate the limited demands of trade unions fairly easily (that is, demands for higher wages or better working conditions, rather than demands for a change in the nature of the society). They argue that in recent years there have been signs that in the future this may not always be the case. If even the limited aspirations of trade unions cannot be accommodated within capitalist society then these unions may be forced to change their stance and demand radical social change. This line of argument can best be seen in the writing of Hyman[38] and Westergaard and Resler.[39]

Hyman argues that in the past employers have been able to give workers higher money wages because there has been sufficient flexibility in the system to allow them to do this. The higher wages have made little real impact on substantial profits and, anyway, higher costs have eventually been regained through higher prices. Hyman believes that the problems faced by capitalist countries in the late 1960s and early 1970s may mean that there is no longer enough flexibility in the system to allow employers to grant even the limited and temporary benefits which workers used to be able to claim.

The moves made by British governments in the late 1960s and early 1970s to 'reform' the system of industrial relations are, according to Hyman, evidence of the extent to which the system is under pressure. The Labour government's White Paper, *In Place of Strife*,[40] and the Conservative government's Industrial Relations Act,[41] he suggests, were introduced because it was believed that as a result of economic crises (especially balance of payments crises) moves had to be made to 'tighten up the system'. An attempt was being made to give the government power to make certain forms of industrial action illegal, because action which in a different situation had posed no real problems was now of major concern.

If, as Hyman believes is possible, the ability of the system to permit trade unions even limited and temporary gains is being reduced, then that could have a significant effect on the views of union members. Importantly it could alert them to the fact that capitalist society cannot really satisfy their aspirations, and lead them to demand and initiate a more radical response on the part of trade unions.

Westergaard and Resler in their discussion note that most commentators argue that because union action is limited to economic action it could never prove a real threat to business rule. According to them this interpretation is erroneous: economic demands are not necessarily any easier to accommodate than demands for workers' control. 'Demands for "worker control" – now in any case more frequently voiced than before – may result in no more than consultation or wage-earner representation on the boards of companies still impelled to pursue profit in capitalist markets. Demands for higher wages may be taken to the point where they challenge the continued viability of private capital.'[42]

Westergaard and Resler also claim that there is some evidence that labour's economic demands in the early 1970s may have been leading in the direction of a challenge to the established order. They note that the miners voted to withhold support for any policy of wage restraint 'so long as the capitalist private profit-making character of British society remains unaltered', and that during the course of a pay dispute nurses 'withdrew their labour from private wards in public hospitals in the hope of ending private fee-paid treatment and the associated privileges of consultants within a health service supposedly dedicated to equality of service for all'.[43] Westergaard and Resler recognise that such examples are only 'straws in the wind' and that in the end the crisis was contained and the capitalist system remained intact. However, they believe that despite the outcome the events of the early 1970s are important in emphasising the vulnerability and inherent instability of the capitalist system. From our point of view importantly they imply that circumstances might arise when trade unions could take part in radical action.

Before leaving the discussion of the views of recent Marxist writers on the impact of trade unions it is worthwhile referring to one more contribution. Work by Anderson[44] is interesting because he takes Hyman's and Westergaard and Resler's optimism a stage further by providing a new twist to the longstanding debate about the roles of union and party in bringing about radical social change. Essentially he challenges the assumption that radical social change can only be initiated by a political party.

Centring his analysis on the contemporary British scene, Anderson argues that the traditional roles of party and union have to some extent been reversed. The British Labour Party, far from being a vehicle for revolutionary change, has become assimilated into capitalism, while the unions have assumed the position of the standard bearer of the working class. He recognises that trade unions can never achieve the level of action of a political party, but for similar reasons they rarely sink to the same depths as a political party.

Currently, Anderson argues, although trade unions are maladapted for aggressive political action, they nevertheless have important political significance. 'The socio-political identity of the European working class is first and foremost incarnate in its trade unions. It experiences itself as a class only through its collective institutions, of which the most elementary is the trade unions. Outside these historic institutions, the working class has purely inert identity, impenetrable even to itself.'[45] Thus, according to Anderson, trade unions everywhere produce working-class consciousness: while this is not the same as socialist consciousness ('the hegemonic vision and will to create a new social order, which only a revolutionary party can create'[46]) it is an essential stage on the way towards it.

Two future developments are viewed as important by Anderson. One is the growth of shop floor activity, often against the official trade union leadership. This is a sign of the way in which rank and file members are trying to regain control over their unions. Such a movement is directed towards both achieving greater internal democracy and ridding unions of capitalist infiltration and domination. The other development has echoes of the comment made by Hyman, for it refers to the nature of recent government economic policy. He argues that the emergence of state-imposed incomes policies means that issues which were previously seen as local will now be seen as national and related, as they are, to the system of production. 'An incomes policy makes capitalism as a system potentially transparent in a sense that it never was previously. The net distribution of the surplus between wages and profits can be seen more visibly and unmistakably: in this sense, wage bargaining can in itself become a case for the abolition of wage slavery.'[47]

It is also worthwhile recording that while Anderson centres on the British experience he argues that his comments have more general relevance. Thus he says that 'the British case is only the most dramatic example of a general trend in the advanced capitalist countries'.[48]

THE POLITICAL IMPLICATIONS OF TRADE UNIONS: THE NON-MARXIST PERSPECTIVE

Many of the currents of thought evident in the Marxist approach to trade unions are mirrored in other writing. C. Wright-Mills probably comes closest to the Marxist tradition in his study of the development of trade unionism in the USA, centring on the way in which the trade union leader operates and maintains his position. His argument is that currently trade unions operate in an unfamiliar political environment. They are led by people with no long-term political vision: rather the principal concern of the union leader is to maintain his own organisation and his position within it.

...the labour leaders allow their unions to evolve into institutions which integrate the industrial worker into a political economy that is changing from laissez-faire to monopoly and to state capitalism with many corporate features. The labour leaders become part of a machinery which keeps them as leaders but makes them the go-betweens of the rank and file workers and the class of owners and managers.[49]

The labour leader thus maintains his position by bargaining on behalf of labour; he provides labour for a certain price. However, if he is to maintain his own creditability then he must supply the labour as and when required. If the labour he has contracted to supply rebels, then his creditability is drawn into question. He thus becomes a 'manager of discontent'.

Such views clearly have a great deal in common with those expressed by many Marxists. They see trade unions being driven, almost inevitably, to become an integral part of the capitalist system. However, as has been noted elsewhere,[50] the view of union leaders as 'managers of discontent' assumes that discontent exists. Union leaders, according to C. Wright-Mills, have to 'whip up discontent', even if they do so only to prove that they can contain it. Without evidence of discontent they have no obvious *raison d'être*.

Lipset's[51] orientation is rather different to that of C. Wright-Mills. He does not share the same view of the current Western political system and is much more willing to see institutions which integrate individuals into the system as valuable. For Lipset, conflict and competition can be valuable if they are kept within certain bounds: they can serve to reduce tension and increase cohesion and solidarity in society. He is therefore keen to see facilities for legitimate opposition within any organisation or system. This is one of the reasons why he has expressed concern about the current internal organisation of trade unions because, unlike the International Typographical Union which he studied, most trade unions have no system of institutionalised opposition.

Despite this concern about the internal organisation of trade unions, Lipset believes that they can be valuable integrating mechanisms in the wider social system. He suggests that trade unions have two central functions in capitalist society. First they 'create a mechanism for the expression of conflict' and second, they integrate workers into the body politic 'by giving them a legitimate means of obtaining their wants'.[52] There is, therefore, more danger to the system if workers are prevented or actively discouraged from forming trade unions than if they are encouraged to do so. Lipset argues that it is 'precisely in those countries where workers have been able to form strong unions and obtain representation in politics that disintegrative forms of political cleavage are least likely to be found': the corollary is that communist movements 'have developed in countries which were most inclined to deny legitimacy to unions and other democratic expressions of working class aspirations'.[53]

Unlike Marxists, then, Lipset is not mourning the fact that trade unions can be used to integrate workers into the capitalist system rather than to bring about revolutionary change. However, to the extent that Lipset views trade unions as integrative organisations, he is mirroring much of their analysis.

Similar comments could be made about the work of the German sociologist, Dahrendorf.[54] He is interested in the nature of conflict in what he terms 'post-capitalist society' or 'advanced industrial society'. His general thesis suggests a reduction in the violence and intensity of conflict in such societies. He also argues that one of the reasons for such a reduction is the isolation of conflict, particularly industrial conflict. If one form of conflict is 'superimposed' on another (say religious or industrial conflict) then such conflict is likely to be more intense and violent than when they are kept separate. Dahrendorf believes that in 'post-capitalist society' industrial conflict is normally isolated from other forms of conflict through institutions like collective bargaining. While this remains the case trade union action in the industrial sphere can have no broad political significance and cannot be said to contribute to revolutionary change.

Dahrendorf also recognises the force of the argument used by Lipset to suggest that far from undermining capitalist society trade unions can help to integrate workers into it. If society recognises the validity of different points of view and therefore the inevitability of conflict, then it can result in greater rather than less stability. Dahrendorf states '... I should not hesitate, on the level of value judgements, to express a strong preference for the concept of societies that recognise conflict as an essential feature of their structure and process'.[55] He goes on to refer to Coser's[56] thesis that conflict can be 'functional' for society: it helps to release tensions and by serving to remove dissociating elements in a relationship may re-establish unity. For Dahrendorf trade unions are an important interest group and it is essential that they be recognised as such. They may promote conflict, but providing such conflict is limited and (as Coser recognised) kept within bounds, it can be functional.

Other commentators have supported the view that the establishment and development of trade unions can lead to a decrease rather than an increase in disruptive conflict. For example, Dubin notes that in the USA 'strike violence has been inversely related to the permanence of unionism'.[57] His explanation is that the development of unionism facilitates the growth of collective bargaining and collective bargaining in turn facilitates the resolution of potentially disruptive conflict.

Dubin's views on the impact of collective bargaining find support in the work of a wide range of other authors (many of whom are associated with the pluralist school in industrial relations). For example, Kerr argues that collective bargaining helps both sides in a dispute to view the issues and the consequences more rationally than would otherwise be the case: thus he says that collective bargaining aids 'rationality – knowledge of costs and consequences – and thus the diplomatic resolution of controversies'.[58] Similarly, Harbison[59] argues that collective bargaining can absorb energy which might otherwise be more destructively directed: collective bargaining, he says, provides a 'drainage channel' for worker dissatisfaction.

An approach which seems to emphasise the integrative functions of trade unions, then, is influential in the non-Marxist as well as in the Marxist tradition. The non-Marxist tradition, though, is if anything more diverse than the Marxist tradition, and it contains many who would disagree with the foregoing analysis. Alan Fox has referred to such people as accepting a 'unitary' frame of reference for industrial relations.[60] They picture industry as a place where different groups may have different roles but nevertheless share a common overall aim. They adopt a 'consensus' view of industrial society and stress the desirability of order.

Such a point of view clearly sees trade unions in a different manner than the pluralist writers referred to earlier. The unitary frame of reference, according to Alan Fox, views trade unions in one of three ways. Trade unions may be seen as an historical carry-over, brought into existence as the result of unenlightened and shortsighted policies on the part of employers who in the past failed to see that the 'humane treatment' of their employees was good business. In such a case trade unions might be tolerated but be seen to have no place in 'enlightened' modern business, except perhaps as a means of improving communications between employers and employees. Alternatively, trade unions may be seen as the result of 'sectional greed' or an imperfect understanding by employees of where their own best interests lie. Again unions might be endured but their rationale would be seen as shaky and their legitimacy dubious. Finally, trade unions, whatever their manifest purposes, may be seen as having the effect of 'serving as power vehicles for those who seek to subvert the existing social order'.[61]

The unitary frame of reference is influential in a range of management and government thinking and action. The British Industrial Relations Act of 1971, for example, showed the influence of the unitary perspective. In the Act, the legal right to join a trade union was balanced by the right not to belong to one: this 'suggests the view that trade unions remain somewhat suspect organisations'.[62] The unitary frame of reference also finds expression in some academic writing: perhaps the best known range of writing which accepts much of the unitary perspective is the human relations school.[63]

In the human relations school conflict is seen as an indication of a malfunctioning of the system. Mayo, whose Hawthorne experiments formed the starting point for the school, saw conflict as pathological: 'it could and must be resolved by developing a sense of shared purpose within industrial organisations'.[64] Essentially Mayo accepted management's definitions of the organisation's main goals and failed to recognise the possibility that workers and managers might have different values. As a result he saw no role for trade unions (as, say, a way of expressing a separate interest, for such separate interests did not exist) and, like much human relations research since, he ignored trade unions.

CONCLUSIONS

Trade unions in Western nations tend to concentrate on economic issues. However, many, though not all, have broader political aspirations. They aim to change or to help to change the nature of society. The strength of this feeling (and whether it is shared by most rank and file members) and the extent of the change desired is not always clear. Nevertheless, because many trade unions openly claim to have political objectives, it is worthwhile examining the ways in which they try to achieve them.

There have always been some people in the trade union movement, and some commentators, who have argued that trade unions should be directly involved in major political action. However, these views (most consistently expressed in the early part of the twentieth century through syndicalism and guild socialism) appear never to have captured the majority view, except possibly during certain periods in France. Western trade unions in the main have preferred to pursue their political objectives indirectly by links with political parties.

Interest, though, has not simply centred on how trade unions pursue their political objectives, but also on whether, if they want, they could ever engage in more radical action and on what political consequences current union action has had. For example, by concentrating on economic issues have trade unions ensured that workers will demand only very limited change to the system and effectively inhibited demands for more radical change?

A number of commentators from a variety of perspectives have put forward the view that not only are trade unions unlikely to initiate radical social change themselves, but that by their actions they also may have reduced the chances of others doing so. This line of thought begins to come through as a fear expressed by some of the Marxist commentators of the early twentieth century and as a hope of many pluralists writing up to the present day. Recently, though, this view has been challenged, not simply by those who hold a unitary perspective but also by some Marxists. These writers have argued that the limited aims and aspirations of unions, essentially their economic aims, may be more difficult to meet in the future. If this is the case then even traditional union action may have more radical implications than has been assumed.

It is important, though, not to move from saying that this could be the case to saying that it necessarily will be the case. Prediction in such matters is difficult, if not impossible. For example, changing economic conditions may create problems for capitalist nations and this may mean that they can no longer meet the limited aspirations of Western trade unions. On the other hand, economic problems may be used as a weapon by the state to secure the cooperation of unions in reducing their demands and therefore reducing the pressure on the system. This was what happened in the early 1970s and, of course, this is just as possible, though no more certain, a future scenario as that suggested by some Marxists.

NOTES

1. Quoted by J.A. Banks, *Trade Unionism*, Collier-Macmillan, London, 1974, p. 73.
2. For a fuller discussion see M.P. Jackson, *Industrial Relations*, Croom Helm, London, 1977.
3. *Quinn* v. *Leatham* [1901] A.C. 495 (HL) 22, 24, 248, 249, 258–60, 267, 269.

4. *Taff Vale Railway Co.* v. *Amalgamated Society of Railway Servants* [1901] A.C. 426 (HL); (1900) *The Times*, 31 August, 22, 214, 226, 227–31, 235, 248, 318, 319.
5. In practice trade unions rarely aim to exert direct influence over MPs except in connection with industrial matters. However, on occasions there have been clashes between a union and a sponsored MP, though the power of the union ultimately to withdraw support is not as important in practice as it may appear at first sight.
6. D.W. Rawson, 'Unions and politics' in P.W.D. Matthews, G.W. Ford (eds), *Australian Trade Unions*, Sunbooks, Melbourne, 1968, p. 177.
7. E. Marx, W. Kendall, *Unions in Europe*, Centre for Contemporary European Studies, University of Sussex, 1971, p. 22.
8. P.M. Brandini, 'Italy: creating a new industrial relations system from the bottom' in S. Barkin (ed.) *Worker Militancy and its Consequences*, Praeger, New York, 1975, p. 85.
9. This distinction is not easy to make, as the contributions of industrial unions are often solicited by the Committee on Political Action.
10. G.K. Wilson, *Unions in American National Politics*, Macmillan, London, 1979.
11. G. Woodcock, 'Syndicalism defined' in G. Woodcook (ed.) *The Anarchist Reader*, Fontana, Glasgow, 1977, p. 208.
12. E. Malatesta, 'Syndicalism: an advocacy' in G. Woodcock, *ibid.*, p. 223.
13. G. Lichtheim, *A Short History of Socialism*, Fontana, Glasgow, 1975, p. 232.
14. H.A. Clegg, *Trade Unionism under Collective Bargaining*, Blackwells, Oxford, 1976, p. 103.
15. See G. Sorel, *Reflections on Violence*, Collier, New York, 1961.
16. Unofficial Reform Committee, *The Miners' Next Step: Being a Scheme for the Reorganisation of the Federation*, Pluto Press, 1973 (reprint), p. 32.
17. H. Pelling, *A History of British Trade Unionism*, Penguin, Harmondsworth, 1971.
18. *Ibid.*, p. 141.
19. *Ibid.*, p. 142.
20. G.D.H. Cole, *Self-Government in Industry*, Hutchinson, London, 1972, p. 38.
21. See M.P. Jackson, *The Price of Coal*, Croom Helm, London, 1974, for wider discussion.

22. G.A. Phillips, *The General Strike*, Weidenfeld & Nicolson, London, 1976, p. 294.
23. D. Guerin, 'Workers' self-management of industry' in M.S. Shatz (ed.), *The Essential Works of Anarchism*, Bantam, New York, 1971.
24. *Op. cit.*, p. 105.
25. F. Engels, 'Labour movements', reprinted in T. Clarke, L. Clements (eds), *Trade Unionism under Capitalism*, Fontana, Glasgow, 1977, p. 40.
26. K. Marx, 'Capital and labour' reprinted in T. Clarke, L. Clements (eds), *ibid.*, p. 55.
27. V.I. Lenin, 'What is to be done?', in T. Clarke, L. Clements (eds), *ibid.*, pp. 64–76.
28. *Ibid.*, p. 64.
29. R. Luxemburg, *The Mass Strike*, Merlin Press, London, 1906.
30. L. Trotsky, 'Marxism and trade unionism', in T. Clarke, L. Clements (eds), *op. cit.*, p. 81.
31. A. Gramsci, 'The Turin workers' councils', reprinted in R. Blackburn (ed.) *Revolution and Class Struggle: A Reader in Marxist Politics*, Fontana, Glasgow, 1977, pp. 374–409.
32. *Ibid.*, p. 383.
33. *Ibid.*, p. 384.
34. *Ibid.*, p. 388.
35. V.L. Allen, *The Sociology of Industrial Relations*, Longman, London, 1971, p. 45.
36. *Ibid.*, p. 46.
37. V.L. Allen, 'The paradox of militancy' in R. Blackburn, A. Cockburn (eds), *The Incompatibles*, Penguin, Harmondsworth, 1967, p. 266.
38. See, for example, R. Hyman, *Marxism and the Sociology of Trade Unionism*, Pluto, London, 1971.
39. J. Westergaard, H. Resler, *Class in a Capitalist Society*, Heinemann, London, 1975.
40. Department of Employment and Productivity, *In Place of Strife*, HMSO, London, 1969, Cmnd 3888.
41. Industrial Relations Act 1971.
42. Westergaard, *op. cit.*, p. 418.
43. Westergaard, *op. cit.*, p. 418.
44. P. Anderson, *'The Limits and Possibilities of Trade Union Action'* in R. Blackburn, A. Cockburn (eds), *op. cit.*
45. *Ibid.*, p. 274.
46. *Ibid.*, p. 274.

47. *Ibid.*, p. 278.
48. *Ibid.*, p. 272.
49. C. Wright-Mills, *New Men of Power: America's Labor Leaders*, Harcourt, New York, 1948.
50. R. Hyman, *op. cit.*
51. S.M. Lipset, 'Political sociology', in R.K. Merton, L. Broom, L.S. Cottrell, Jr. (eds), *Sociology Today*, New York, 1965, pp. 81–114.
52. *Ibid.*, p. 111.
53. *Ibid.*, p. 113.
54. R. Dahrendorf, *Class and Class Conflict in Industrial Society*, Routledge & Kegan Paul, London, 1959.
55. *Ibid.*, p. 206.
56. L. Coser, *The Functions of Social Conflict*, Routledge & Kegan Paul, London, 1956.
57. R. Dubin, 'Constructive aspects of industrial conflict', in A. Kornhauser, R. Dubin, A.M. Ross (eds), *Industrial Conflict*, McGraw Hill, New York, 1954, p. 46.
58. C. Kerr, 'Industrial conflict and its mediation', *American Journal of Sociology*, vol. LX (1954), p. 199.
59. F.H. Harbison, 'Collective bargaining and American capitalism' in A. Kornhauser, R. Dubin, A.M. Ross (eds), *op. cit.*, pp. 270–79.
60. A. Fox, 'Industrial relations: a social critique of pluralist ideology', in J. Child (ed.), *Man and Organisation*, Allen & Unwin, London, 1973, pp. 185–233. See also A. Fox, *Industrial Sociology and Industrial Relations*, Research Paper 3, Royal Commission on Trade Unions and Employers' Associations, HMSO, London, 1966.
61. A. Fox, 1973, *op. cit.*, p. 190.
62. *Ibid.*, p. 200.
63. The title given to a variety of studies of the social psychology of industry, dating from E. Mayo's Hawthorne experiments.
64. S.R. Parker *et al.*, *The Sociology of Industry*, Allen & Unwin, London, 1972, pp. 95–96.

Chapter eight
TRADE UNIONS AND GOVERNMENTS : NEW DIRECTIONS?

Trade unions have never been able to act without governments taking an interest in what they do and on occasions governments have sought to restrict trade union policies and action. At the same time trade unions have sought the assistance of governments in achieving certain of their objectives. The relationships between trade unions and governments, then, are complicated and the pattern varies and has varied over time and between countries. However, it is possible to isolate some of the major features of such relationships. One is the way in which unions have sought the assistance of governments in achieving safeguards for their members, principally through the enforcement of minimum terms and conditions of employment. Another is the way in which governments have taken an interest in the conduct of collective bargaining. A third is the way in which governments have taken an interest in the results of collective bargaining, particularly the wage agreements. Recently the increasing interest taken by Western governments in directing the economy has meant that some have tried to forge a closer alliance with trade unions.

LINKS WITH GOVERNMENT ACTION IN SETTING DOWN MINIMUM TERMS AND CONDITIONS

While much union activity to improve the wages and working conditions of their members has centred on bargaining with employers and employers' associations some has also been linked to government action. Generally such government action has been strongest in the area of minimum terms and conditions of employment.

In Britain, government action in this area dates back to the nineteenth century. One strand involves the government in regulating working conditions by laying down the rules for the notification of accidents and industrial diseases, the proper provision of ventilation and sanitation and maximum hours of work. These areas are covered by a variety of different pieces of legislation, such as the Mines Acts and Factories Acts. The earliest Mines Acts were concerned to regulate and then prohibit the employment of women and children underground and this concern is still evident in recent legislation like the 1961 Factory Act (which limited the working hours of women in factories to nine each day and forty-eight in a week as well as prohibiting the employment of women at night unless special exemption has been obtained). Although much of the early legislation was inspired by a concern for the welfare of women and children, coverage has now been expanded to the work community as a whole.

Another strand of government action in this area in Britain deals with minimum wages. Currently this is dealt with through the provisions of Wages Councils and associated legislation and the Fair Wages Resolutions of the House of Commons. Wages Councils are statutory bodies, set up in their modern form by the Wages Council Act of 1945 and composed of equal numbers of employers and employees' representatives, which have the power to lay down minimum wages for the industries they cover. They have been established in areas where trade unions have been weak and unable· to operate effectively. Initially they were concentrated in what were known as 'sweated trades' (trade boards, the early equivalents of wages councils, were set up in 1909 by the Trade Boards Act and covered only four trades, tailoring, paper-box making, machine-made lace and net finishing and chain making, where wages and working conditions were scandalously poor). Subsequently the industrial coverage of this legislation was extended, though since the Second World War this trend has been reversed, most dramatically since the criticisms of the Donovan report[1] (in the ten years following the publication of the report fourteen Wages Councils were abolished). The Fair Wages Resolutions of the House of Commons were first introduced in 1891 to ensure that any employer who contracted with the government had to observe terms and conditions of employment not less favourable than those established for the trade or industry in the district where the work was carried out by machinery of negotiation or arbitration'.[2] Initially the Resolutions only applied to wages but those passed in 1909 and 1946 extended the cover to other areas including hours, work and trade union membership.

As well as laying down minimum wages in such ways, British governments have also intervened to allow employees to ensure that they are paid the same wages as other workers in the same industry and area. Thus, section 8 of the Terms and Conditions of Employment Act of 1959 said that where it could be shown that employers' and employees' organisations had agreed on terms and conditions of employment to be applied to a particular industry, or part of an industry, then if an employer in that industry was not observing those conditions a case could be presented to an industrial court who would order that the employer should do so: enforcement would be by the court stating that these provisions were to be an implied term of the contract of employment. These provisions have now been taken over by the 1959 Act's successor in this area, the Employment Protection Act of 1975 (the role of the industrial court is now undertaken by the Central Arbitration Committee).

While the British government (and others who have introduced similar legislation and policies) clearly have had an important role to play in establishing minimum wages and working conditions, even in this area the unions still have had an important function. Much of the legislation was only introduced following union pressure: frequently unions persuaded a number of employers in an industry to accept certain conditions of work and then used this as a way of putting pressure on the government to introduce legislation. Certainly the early Mines and Factories Acts followed extensive union as well as more general pressure. The unions also have had a role to play in enforcing the legislation. For instance, although the Wages Councils' rates are backed up by an official inspectorate, this inspectorate is not large enough to be able to police the system by itself effectively, and in practice there is evidence of widespread evasion of the statutory rates.[3] The unions, therefore, have had a role to play in reinforcing the inspectorate, though it has to be added that because the areas covered by Wages Councils are those where union organisation is weak, often they have not been able to do so very effectively. Under the recent health and safety legislation[4] unions have a similar policing role to play. The legislation allows unions to appoint safety representatives who have the right to carry out inspections and report defects. Again they are supplementing other work in the area, though they are likely to be more successful in doing so than they have been in the Wages Council field.

GOVERNMENT INTERVENTION IN COLLECTIVE BARGAINING

Trade unions, then, have sometimes sought the assistance of governments in enforcing minimum terms and conditions of employment. Governments have also intervened in another area of interest to trade unions, the way in which collective bargaining is carried out. The extent to which governments have intervened in this area has varied, and so too has the union reaction.

Traditionally, the level of government intervention in the way collective bargaining has been carried out has been the lowest in Britain of any of the major Western nations. Kahn Freund's often quoted statement:

There is perhaps, no major country in the world in which the law has played a less significant role in the shaping of (industrial) relations than in Great Britain and in which today the law and the legal profession has less to do with labour relations.[5]

accurately described the position prior to the 1960s. Apart from the two wartime periods (when an element of compulsory arbitration was introduced through the 1915 Munitions of War Act and the 1940 Conditions of Employment and National Arbitration Order) governments left trade unions and employers to settle disputes themselves, usually being willing to offer help or guidance (through the officially sponsored conciliation and mediation services) but only if it was asked for by the parties concerned. Similarly industrial relations legislation seemed to be more concerned with keeping the law out of such matters than anything else. Thus, the important Trade Union Act of 1871 was passed in an attempt to prevent trade unions from being declared 'unlawful bodies' and being sued for acting 'in restraint of trade', while the Conspiracy and Protection of Property Act of 1875 attempted to prevent unions being sued for 'criminal conspiracy' as the result of strike action, and the Trade Disputes Act of 1906 and the Trade Union Act of 1913 were introduced to reverse the attempts of the judiciary to interfere in trade union affairs. With one or two minor deviations during the interwar years this pattern held until the 1960s. Since the 1960s the position has changed a little. The 1971 Industrial Relations Act permitted governments to intervene in industrial disputes where the national interest was threatened and to regulate trade union affairs. Coming, as it did, so swiftly after the previous Labour government's White Paper, *In Place of Strife*,[6] which followed a similar though not identical line, the 1971 Act seemed to herald a new approach to intervention in collective bargaining by British governments. However, the repeal of the 1971 Act in 1974 and subsequent actions and statements by both major British political parties[7] lead one to question whether the deviation was of long term or merely short term significance.

The clearest contrast to government intervention in collective bargaining in Britain can be seen by looking at North America. In the USA, for example, since the 1930s at least, governments have intervened in collective bargaining in a major way. The 1935 Wagner Act laid down the procedure for the registration of bargaining units and the recognition of bargaining rights. Trade unions who were able to prove that they had the support of the workforce (through a ballot organised by the National Labour Relations Board) were able to force an employer to bargain with them over a specified range of subjects. A later piece of legislation, the Taft-Hartley Act of 1947, showed government willingness to intervene in other areas of collective bargaining. In this case the government was able to intervene when bargaining seemed to have broken down and as a result national safety or well-being was imperilled, and to impose a 'cooling-off' period during which a trade union could be forced to withdraw from strike action. The 1947 Act also showed the government's willingness to intervene in the internal affairs of trade unions, and the powers given to them in this area were extended twelve years later by the 1959 Landrum-Griffin Act.

In many other Western democracies governments intervene in collective bargaining, and most come closer to the USA than the British model. For example, in Australia the system of compulsory arbitration is so important that some commentators have argued that effectively it has superseded collective bargaining: others, noting that the parties frequently bargain about the application and interpretation of arbitration awards, would not go this far but would accept that the level of government intervention is substantial and important. Similarly in West Germany collective bargaining has a legal basis (through a series of Collective Agreement Acts in 1949, 1952 and 1969) and collective agreements can be legally enforced. In other Western European nations the details differ but the extent of government intervention in collective bargaining clearly is greater than in Britain.

The reaction of the trade union movements in these countries to the different levels of government intervention in collective bargaining is interesting. In Britain the trade unions historically have proclaimed their faith in 'voluntary collective bargaining'. Flanders[8] has noted that Britain has never had a truly voluntary system of industrial relations and trade unions have never proposed that it should have: for example, they have supported government intervention to restrict the right of employers to sue trade unions as the result of industrial disputes. What voluntarism has meant to British trade union leaders is a minimum role for the state and action by the state when other methods have failed. It is also clear that the notion of voluntarism and 'free collective bargaining' has had and still retains a powerful emotional appeal for British trade union leaders. During the dispute over *In Place of Strife*[9] and the 1971 Industrial Relations Act, trade union leaders frequently claimed to be fighting to preserve 'free collective bargaining'.

On the other hand trade unions in the USA have adopted a rather different approach. Initially, prior to the major legislation of the 1930s, they, like the British trade unions, opposed widespread state intervention in collective bargaining. However, experience of the Wagner Act persuaded them that state intervention could be a valuable aid, and even after the less favourable experience with the legislation of the post Second World War years, USA trade unions have retained a generally sympathetic attitude towards governmental intervention in collective bargaining. A similar pattern can be seen in union reaction in one of the other countries where government intervention in collective bargaining has been important, Australia. In Australia trade unions initially faced compulsory arbitration with some scepticism but experience of it persuaded them to modify their stance: in fact, in some instances they have argued for its extension.

The contrast between the attitude of British trade unions towards the White Paper *In Place of Strife* and the 1971 Industrial Relations Act on the one hand, and the attitude of trade union movements in countries like the USA and Australia towards government intervention in collective bargaining on the other, has excited a number of comments. In part the explanation for the difference in attitude can be linked to the benefits the trade union movements have gained from government intervention. British trade unions were well established by the 1960s with almost half of the working population in membership. They had fought for, and to a large degree obtained, recognition and bargaining rights from employers. Government intervention, certainly of the kind proposed, only seemed likely to weaken their power. USA and Australian trade unions were less well established when their governments took the initiative and intervened in collective bargaining in the 1930s and towards the end of the nineteenth century respectively. Government intervention offered to increase union power rather than decrease it: later action changed things somewhat but the unions concerned still believed that on balance they gained more than they lost from state intervention.

The balance of advantage for the trade union thus clearly seems to be an important consideration in explaining union attitudes towards government intervention in collective bargaining. However, the issue cannot be disposed of quite so simply. British trade unions did not only oppose government intervention in the late 1960s and early 1970s because on balance it seemed to them likely to weaken their power, though undoubtedly this was an important consideration: they also opposed government intervention because, as Flanders argues,[10] they had an emotional attachment to and faith in the virtues of voluntarism. In part they were opposing a change which seemed to them likely to introduce an alien and unacceptable system of industrial relations in place of one which had been fought for and achieved over a century of activity by British trade unionists.

Clegg[11] has argued that the pattern and level of government intervention in collective bargaining has been important in determining the structure of bargaining in the country concerned (he does not claim it is the only factor, others include the structure of management and the attitude of employers, but he does claim it is an important one). He highlights the experiences in the USA, Australia and West Germany as providing particularly good examples. In the USA the Wagner Act played an important role in encouraging the development of plant bargaining (now the dominant kind of bargaining in the USA); in Australia the system of compulsory arbitration reinforced the system of industry-wide bargaining and widened the scope of bargaining topics; the West German works council legislation put important restraints on industrial conflict at that level and as a result has influenced the way bargaining disputes have been resolved. In none of these cases were the precise results the intention of the legislators: nevertheless, the consequences of the legislation, even if unintended, were important in shaping collective bargaining in those countries.

INCOMES POLICIES

Government intervention in collective bargaining has had important, and Clegg would argue crucial, consequences for the development of bargaining and trade unionism. However, the discussion so far has centred on the role of governments in determining minimum terms and conditions of employment and on the way in which they intervene in the bargaining process. There is, though, another form of government intervention which has become increasingly important: that is, intervention to affect the result of any bargaining that may take place. This discussion is best entered by looking at the role of governments in introducing incomes policies.

Incomes policies have a long history; some would argue that the policies introduced by the British government to restrict wage rises during the First World War can be seen in this light. However, Towers, using the definition of incomes policy which says that it 'is taken to mean measures which seek to intervene directly in the process of income determination and the working of labour markets for the purpose of moderating the rate of price inflation, controlling the distribution of incomes, and increasing the efficiency with which labour resources are used and allocated in the economy'[12] is able to argue that incomes policies (in his more sophisticated form) did not begin in Britain until after the Second World War. He talks about four phases of incomes policy in Britain.

The first is from the end of the Second World War until 1964. This phase begins with the White Paper of 1944 which related the question of full employment to inflation and incomes policies, continued with the wage restraint introduced by the Labour government between 1948 and 1950 and the Conservative government in 1956 and concluded with the attempts to introduce a permanent incomes policy between 1961 and 1964 (which included the 'pay pause' of 1961, the work of the short-lived National Incomes Commission and the more durable National Economic Development Council, and the 'guiding light' under which pay increases were to average between 3 and 3.5 per cent). Towers argues that though much of the machinery and policy established during this period was abandoned after a relatively short period, it was part of a 'learning process' and established the framework upon which incomes policies developed in the sixties and seventies.

The second phase was from 1964 to 1970, when incomes policy developed through three distinct stages. The first was from December 1964 to June 1966, when the voluntary agreement of both sides of industry was relied upon to limit rises in incomes to permit controlled economic growth. The second was from July 1966 to December 1969, when statutory controls were attempted, initially through a 'standstill' on all incomes, then through a period of 'severe restraint' and only towards the end of the stage relaxing further to permit more substantial wage increases. The third was from January to June 1970, when a second attempt was made to gain voluntary restraint on rises in incomes. Towers comments that by 'any standard the 1964–70 phase was a remarkably determined and sustained attempt to achieve an effective incomes policy'.[13] It was linked to severe economic problems, especially recurring balance of payments crises. The establishment of the National Board for Prices and Incomes to try to guide and monitor incomes policy can be seen as a consolidation of earlier experiments with similar bodies and initially was linked to the attempt to gain the voluntary co-operation of both sides of industry.

The third phase was from 1972 to 1974, when the Conservative government of Edward Heath reversed its earlier opposition to incomes policies. Stage one of the policy lasted from November 1972 until March 1973 and involved a 90 day standstill on prices, rents, dividends and pay with the possibility of an extension for a further 60 days. Stage two lasted from April 1973 to November 1973 and pay increases were limited to 4 per cent plus £1 a week, with a ceiling of £250 a year. Stage three lasted from December 1973 until June 1974 and the earlier pay increase limits were altered to 7 per cent or £2.25 a week with a ceiling of £300 a year. Policy during this phase was strongly influenced by the economic problems arising from the 'oil crises'. Thus, it was similar to earlier phases in that it was linked to an economic crisis (albeit of a different origin); the use of the Pay Board to implement policy clearly had echoes of earlier initiatives.

The fourth phase identified by Towers covered the period after 1974 until 1978. In practice this phase is somewhat different to the earlier ones, particularly in terms of the trade union response, and so will be dealt with later separately.

Britain has not been alone in showing interest in incomes policies in the post Second World War years. Most other Western nations have introduced incomes policies at one time or another during this period. Neither has Britain been alone in experiencing problems. Few incomes policies have survived long; even the Dutch experiment which was hailed as a 'success' by many external commentators eventually broke down.

In many ways, though, the problems and failures of incomes policies are not as important for trade unions as the fact that despite such setbacks, few governments have abandoned them altogether. In the early 1970s, for example, most Western governments returned to incomes policies of one type of another, as one of the responses to the economic problems caused by the oil crisis. This was the case even in those nations where governments were fiercely opposed to state intervention in the economy or where they had been elected on a platform which specifically opposed incomes policies. For example, in the USA the Republican and anti-interventionist government headed by Richard Nixon introduced a statutory price and wages freeze in August 1971 which was later modified, but which continued through guidelines for wage increases that were effective until 1973.

In many instances the response of trade unions has been simply to oppose the controls imposed; usually this opposition has been successful in bringing about the eventual collapse of the policy. In some ways trade union opposition is a 'gut' reaction: in other ways it is a realisation that controls over incomes restrict their freedom to bargain and thus interfere with one of their central functions much more than other aspects of government intervention. A number of writers have questioned what the role of trade unions would be if incomes policies became effective and as a result unions had no real role in wage bargaining.

However, there are a number of examples from the mid 1970s of where trade unions have adopted rather a different approach to incomes policies. Rather than simply oppose them they sought to extract from government a price for their support. This approach is particularly interesting because according to some commentators[14] it was the result of the growing strength of the trade union movement. The trade union movement, from this point of view, had succeeded in defeating earlier attempts to control incomes and now was able to argue that any moves in this direction needed its support if they were to succeed. It is also interesting because the price demanded for co-operation was action on a range of issues with which unions previously had not been centrally and directly concerned.

This is an area worthy of detailed consideration, for it presents evidence of a potentially new way of ordering union/government relations. The best example to refer to for illustration is taken from Britain.

BRITAIN: THE SOCIAL CONTRACT

The social contract (or social compact as it was sometimes referred to) had its origins in discussion between the Labour Party while in opposition between 1970 and 1974 and the trade unions. These discussions were referred to and made an important part of the Labour Party's 1974 election manifesto.

The Labour Party's victory in the 1974 general election meant that the 'social contract' was to have more than propaganda importance. For the following three years the 'social contract' held the centre of the national industrial stage. One crucial part of it was an agreement between the TUC and the government over wage and price restraint. The details of this part of the agreement changed as new targets were set each year: in the first year, 1974, the agreement simply said that there was little scope for real increases in consumption but left individual unions the freedom to negotiate within this general guideline; in 1975 more precise limits were laid down of increases of £6 a week except for people earning more than £8,500 a year; in 1976 the weekly figure was replaced by a guideline suggesting wage increases of no more than 6.5 per cent.

However, the social contract was not simply a vehicle for wage restraint: this is why it was such an important development from incomes policy. In return for wage restraint the government agreed to repeal certain industrial relations legislation, to introduce a new economic strategy and to introduce a range of social service legislation.

As a vehicle for wage restraint the social contract had some success. During its first year of operation it seemed to have little impact. It was implemented, though, during a period of fast rising inflation (which reached levels exceeding 20 per cent by early 1975) and against a background of a previous period of fairly rigid wages policy. The following two years were much more successful. Wage rises were reduced, eventually to a level below that current for price rises. Again the background was important. During the previous twelve months Britain's economic position had worsened considerably and union leaders clearly believed that the description of the situation as a 'crisis' was apt.

The social contract also had some success in ensuring some union involvement in a range of areas which had not previously been their central direct concern. The breadth of vision of the contract is probably best indicated by reference to the 1976 TUC – Labour Party agreement. This dealt with a number of issues which were close to the traditional interests of trade unions. For example, it discussed the need to expand the economy, the desirability of re-establishing full employment and ways of increasing industrial democracy. But it also dealt with a range of issues which were far from the traditional wage bargaining area, covering the whole field of social policy from pensions to housing, family poverty to education.

Of course British trade unions have not totally ignored such issues before. Their close links with the Labour Party have ensured their involvement. Many unions have statements in their objectives about social justice, the nature of society, and even specific items of social policy. However, in the past they have largely assigned those matters to a separate category from industrial issues: general social questions have been pursued through the strong links many unions have with the Labour Party. The novel feature of the social contract is that they were made part of the wage bargaining package.

The social contract has been questioned and attacked from a variety of perspectives. Some comments have been concerned about the detail of its operation. For example, Taylor[15] has argued that although the trade unions consulted and reached an agreement with the government on broad social and economic matters, in practice their influence on policy decisions was limited. Other commentators have looked at the broader impact of the initiative. For example, some Marxists saw the contract as simply another way of maintaining the 'status quo': thus, Hyman and Brough[16] argued that it offered only a very marginal challenge to the powers and privilege of capital. On a similar level, but from a different standpoint, pluralists expressed concern about the contract because they believed that it could jeopardise trade union independence. Clegg argued that the social contract, if it was to be seen as more than a limited political device, had to be viewed as a 'continuous partnership' between unions and government. However, he said that 'it is not easy to find a place for trade union independence in a model of permanent partnership between trade unions and the government, for such an arrangement is perilously close to the transformation of the unions into agencies of the state'.[17]

On the other hand, some commentators have been far more optimistic. Fatchett and Whittingham argued that something like the social contract by 'broadening the scope of relevance in industrial relations terms ... possesses the potential to reshape the parameters of collective bargaining'.[18] Issues which previously were considered irrelevant to, or inadmissable in, collective bargaining could be discussed. Further, Fatchett and Whittingham argued that the social contract offered trade unions the potential to achieve real change in society. Traditionally unions' ambitions had been limited to consolidating and improving the lot of particular sections of workers. One result was that unions were written off by radical political theorists as a potential vehicle for revolution. However, the social contract, because it demanded a widening of union objectives from immediate and sectional to more general class-based aspirations, increased the potential of unions as vehicles for major social change.

Fatchett and Whittingham recognised dangers. The social contract offered unions the opportunity to have more influence but it also brought tensions and dilemmas: the influence may have been achieved at the cost of them being perceived as agents of incomes control. They also recognised that devices like the contract could lead to greater centralisation within unions. If that were to happen then it could never achieve its full potential. 'But if the Social Contract were to become more the property of trade union members and to voice their aspirations, it would then be much more than the short term expedient on wages which some have characterised it.'[19]

Central to Fatchett and Whittingham's argument was that the social contract was not a fixed programme. It was something which could be developed and something which offered potential. The broadening of the scope of collective bargaining would be an important opportunity and according to them it is this, not the detail of the 1974–77 agreement between the Labour Party and trade unions, which characterised the contract.

SIMILAR DEVELOPMENTS IN OTHER COUNTRIES

Perhaps the closest parallel to the 'social contract' outside Britain can be seen in the Netherlands. The Dutch case is interesting because, as has been noted, after the Second World War the Netherlands was able to boast one of the most successful national incomes policies. However, by the late 1950s effectively it has been abandoned. The mid 1960s were years of development and at times disorganisation in Dutch industrial relations. The government, often with the sympathy of the official union leaders but with the suspicion of many rank and file union members, tried to regain control of wage fixing. Their success was limited, and certainly by the early 1970s nothing as integrated and stable as the post Second World War system had been established.

The economic crises of the early 1970s persuaded many of the need to find a new and effective system and by 1972 the major trade unions had entered into discussions with the government and the employers on a 'wage-price programme'. The discussions were complicated by the political instability during this period but eventually led to the conclusion of what writers have referred to, in English translations, as a 'social contract'. Although the details of the contract differed from its British counterpart, the central idea was similar. The trade unions indicated 'their willingness to negotiate an agreement with the government which would set limits to wage increases, in return for which the government would introduce and support desired changes in social legislation'.[20]

The Dutch social contract had a much shorter history than the British example. Disagreement over the way to deal with differentials between higher and lower paid workers, a series of strikes, and the precarious political situation, meant that the contract was not renewed in 1974 or in 1975. In practice, however, the government was able to impose limits on wage increases in those years which were broadly accepted, because of the problems caused by the oil crisis. Nevertheless, despite later discussions on a possible accord between the unions and employers at the central level, the social contract has not since been operative and the government has relaxed its hold over wage increase levels.

In its detailed operation, then, it is difficult to argue that the social contract in the Netherlands proved to be success. Yet, Peper[21] has argued that it at least provides one model for future development and one way in which government policy and administration might be related to the total system of collective bargaining. Of course, this does not mean that there is no concern about moves that might be made in such a direction. As in Britain, concern is expressed from within the trade union movement about the desirability of any co-operation with government attempts to limit wage rises and interfere in collective bargaining. Concern is also expressed by other parties. Some see trade union bargaining over broad social and economic policies as a threat to traditional democratic procedures: 'some people object to what they see as an infringement by the trade unions on the prerogative of the parliament'.[22]

Apart from the Netherlands, the developments in the West which come closest to the idea of the social contract are to be found in the Scandinavian countries. In 1976 in Norway a multipartite agreement was concluded which provided a framework for all sectors and covered both social and economic issues. The terms of the agreement provided for increases in disposable incomes of 3.7 per cent (higher for pensioners and farmers), a reduction in the working week (from 42.5 to 40 hours), a 2 per cent reduction in taxes (graduated in favour of low income groups), improvements in family allowances and social security benefits, and food subsidies. The Swedish agreements between the employers, unions and governments covering 1974 to 1976 similarly dealt with work and non-work issues. As well as dealing with wage rises, hours of work and employer accident liability, they also led to government action over a range of social issues, relating, for example, to the pensionable age, child and housing allowances. The Swedish agreements, though, were different to those in other countries in that they were the result of an evolution of arrangements for tripartite bargaining which had existed for many years rather than simply a reaction to the economic problems of the 1970s.

The range of bargaining on non-work issues in Western nations is usefully summarised by Barkin in two publications. He argues that although the British social contract is 'the most far reaching new instrument in industrial relations', it 'has a parallel in seven other European countries'[23] (three of them have been referred to above, the Netherlands, Norway and Sweden: he adds four more, Austria, Denmark, Belgium and Finland). The extension of bargaining of the kind seen in Britain with the social contract, then, is by no means necessarily restricted to a particular period in British history, or just to Britain, and the issues which the extension raises have general relevance.

PATTERNS OF GOVERNMENT, TRADE UNION RELATIONS

Crouch, in a variety of publications,[24] has examined the main alternatives available in the ordering of relations between the state and trade unions. He outlines four main possibilities. These are combinations of two separate choices, each of which open up two different alternatives. First, are trade unions to remain powerful, autonomous and decentralised, or not? Second, is the system going to develop in a liberal or corporatist direction? The options opened up by these choices are illustrated in Fig. 1. It is worthwhile looking in turn at what each of the four options implies.

The first option, free collective bargaining, is the preferred option of the trade unions, certainly by tradition of British unions. It implies limited government intervention in industrial relations and a strong trade union movement. It is likely to flourish during times of national prosperity. The second option, neo-*laissez-faire* has

Figure 1: Relations between Trade Unions and the State

Nature of System	Position of Trade Unions	
	Strong	Weak
Liberal	1. Free Collective Bargaining	2. Neo-*laissez-faire*
Corporatist	4. Bargained Corporatism	3. Corporatism.

Source: C. Crouch, *The Politics of Industrial Relations*, Manchester U.P., Manchester, 1979.

some similarities to free collective bargaining. The state maintains a low profile as far as industrial relations are concerned. However, in practice it is interested to influence developments in industrial relations by indirect means, principally the control of the money supply, the level of state spending, and the level of unemployment. These measures can be used to reduce union power and thus effect the outcome of what might otherwise be seen as free collective bargaining. It should also be recognised that the *laissez-faire* option is not simply one involving economic policy but might also involve practical action (measures that aim to increase 'industrial freedom', like the 1971 Industrial Relations Act) designed to buttress economic policy. The third option, corporatism, or the corporate state, 'has its origins in nineteenth century Roman Catholic thought' and is built on 'the close integration of political, economic and moral forces'.[25] It implies a weak trade union movement, because trade union leaders use the strength of their organisations to restrain and control their members, to fit it with the national consensus rather than their own sectional aims. It also implies strong central state direction and control. The fourth option, bargained corporatism, occurs when the state pursues a strong central course but has to bargain with a strong trade union movement and make concessions to get its co-operation. Unions, in effect, are offered greater political influence in return for accepting greater state interference and control.

Examples of all four options can be seen in recent industrial relations experience. The first option, free collective bargaining, was most characteristic of the early post Second World War years in Britain. The government intervened in industrial relations but played a minimum role, concentrating on establishing minimum terms and conditions of employment and the bounds of acceptable action. The second option, neo-*laissez-faire*, has been pursued to

some extent by a number of British Conservative Party governments, but in terms of economic policy has been most characteristic of the Thatcher government of the late 1970s and early 1980s.
Possibly the best British example of the political manifestations of
this option can be seen in the 1971 Industrial Relations Act: elsewhere it can be seen in the many different attempts to control collective bargaining itself. The third option, corporatism, finds
echoes in post Second World War West Germany, where the trade
union movement has been one of the most co-operative with the
state. The fourth option, bargained corporatism, can be seen in the
social contracts negotiated in Britain and the Netherlands in the
1970s, but has echoes in the various attempts to introduce similar
devices and incomes policies elsewhere.

One of the problems with Crouch's alternatives, however, is that
frequently the options are not found in their pure form: in most
instances governments have used a mixture of approaches and
stances. For example, the British Labour government of the mid
1970s used both monetary and public spending controls (which are
associated with the neo-*laissez-faire* option) at the same time as they
negotiated versions of the social contract (which is associated with
bargained corporatism). Nevertheless, Crouch's alternatives do
point to possible directions and mixtures of government policy and
union reaction and as such enable one to illustrate a number of the
different possible arrangements of state/trade union relations. They
also, as Crouch claims, allow one to 'make sense of several am-
biguities of contemporary political divisions: for example, the
occasional consensus between advocates of *laissez-faire* and of
free collective bargaining (an alliance of those rejecting corporatism)'.[26]

It would not be helpful to try to predict the future direction of
state/trade union relations. It might, though, be worthwhile to
point to some of the factors that could determine such directions.
One of the factors which will help to determine the extent to which
free collective bargaining can be pursued is the economic environment in the country concerned or affecting the country concerned
at any particular time. In the immediate post Second World War
years in Britain prosperity increased and inflation was contained
because of the scope for growth. Nevertheless, it needs to be re-
membered that free collective bargaining during part of the immediate post Second World War years was controlled through a
government/TUC agreement to restrict wage rises. Later, the economic consequences of free collective bargaining, particularly infla-

tion, led subsequent governments to try to control the process. What level of inflation a nation can stand is clearly a matter for debate but the fear of the effects of inflation have undoubtedly led governments and others to believe that the consequences of free collective bargaining are unacceptable.

The second option, neo-*laissez-faire*, may be constrained by the social consequences of the economic policy. In order to weaken the power of trade unions by economic policy alone, governments may have to pursue their policy to lengths which bring unacceptable social consequences, such as those associated with a high level of unemployment. Any move to use political means to control trade union power may also raise problems. It may not be so much that particular devices will produce particular reactions: rather it may be that violent moves in a new direction may be seen as an attack on established rights and bring a violent confrontation. Arguably this was what happened with the British Industrial Relations Act which tried to introduce measures accepted in other countries but unknown in Britain.

The third option, corporatism, relies on a trade union organisation which is able to control rank and file members. In West Germany the main trade union organisations appeared to be able to offer a united but disciplined membership in the post Second World War years. Comparatively, the West German trade union organisation is highly professionalised and efficient. Yet, as has been noted, by the end of the 1960s there were signs of unrest amongst rank and file members about the policy pursued by the official leadership. In Britain the official leadership has never been able to control the rank and file membership to anything like the extent of its West German counterpart. The extent of decentralisation and the growing importance of shop floor organisation has been one of the factors that has made corporatism in its pure form difficult to achieve in Britain.

The fourth option, bargained corporatism, is limited by two factors in particular. The first is the willingness or otherwise of the government to enter into a bargain with the trade union movement. Bargained corporatism involves giving the trade union movement greater political influence than they otherwise would have had. Some governments are likely to view this as an unacceptable reduction in the sovereignty of an elected Parliament. This was a criticism frequently heard in the debates over the social contracts in Britain and the Netherlands. Ths second factor is the ability of the trade union leadership to persuade its membership that it is worth trading in some of their traditional practices and powers for a greater say in broader political matters.

There is evidence that in the British case in the post 1979 period, both of these factors have worked against an extension, or even a maintenance, of the degree of bargained corporatism previously achieved. The Conservative victory at the general election in May 1979 brought the Thatcher government to power, with its commitment to the market economy and a reduction in union influence. For their part, many trade unionists seemed to lose interest in what we have termed 'bargained corporatism', to such an extent that a TUC resolution passed in September 1980 attempted to prevent union leaders even discussing incomes policies and related issues with governments. However, Thomson[27], writing in October 1979, questioned whether indicators like this should be viewed as having long-term significance. According to Thomson, two items are likely to prevent bargained corporatism being abandoned as a long-term strategy by British governments. One is that he believes that there will be strong pressure on any government 'to forge a consensus amongst the major interest groups' and, if it does so (especially if in trying to do so it introduces an incomes policy) the price will be the 'incorporation of the union movement'. The other is that despite the changes that have occurred over the last decade or so, the net result 'has been a strengthening of union influence that will not easily be eroded'.[28] As far as the union movement itself is concerned, Thomson recognises the pressures on the leadership to withdraw from close co-operation with governments. Such pressures might result in 'a straining of the relationships among the various centres of power in the union movement, especially if the leadership shows signs of becoming incorporated and compromised by involvement in rational decision making'.[29] However, Thomson argues that despite problems and temporary withdrawals, in the long term the union movement will retain its interest in close relations with governments: thus, he says, 'all signs indicate that the union leadership will have to continue to strike an uneasy balance among its power vis-à-vis government and industry, its responsibility to both the larger society and its members, and its authority over the latter'.[30]

CONCLUSIONS

Governments never have left trade unions alone, completely free to pursue their central aim, the improvement of the terms and conditions of service of their members, nor in practice have many trade unions ever demanded that this should be the case. To the contrary, trade unions in many countries have welcomed and even encouraged government involvement in particular areas. For example, in Britain unions have welcomed government involvement to establish safety and health standards and to enforce minimum levels of pay, and in the USA unions have welcomed government involvement to specify and if necessary enforce bargaining units and arrangements.

However, unions in all Western nations have been rather more sceptical about government intervention to control the agreements reached between employers and themselves over wage levels. Nevertheless, incomes policies have grown in popularity and have been tried at one time or another in virtually all Western nations since the Second World War.

The moves made by unions in the mid 1970s, for example in Britain and the Netherlands through social contracts, to demand a price for their co-operation in incomes restraint, what has been termed 'bargained corporatism', raised interesting possibilities. If pursued on a long-term basis they could result in much closer co-operation between unions and governments. In practice the strength of such arrangements is bound to fluctuate given the political orientations and affiliations of the unions and the changing political complexions of Western governments. Nevertheless, even as a short-term device these arrangements represent an interesting extension of union policy and attitude towards incomes restraint. As such they represent one of a number of possible ways of accommodating the inevitable tension between governments and trade unions.

NOTES

1. Royal Commission on Trade Unions and Employers' Associations, 1965–68, *Report*, HMSO, London, 1968, Cmnd 3623.
2. E.G.A. Armstrong, 'The role of the state' in B. Barrett, E. Rhodes, J. Beirshon, *Industrial Relations and the Wider Society*, Collier-Macmillan, London, 1975, p. 114.
3. A number of studies of the application of wages councils' rates show widespread evasion. The number of inspectors appointed make effective policing virtually impossible.
4. In particular through the appointment of union safety representatives.

5. O. Kahn Freund, in A. Flanders, H.A. Clegg (eds), *The System of Industrial Relations in Great Britain*, Blackwell, Oxford, 1953, p. 44.
6. Department of Employment and Productivity, *In Place of Strife*, HMSO, London, 1969, Cmnd 3888.
7. The legislation introduced by the Conservative Government in 1980 does not contradict this statement, but future events might raise more doubts.
8. A. Flanders, 'The tradition of voluntarism', *British Journal of Industrial Relations*, vol. XII (1974), no. 3, pp. 352–70.
9. *Op. cit.*
10. A. Flanders, 1974, *op. cit.*
11. H. Clegg, *Trade Unionism under Collective Bargaining*, Blackwell, Oxford, 1976.
12. B. Towers, *British Incomes Policy*, Occasional Papers in Industrial Relations, Universities of Leeds and Nottingham, 1978, p. 3.
13. *Ibid.*, p. 13.
14. See A.W.J. Thomson, 'Trade unions and the corporate state in Britain', *Industrial and Labor Relations Review*, vol. 33 (1979), no. 1, pp. 36–54.
15. R. Taylor, *Labour and the Social Contract*, Fabian Tract 458, Civic Press, Glasgow 1978.
16. R. Hyman, I. Brough, *Social Values and Industrial Relations: A Study of Fairness and Inequality*, Blackwell, Oxford, 1975.
17. H.A. Clegg, *The System of Industrial Relations in Great Britain*, Blackwell, Oxford, 1975, p. 504.
18. D.J. Fatchett, W.M. Whittingham, 'Other aspects of the social contract', *Industrial Relations Journal*, vol. 9 (1978/9), no. 4, p. 61.
19. *Ibid.*, p. 62.
20. W. Albeda, 'Changing industrial relations in the Netherlands', *Industrial Relations*, vol. 16 (1977), no. 2, p. 142.
21. B. Peper, 'The Netherlands : From an ordered harmonic to a bargaining relationship', in S. Barkin (ed.) *Worker Militancy and its Consequences, 1965–75*, Praeger, New York, 1975, pp. 118–53.
22. *Ibid.*, p. 149.
23. S. Barkin, 'Social Contracts in Europe', *Free Labour World*, May-June 1977, p. 6.
24. C. Crouch, *The Politics of Industrial Relations*, Manchester U.P., 1979.

25. *Ibid.*, pp. 123–24.
26. C. Crouch, *Class Conflict and the Industrial Relations Crisis*, Heinemann, London, 1977, p. 265.
27. *Op. cit.*
28. *Ibid.*, p. 54.
29. *Ibid.*, p. 51.
30. *Ibid.*, p. 52.

Chapter nine

CONCLUSIONS: TRADE UNIONS AS MATURE
ORGANISATIONS

CHANGE AND DEVELOPMENT

A hundred years ago trade unions in Britain were in their infancy, restricted to craft workers and largely conservative bodies. In the USA unions confined their recruitment to skilled workers, effectively excluding unskilled manual workers from their ranks. The position was broadly similar in other parts of Western Europe, in Canada, and in Australia. Since then trade unions have broadened their horizons, and although in some countries they still only organise a minority of the workforce, nevertheless they play an important role on the industrial and political stage in all Western democracies.

Trade unions never have been, nor ever could be, static organisations. They have changed and developed and will continue to do so. In part the way they change will be a response to the environment in which they operate. They are affected, for example, by economic conditions. There is little doubt that a buoyant economy gives unions much more scope to bargain and to press home their demands; it has been noted that in such conditions employers may be willing to give into union requests for, say, higher wages, or better conditions, because they know that the increased costs can be recouped through higher prices and that it is unlikely that their market share will be adversely affected. At the same time, buoyant economic conditions seem to increase the likelihood of workplace bargaining and this can present a challenge to the union, in some instances threatening the unity of the organisation.

Similarly, unions will be affected by government policy. Governments can encourage or discourage recognition, through direct example in the public sector and by the use of legislation. Reference has been made to the emphasis which Bain[1] has placed on this factor when considering the recognition of white collar unions.

These are only two aspects of a varied environment. Others include technology and technological change, market conditions, employer orientations and the attitudes of the wider public. One does not need to accept the systems approach to the study of industrial relations to note that all of these factors are interrelated and, singly or in combination, have had and will continue to have an effect on trade unions.

However, while the environment in which trade unions operate has been and will continue to be important for them, it is vital not to overestimate its importance. Within given environmental conditions, unions and their leaders retain some room for manoeuvre. In the past the philosophy and policy of union leaders has been important in determining the development of their organisations. Trade unionism in the USA, for example, developed in the first part of the twentieth century along lines determined by a group of relatively conservative leaders who failed to seize the opportunities to unionise unskilled manual workers. However, this is not to argue that with different leaders USA unions would have developed, say, along the lines of British unions. For one thing it is unlikely that leaders of the type who dominated British unions at the beginning of the twentieth century could have emerged in the USA; it was not only in trade unions that the USA differed from Britain in this period, but also in its politics and industrial structure and, in part at least, USA unions and the type of leaders they appointed were a reflection of the political and industrial conditions. However, the success of the CIO in the 1930s and 1940s showed that a different type of union leader and union policy could emerge in the USA. Again in part the emergence of such new leaders and policies was a reflection of changed conditions (economic and political) but there is little doubt that the USA union movement was slower to respond to such conditions and change its own orientation to meet the new conditions than it might have been, because of the nature (and institution) of the AFL leadership.

Similarly, the development of trade unions in Britain in part reflects the political and economic environment in which they have operated. The strong links between the Labour Party and the trade unions are a crucial aspect of this environment. Yet the links have been shaped and at times fostered by prominent union leaders. Bevin was one of the most important British union leaders of the first part of the twentieth century and there is little doubt that his political orientation helped to shape the outlook of his union and of the whole movement: in turn the orientation of the union movement had an important influence on the development of the Labour Party. More recently the role played by union leaders like Jack Jones and Hugh Scanlon was important in re-establishing the links between the trade unions and the Labour Party after the strains encountered in the late 1960s. This is not to suggest that without the activity of such leaders the traditional links between the trade unions and the Labour Party would have been completely broken, but it might have taken longer for the conflict to subside; if this had been the case then the future of the Labour Party might have been different, and undoubtedly this would have affected trade unions themselves.

Trade unions, then, are not completely constrained by their environment; there is some freedom of action and limited choice. If they pursue policies which are completely out of tune with their environment then such policies will fail to bring the hoped-for results, but it is not inevitable that they will seize opportunities when they are offered by their environment as soon as or in the way that they could do.

Similarly, the environment in which trade unions operate is not something abstract and completely separate from them. At points they are closely linked to and overlap with it. Note has already been taken, for example, that trade union action can affect the economic environment: trade union attitudes to work rules and practices can affect economic growth. In the same way union attitudes and action can affect another aspect of their environment, the orientation of the wider public. The relatively hostile public attitude towards trade unions in Britain in 1978 was in part a response to the activity of particular trade unionists, for instance the aggressive picketing during the lorry drivers' dispute. In turn this hostile public attitude had an affect on another aspect of the environment of trade unions, government policy. In the particular case cited, it made it easier for the government to propose legislation to restrict union activity.

Further, trade union reaction at any particular point in time, to any proposal, problem or development, may be constrained by the history of that union and the union movement. The current organisational structures of unions have evolved over many years and determine lines of action and power relationships. Such factors exert an important influence on policy and future direction. For example, attempts to rationalise the trade union movement have been affected by the history and current organisational form of the bodies concerned. In Britain, mergers between unions like the

National Union of Railwaymen and the Associated Society of Locomotive Engineers and Fireman are unlikely in the near future, not because such mergers would be illogical on operational grounds but because of the history of hostility between the two unions. Similarly, many proposed mergers have failed because the unions concerned had built up their own hierarchies, and the people occupying senior positions either feared that they would lose their seniority or opposed their opposite numbers on personal grounds.

It is not accidental that the most dramatic rationalisation of a trade union movement occurred in West Germany, and that it occurred after the Second World War, at the insistence of the occupying forces and after the virtual destruction of the old trade union movement by the Nazis. However, it also needs to be recalled that the move to create a more unified trade union movement in West Germany was not simply one insisted on by the occupying forces: the idea also found favour with the West German trade union leaders because of the history of the union movement in the 1930s. They believed that the divisions within the union movement were one of the reasons why the unions were unable to prevent the rise of National Socialism.

Of course, to note the importance of history is not to argue that in the future trade unions cannot or will not change. To the contrary, as has been noted, trade unions are bound to change. The direction and pace of change, though, is likely to be affected by their history and their current organisational form, just as it will be affected by their environment, the demands made by their members and new ideas.

PROBLEMS OF MATURE ORGANISATIONS

It has been argued that attempts to predict the direction of future developments are futile. No social phenomenon reacts to stimuli in a predictable enough fashion to permit forecasts to be made with any reasonable level of accuracy. Prediction is futile because not only is the environment in which unions will have to operate uncertain, but so too is the reaction of key personnel, and the future direction of unions depends on both their environment and their reactions to it.

However, it is possible to indicate the areas in which problems are likely to arise in the future, if not the way in which they are likely to be solved. In this context it is important to recognise the extent of the changes that have taken place to the nature of unions in industrially developed nations this century. Many authors have pointed out that unions are no longer primarily concerned with fighting the kind of battles that preoccupied them at the beginning of the century: they are no longer emerging but are now mature organisations. Thus, as long ago as the 1950s, Harbison, discussing the position of unions in the USA was able to note that: 'The problems confronting the newly organised unions which were struggling in the thirties to establish beachheads in industries long characterised by hostility to organised labour are not the same as those faced today by strong, stable and secure labor organisations'[2] while Lester, also discussing the position of unions in the USA at the same time, said: 'The formative stage of American unionism is now largely completed. The union empires have largely been built. Organised labor in this country has acquired its chief institutional characteristics.'[3]

If these comments were appropriate for a country like the USA then they were even more appropriate for many Western European nations and Australia, where union movements had a longer and firmer history.

Linked to this, a number of authors have noted changes in the pattern of industrial conflict. The bitter battles involving protracted strike action over recognition which were a feature of the early stages of unionisation are said to occur far less frequently today. One of the reasons for this reduction in violence could be a reduction in the intensity of the opposition of American employers to unionisation and union policy. Another reason, as writers like Dahrendorf[4] have pointed out, could be the institutionalisation of industrial conflict and its separation from other spheres of social conflict.

The discussion of changes in the nature of industrial conflict is taken a further stage by Ross and Hartman[5] when they suggest changes in the pattern of strikes in Western nations. In the early stages of union development unions engaged in strike action to gain recognition: in parallel, and then later, strike action was used by unions to gain economic benefits. However, Ross and Hartman argue that unions have used the strike weapon less frequently in recent years because they have believed that their objectives could be gained just as well, and possibly better, through political rather than strike action.

None of these comments should be accepted uncritically. For example, it would be difficult to accept the idea that the use of the strike weapon is being abandoned by trade unions. In Britain although it is fair to point out that the use of the long-drawn-out national strike by trade unions has declined since the 1930s, it has been replaced by the more frequent use of the shorter, local and often unofficial strike. The result may have been a decrease in the number of working days lost through strikes, if the pre and post Second World War years are compared, but that has been accompanied by an increase in the number of strikes. Further, there is some evidence of more frequent use of the long national official strike by British trade unions in the 1970s than was the case in the 1950s and 1960s (in 1971 and 1972 about three-quarters of all days lost through strikes were lost as the result of official strikes and on average strikes lasted for about 13 days compared to between 4 and 5 days during the 1950s and 1960s). In other countries the details differ but there is evidence that the use of the strike weapon by trade unions has by no means disappeared and of a general trend towards the increased use of the strike weapon in Western nations in the early 1970s.

It is also worthwhile noting that even if one could show a reduction in strike activity, this would not necessarily mean that trade unions had abandoned the use of industrial conflict as a way of achieving their objectives. The strike weapon is only one manifestation of industrial conflict: overtime bans, output restrictions, factory occupations are simply examples of a range of alternatives that can be used. In particular economic conditions such alternatives may appear to trade unions to be preferable forms of action to strikes.

In a similar way the assertions about the reduction in violence need to be treated with caution. While it may be true that the level of violence associated with industrial conflict declined in the post Second World War years, violence has by no means been absent. Although Taft and Ross[6] placed emphasis on a decrease in such violence, they recognised that there were serious violent incidents in the USA in the 1960s. Note has been made in an earlier chapter of the violence associated with the industrial conflict in France in 1968.

Again, while unions may have been less preoccupied with recognition issues after the Second World War than was the case in the last part of the nineteenth and first part of the twentieth century, such issues were far from being completely absent from the industrial scene in the mid twentieth century. Earlier the recognition dispute at Grunwicks[7] was referred to and this illustrates both the difficulties that some unions still face in gaining bargaining rights, and the way in which violence can easily erupt in industrial disputes.

Caution, then, needs to be exercised in interpreting trends. It is clear that unions still face recognition problems, still use the strike weapon extensively, and at times industrial conflict still is associated with violence. Nevertheless, this should not be allowed to deflect from appreciation that trade unions are working in a different environment than was the case at the beginning of this century, that they have become more adept at using political pressure and that more generally they are now having to face the kind of problems associated with mature organisations. These problems include one cluster related to the size of the organisation, others deriving from the increasingly close relationships between many unions and employing organisations, and others deriving from the need to work in a political environment, sometimes leading unions to forge fairly close relations with governments. Each of these issues would repay a little more attention.

Unions vary tremendously in their size. In countries like West Germany there are relatively few unions but a high proportion are large by international standards. In countries like Britain and the USA there are a number of very large unions but also a large number of very small ones. However, in these countries there has been a trend towards amalgamation, with a consequent reduction in the number and increase in the size of the unions remaining.

An increase in the size of trade unions can cause problems, for it can raise difficulties for relationships between union leaders and rank and file members. One does not have to accept Michels' 'iron law of oligarchy'[8] to recognise that large scale organisations face particular problems in this area. In some instances the problems may be caused by little more than poor communications; in others the problems may be the result of leaders and rank and file members growing apart socially and in terms of their frames of reference.

To some degree, the development of unofficial workplace bargaining can be seen as a reaction to the increasing size of unions. Of course, this has not been the only factor: others have included changing economic conditions, the increase in the size of the firm and technological developments. However, in some instances the increase in the size of the union organisation and the remoteness between union leaders and rank and file has played a part.

None of this is to suggest that size by itself poses insuperable disadvantages. Clearly, from the point of view of bargaining and the provision of services size can be an important advantage

However, this does not detract from the fact that size at least poses its own problems and ones which are likely to feature strongly in the future.

Similarly in the future union relations with managements are likely to be the cause of problems and debate. If unions co-operate closely with management is this likely to lead to a loss of their independence? On the other hand, if unions refuse to co-operate with managements then are they passing over the opportunity to exert influence on behalf of their members on issues which clearly are of concern to them? Such questions are likely to be brought into focus when industrial democracy is discussed.

Public discussion of industrial democracy in Britain was re-started in the late 1970s with the publication of the majority report of the Bullock Committee.[9] This suggested that a new form of government should be introduced in all private companies with more than 2,000 employees; it was based on what was called the $2X + Y$ formula. According to this formula company boards would be formed with equal numbers of shareholders and employee representatives, along with an unequal number of independent members. Crucially, the employee representatives were to be selected by the trade unions in the enterprise.

British trade unions differed in their reaction to this report. The majority, including Britain's largest union, the Transport and General Workers Union, whose leader Jack Jones was an influential member of the committee, accepted the report on the basis that it would give them a greater say in the way the enterprise was run and thus enable them to defend the interests of their members more effectively. The trade unions believed that they could exercise this influence and yet retain their independence by ensuring that their representatives would not be tied too closely to them: the representatives would not be mandated on particular issues and therefore could not be assumed to be putting forward union policy. Thus, it would not be inconceivable for a union to oppose decisions taken by an enterprise with which their representatives concurred.

Not all unions accepted this line of argument. Some believed that the links between the representative and the union would be so strong, whatever the theory, that the union would soon become closely linked to the management of the enterprise. In taking this line unions like the General and Municipal Workers Union were following what was the dominant view in the British trade union movement from the end of the 1920s up until 1965. They were also accepting the argument of many pluralist writers, like Clegg,[10] who argued that trade union independence was of paramount importance and was a better guarantee of democracy than special participative schemes. In practice, the debate over the Bullock Committee report has now lost some of its force because the report itself has lost its political backing. Nevertheless, the debate over the issues raised remains important.

Of course, not only British unions have had to face such choices in connection with industrial democracy. Trade unions in West Germany have participated in schemes of industrial democracy for many years. The scheme of co-determination in the coal and steel industries is the most important and has endured, with minor changes, since the end of the Second World War. Interestingly, this scheme is accepted even by some of the critics of the majority report of the Bullock Committee in Britain, for it is recognised that because of the way in which it has been approached by the trade unions it has not impaired their independence.

Rather more difficult issues are raised by the experience of trade unions in Yugoslavia. Their experience with workers' councils has raised a number of questions. Crucially, writers like Kolaja[11] have argued that because of their close association with the workers' councils the unions have lost their independence and ceased to be able to defend workers' interests. At the same time some would argue that the main beneficiaries of the scheme have not been the shop floor workers but professional managers who have gained greater freedom of action.

Of course, discussion of union relationships with management should not be confined simply to consideration of full-blown schemes of industrial democracy. Such schemes often call for the most extensive co-operation but other looser devices also raise important questions and are widely used. Joint consultation and worker participation, for example, are found throughout substantial parts of industry in Western democracies. They are looser forms of association than industrial democracy because the workers, or their representatives, who are involved in such arrangements hold little executive power. In the case of joint consultation the arrangement is specially devised to ensure that management retains the ultimate responsibility for executive decisions. As a result there is less danger of union independence being compromised. Nevertheless this danger is not totally absent, particularly if unions nominate or control the workers' representatives: on the other hand if they do not do this then there is the danger that the workers' representatives will rival the union for the allegiance of the workers.

Union relations with governments rather than managements raise problems just as complicated. Unions have welcomed the opportunity to be involved in discussions with governments, to join advisory committees and the like in the past because they have seen this as a way of influencing policy and furthering the interests of their members. Such communications and discussions with governments have a long history and are by no means a recent phenomenon. Nevertheless the extent of such communications and discussions has increased in recent years for two reasons. First, governments have consulted all shades of opinion increasingly in recent years, and trade unions have simply benefited from this general trend. Second, trade unions, as they have matured, have been seen (and in part have sought to be seen) as responsible bodies who ought to be consulted over important economic and social matters.

The concern of many Western governments since the Second World War to exert greater control over the direction of their economies has brought another factor into play. If governments want to control the economy then they have to seek to control unions but, as Thomson[12] has argued, in most instances they have discovered that it is difficult to do so in the long term without the co-operation of the trade unions. The social contracts which were a feature of some countries in the 1970s were one result of this.

Relations with governments, whether they remain simply at the discussion and consultation level or whether they extend to formal social contract type arrangements, raise problems as well as possibilities for trade unions. The problems, in essence, are very similar to those raised in relationships between unions and management. A refusal to enter into discussions or agreements may mean that unions lose the opportunity to influence events in a way that will benefit their members: a willingness to do so may lead to their incorporation into the capitalist state and a loss of independence. Similarly, as with relationships between unions and management, there is not necessarily any blanket answer to the dilemmas facing union/government relationships. The strength of the particular union, the nature of the relations between union members and rank and file, and the policies of the government may all have an effect and influence the choice of one course of action rather than another.

The problems outlined above are simply three that are likely to face unions 'as mature organisations'. However, they are three of the more important ones, and the reaction to them undoubtedly will help to shape the kind of union movement that will develop over the next hundred years.

NOTES

1. G.S. Bain, *The Growth of White Collar Unionism*, Oxford U. P. London, 1970.
2. F.H. Harbison, Forword to R.A. Lester, *As Unions Mature*, Princeton U.P., Princeton, 1958, p. 4.
3. *Ibid.*, pp. 154–55.
4. R. Dahrendorf, *Class and Class Conflict in Industrial Society*, Routledge & Kegan Paul, London, 1968.
5. A.M. Ross, P.T. Hartman, *Changing Patterns of Industrial Conflict*, Wiley, New York, 1960.
6. P. Taft, P. Ross, 'American labor violence: its causes, character and outcome', in H.E. Graham, T.R. Gurr (eds), *Violence in America*, Bantam, New York, 1969.
7. See Chapter 7, p. 138.
8. R. Michels, *Political Parties*, Dover, New York, 1959.
9. Report of the Committee of Inquiry on Industrial Democracy, HMSO, London, 1977, Cmnd 6706.
10. H.A. Clegg, *A New Approach to Industrial Democracy*, Blackwell, Oxford, 1963.
11. J. Kolaja, *Workers' Councils: The Yugoslav Experience*, Tavistock, London, 1965.
12. A.W.J. Thomson, 'Trade unions and the corporate state in Britain', *Industrial and Labor Relations Review*, vol. 33 (1979), no. 1, pp. 36–54.

BIBLIOGRAPHY

ADAMS, R.J. (1975) *The Growth of White Collar Unionism in Britain and Sweden: A Comparative Investigation*, Industrial Relations Research Institute, University of Wisconsin

ADAMS, R.J. (1975) 'The recognition of white collar unions', *British Journal of Industrial Relations*, vol. XIII, no. 1, pp. 102–6

ADAMS, R.J. (1977) 'Bain's theory of white collar union growth: a conceptual critique', *British Journal of Industrial Relations*, vol. XV, no. 3, pp. 317–21

ALBEDA, W. (1971) 'Recent trends in collective bargaining in the Netherlands', *International Labour Review*, vol. 103, pp. 247–68

ALBEDA, W. (1977) 'Changing industrial relations in the Netherlands', *Industrial Relations*, vol. 16, no. 2, pp. 133–44

ALLEN, V.L. (1954) *Power in Trade Unions*, Longmans, Green, London

ALLEN, V.L. (1967) 'The paradox of militancy' in Blackburn, R., Cockburn, A. (eds), *The Incompatibles*, Penguin, Harmondsworth

ALLEN, V.L. (1971) *The Sociology of Industrial Relations*, Longmans, London

ALLEN, V.L. (1975) 'Trade unions: an analytical framework' in Barrett, B. *et al.* (eds), *Industrial Relations in the Wider Society*, Collier-Macmillan, London

ANDERSON, P. (1967) 'The limits and possibilities of trade union action', in Blackburn, R., Cockburn, A. (eds), *The Incompatibles*, Penguin, Harmondsworth

ARMSTRONG, E.G.A. (1975) 'The role of the state' in Barrett, B., *et al.* (eds), *Industrial Relations and the Wider Society*, Collier-Macmillan, London

BAIN, G.S. (1970) *The Growth of White Collar Unionism*, Oxford U. P., London

BAIN, G.S. (1978) Nov/Dec 'Union growth and public policy in Canada', *The Labour Gazette*, vol. LXXVIII, pp. 529–37

BAIN, G.S., CLEGG, H.A. (1974) 'A strategy for industrial relations research in Great Britain', *British Journal of Industrial Relations* vol. XII, no. 1

BAIN, G.S., ELSHEIKH, F. (1976) *Union Growth and the Business Cycle: An Econometric Analysis*, Blackwell, Oxford

BAIN, G.S., PRICE, R. (1972) 'Who is a white collar employee?', *British Journal of Industrial Relations*, vol. X, no. 3, pp. 325–39

BANKS, J.A. (1972) *Social Movements*, Macmillan, London

BANKS, J.A. (1974) *Trade Unionism*, Collier-Macmillan, London

BARBASH, J. (1967) *American Unions*, Random House, New York

BARKIN, S. (1977) 'Social contracts in Europe', *Free Labour World*, May/June, pp. 6–9

BELL, D. (1960) 'Union growth and structural cycles' in Galenson, W., Lipset, S.M. (eds), *Labour and Trade Unionism*, Wiley, New York

BERGMANN, J., MULLER-JENTSCH, W. (1975) 'The Federal Republic of Germany: Co-operative unionism and dual bargaining system challenged' in Barkin, S. (ed.), *Worker Militancy and its Consequences, 1965–75*, Praeger, New York

BLACKBURN, R.M. (1967) *Union Character and Social Class: A Study of White Collar Unionism*, Batsford, London

BLANPAIN, R. (1971) 'Recent trends in collective bargaining in Belgium', *International Labour Review*, vol. 104, pp. 111–30

BRANDINI, P.M. (1975) 'Italy: creating a new system of industrial relations from the bottom', in Barkin, S. (ed.), *Worker Militancy and its Consequences, 1965–75*, Praeger, New York

BROOMWICH, L. (1959) *Union Constitutions*, The Fund for the Republic, New York

BROWN, E.C. (1966) *Soviet Trade Unions and Labour Relations*, Harvard U.P., Cambridge (Mass.)

BROWN, W., EBSWORTH, R., TERRY, M. (1978) 'Factors shaping shop steward organisation in Britain', *British Journal of Industrial Relations*, vol. XVI, no. 2, pp. 139–58

BUKHARIN, N. (1925) *Historical Materialism: A System of Sociology*, International Publishers, New York

BULLOCK, A. (1960) *The Life and Times of Ernest Bevin*, Heinemann, London

BURKITT, B., BOWERS, D. (1979) *Trade Unions and the Economy*, Macmillan, London

CAMERON, G.C., ELDRIDGE, J.E.T. (1968) 'Unofficial strikes' in

Eldridge, J.E.T. *Industrial Disputes*, Routledge & Kegan Paul, London

CHAMBERLAIN, N.W., CULLEN, D.E., LEWIN, D. (1980) *The Labor Sector*, McGraw-Hill, New York

CHILO, J., LOVERIDGE, R., WARNER, M. (1973) 'Towards an organisational study of trade unions' *Sociology*, vol. 7, pp. 71–91

CLEGG, H.A. (1954) *General Union*, Blackwell, Oxford

CLEGG, H.A. (1963) *A New Approach to Industrial Democracy*, Blackwell, Oxford

CLEGG, H.A. (1976) *Trade Unionism Under Collective Bargaining*, Blackwell, Oxford

CLEGG, H.A., KILLICK, A.J., ADAMS, R. (1961) *Trade Union Officers*, Blackwell, Oxford

COATES, K., TOPHAM, T. (1970) *Workers' Control*, Panther, London

Commission on Industrial Relations (1974) *Workplace Participation and Collective Bargaining in Europe*, HMSO, London

Committee of Inquiry on Industrial Democracy (1977) *Report*, HMSO, London, Cmnd 6706

Committee on the Relations Between Employers and Employed (1916–18) *Reports*, HMSO, London cd 8606, 9001, 9002, 9099, 9153

COLE, G.D.H. (1923) *Workshop Organisation*, Oxford U.P., Oxford

COLE, G.D.H. (1953) *An Introduction to Trade Unionism*, Allen & Unwin

COLE, G.D.H. (1972) *Self-Government in Industry*, Hutchinson, London

COLEMAN, J.R. (1955) 'The compulsive pressures of union democracy' *American Journal of Sociology*, vol. 61, no. 6, pp. 519–26

COSER, L. (1956) *The Functions of Social Conflict*, Routledge & Kegan Paul, London

CROMPTON, R. (1976) 'Approaches to the study of white collar unionism', *Sociology*, vol. 10, no. 3, pp. 407–24

CROMPTON, R. (1979) 'Trade unionism and the insurance clerk', *Sociology*, vol. 13, no. 3, pp. 403–25

CROSLAND, C.A.R. (1956) *The Future of Socialism*, Cape, London

CROUCH, C. (1977) *Class Conflict and the Industrial Relations Crisis*, Heinemann, London

CROUCH, C. (1979) *The Politics of Industrial Relations*, Manchester U.P., Manchester

CYRIAX, G., OAKESHOTT, R. (1960) *The Bargainers*, Faber, London

DAHL, R.A. (1958) 'A critique of the ruling elite model', *American Political Science Review*, vol. 52, pp. 463–69

DAHRENDORF, R. (1959) *Class and Class Conflict in Industrial Society*, Routledge & Kegan Paul, London

DAVIES, H.B. (1972) 'The theory of union growth' in McCarthy, W.E.J. (ed.), *Trade Unions*, Penguin, Harmondsworth

DEMERY, D., McNABB, R. (1978) 'The effects of demand on the union relative wage effect in the United Kingdom', *British Journal of Industrial Relations*, vol. XXI, no. 3, pp. 303–8

Department of Employment and Productivity (1969) *In Place of Strife*, HMSO, London, Cmnd 3888

DUBIN, R. (1954) 'Constructive aspects of industrial conflict' in Kornhauser, A., Dubin, R., Ross, A.M., *Industrial Conflict*, McGraw-Hill, New York

EDELSTEIN, J.D. (1967) 'An organisational theory of union democracy', *American Sociological Review*, vol. 32, pp. 19–31

EDELSTEIN, J.D., WARNER, M. (1979) *Comparative Union Democracy*, Transaction Books, New Brunswick

ELDRIDGE, J.E.T. (1973) *Sociology and Industrial Life*, Nelson, London

ELSHEIKH, F., BAIN, G.S. (1978) 'American trade union growth: An alternative model', *Industrial Relations*, vol. 17, no. 1, pp. 95–99

ELSHEIKH, F., BAIN, G.S. (1978) 'Union growth: a reply' *British Journal of Industrial Relations*, vol. XVI, no. 2, pp. 99–102

ENGELS, F. (1977) 'Labour movements' in Clarke, T., Clements, L. (eds), *Trade Unionism Under Capitalism*, Fontana, Glasgow

FATCHETT, D.J., WHITTINGHAM, W.M. (1978/79) 'Other aspects of the social contract', *Industrial Relations Journal*, vol. 9, no. 4

FINLAY, J.E. (1972) *The Corrupt Kingdom*, Simon & Shuster, New York

FLANDERS, A. (1967) *Collective Bargaining*, Faber & Faber, London

FLANDERS, A. (1968) *Trade Unions*, Hutchinson, London

FLANDERS, A. (1974) 'The tradition of voluntarism' *British Journal of Industrial Relations*, vol. XII, no. 3, pp. 352–70

FLANDERS, A., CLEGG, H.A. (eds) (1953) *The System of Industrial Relations in Great Britain*, Blackwell, Oxford

FOX, A. (1966) *Industrial Sociology and Industrial Relations*, Research Paper No. 3, Royal Commission on Trade Unions and Employers' Associations, HMSO, London

FOX, A. (1972) *A Sociology of Work in Industry*, Collier-Macmillan, London

FOX, A. (1973) 'Industrial relations: a social critique of pluralist ideology' in Child, J. (ed.) *Man and Organisation*, Allen &

Unwin, London

FOX, A., FLANDERS, A (1969) 'The reform of collective bargaining: from Donovan to Durkheim', *British Journal of Industrial Relations*, vol. VII, no. 2, pp. 151–80

GIUGNI, G. (1971) 'Recent trends in collective bargaining in Italy', *International Labour Review*, vol. 104, pp. 307–28

GOLDTHORPE, J.H. (1964) 'Social stratification in industrial society' in Halmos, P. (ed.), *The Development of Industrial Societies*, Sociological Review Monograph No. 8, University of Keele

GOLDTHORPE, J.H., LOCKWOOD, D., BECHHOFER, F., PLATT, J. (1968) *The Affluent Worker: Industrial Attitudes and Behaviour*, Cambridge U.P., London

GOLDSTEIN, J. (1952) *The Government of a British Trade Union*, Free Press, Glencoe

GOODMAN, J.F.B., WHITTINGHAM, T.G. (1969) *Shop Stewards in British Industry*, McGraw-Hill, London

GRAMSCI, A. (1977) 'The Turin workers' Councils', in Blackburn, R. (ed.), *Revolution and Class Struggle: A Reader in Marxist Politics*, Fontana, Glasgow

GUERIN, D. (1971) 'Workers' self-management of industry' in Shatz, M.S. (ed.), *The Essential Works of Anarchism*, Bantam, New York

HALL, B. (ed.) (1972) *Autocracy and Insurgency in Organised Labor*, Transaction Books, New Brunswick

HARBISON, F.H. (1954) 'Collective bargaining and American capitalism' in Kornhauser, A., Dubin, R., Ross, A.M. (eds), *Industrial Conflict*, McGraw Hill, New York

HILL, S. (1974) 'Norms, groups and power: the sociology of workplace industrial relations', *British Journal of Industrial Relations*, vol. XII, no. 2, pp. 213–35

HINES, A.G. (1964) 'Trade unions and wage inflation in the United Kingdom 1893–1961', *Review of Economic Studies*, vol. XXI, pp. 221–52

HINES, A.G. (1969) 'Wage inflation in the United Kingdom, 1948–1962: a disaggregated study', *Economic Journal*, vol. 9, pp. 66–89

HINTON, J. (1973) *The First Shop Stewards' Movement*, Allen & Unwin, London

HOWELLS, J.M., WOODFIELD, A.E. (1970) 'The ability of managers and trade union officers to predict workers preferences', *British Journal of Industrial Relations*, vol. VIII, no. 2, pp. 237–51

HUGHES, J. (1968) *Trade Union Structure and Government*, Research

Paper 5, Part 2, Royal Commission on Trade Unions and Employers' Associations, 1965–68, HMSO, London

HYMAN, R. (1975) *Industrial Relations: A Marxist Introduction*, Macmillan, London

HYMAN, R. (1975) *Marxism and the Sociology of Trade Unionism*, Pluto, London

HYMAN, R., BROUGH, I (1975) *Social Values and Industrial Relations: A Study of Fairness and Inequality*, Blackwell, Oxford

International Labour Office (1961) *The Trade Union Situation in the United Kingdom*, ILO, Geneva

JACKSON, D., TURNER, H.A., WILKINSON, F. (1975) Do Trade Unions Cause Inflation? Cambridge U.P., London

JACKSON, M.P. (1973) *Labour Relations on the Docks*, Saxon House, Farnborough

JACKSON, M.P. (1974) *The Price of Coal*, Croom Helm, London

JACKSON, M.P. (1977) *Industrial Relations*, Croom Helm, London

JAMES, R.C., JAMES, E.D. (1965) *Hoffa and the Teamsters*, D. Van Nostrand, Princeton

JAMIESON, S. (1973) *Industrial Relations in Canada*, Macmillan, Toronto

JOHNSON, H.G., MIESZKOWSKI, P. (1970) 'The effects of unionisation on the distribution of income: a general equilibrium approach' *Quarterly Journal of Economics*, vol. XXXIV, no. 4, pp. 537–61

KELSALL, R.K., LOCKWOOD, D., TROPP, A. (1956) 'The new middle class in the power structure of Great Britain', Transactions of the Third World Congress of Sociology

KENDALL, W. (1975) *The Labour Movement in Europe*, Allen Lane, London

KERR, C. (1954) 'Industrial conflict and its mediation', *American Journal of Sociology*, vol. LX, pp. 230–45

KERR, C. (1957) *Unions and Union Leaders of their Own Choosing*, The Fund for the Republic, New York

KERR, C., DUNLOP, J.T., HARBISON, F.H., MAYERS, C.A. (1962) *Industrialism and Industrial Man*, Heinemann, London

KEYNES, J.E. (1939) 'Relative movements of real wages and output' *Economic Journal*, vol. 49, pp. 34–51

KOLAJA, J. (1965) *Workers' Councils: The Yugoslav Experience*, Tavistock, London

KORPI, W. (1978) 'Workplace bargaining, the law and unofficial strikes: the case of strikes', *British Journal of Industrial Relations*, vol. XVI, no. 3, pp. 355–68

LANE, T. (1974) *The Union Makes Us Strong*, Arrow, London

LEIBERSON, W.M. (1959) *American Trade Union Democracy*, Columbia U.P., New York

LENIN, V.I. (1977) 'What is to be done?' in Clarke, T., Clements, L. (eds) *Trade Unionism Under Capitalism*, Fontana, Glasgow

LENSKI, G.E. (1966) *Power and Privilege*, McGraw-Hill, New York

LESTER, R.A. (1958) *As Unions Mature*, Princeton U.P., Princeton

LEWIS, H.G. (1965) *Unionism and Relative Wages in the United States*, Chicago U.P., Chicago

LICHTHEIM, G. (1975) *A Short History of Socialism*, Fontana, Glasgow

LIPSET, S.M., TROW, M.A., COLEMAN, J.S. (1956) *Union Democracy*, Free Press, New York

LIPSET, S.M. (1965) 'Political sociology' in Merton, R.K., Broom, L., Cottrell, L.S. Jnr. (eds), *Sociology Today*, New York

LOCKWOOD, D. (1958) *The Blackcoated Worker*, Allen & Unwin, London

LOCKWOOD, D. (1966) 'Sources of variation in working class images of society', *Sociological Review*, vol. 14, no. 3, pp. 249–67

LOVERIDGE, R. (1972) 'Occupational change and the development of interest groups among white collar workers in the UK: a long term model', *British Journal of Industrial Relations*, vol. X, no. 3, pp. 340–65

LUMLEY, R. (1973) *White Collar Unionism in Britain*, Methuen, London

LUPTON, T. (1963) *On the Shop Floor*, Pergamon, Oxford

LUXEMBURG, R. (1906) *The Mass Strike*, Merlin Press, London

McCARTHY, W.E.J. (1964) *The Closed Shop in Britain*, Blackwell, Oxford

McCARTHY, W.E.J. (1966) *The Role of Shop Stewards in British Industrial Relations*, Royal Commission on Trade Unions and Employers' Association Research Paper 1, HMSO, London

McCARTHY, W.E.J., PARKER, S.R. (1968) *Shop Stewards and Workshop Relations*, Royal Commission on Trade Unions and Employers' Associations, 1965–68, Research Paper 10, HMSO, London

McCARTHY, W.E.J., PARKER, P.A.L., HAWES, W.R., LUMB, A.L. (1971) *The Reform of Collective Bargaining at Plant and Company Level*, Department of Employment Manpower Papers No. 5, HMSO, London

MAGRATH, C.P. (1958–59) 'Democracy in overalls: the futile quest for union democracy', *Industrial and Labor Relations Review*, vol. 12, pp. 503–25

MALATESTA, E. (1977) 'Syndicalism: an advocacy' in Woodcock, G. (ed.) *The Anarchist Reader*, Fontana, Glasgow

MARTIN, R. (1968) 'Union democracy: an explanatory framework', *Sociology*, vol. 2, pp. 205–20

MARX, E., KENDALL, W. (1971) *Unions in Europe*, Centre for Contemporary European Studies, University of Sussex

MARX, K. (1977) 'Capital and labour' in Clarke, T., Clements, L. (eds), *Trade Unionism Under Capitalism*, Fontana, Glasgow

MAYO, E. (1946) *The Human Problems of Industrial Civilisation*, Harvard U.P., Cambridge (Mass.)

MICHELS, R. (1962) *Political Parties*, Free Press, New York

MILLER, D. (1978) 'Trade union workplace representation in the Federal Republic of Germany: an analysis of post war Vertrauensleute policy of the German metalworkers' union (1952–77)', *British Journal of Industrial Relations*, vol. XVl, no. 3, pp. 335–54

MILLS, C. WRIGHT (1948) *The New Men of Power*, Harcourt Brace, New York

MILLS, C. WRIGHT (1959) *The Power Elite*, Oxford U. P., New York

MOORE, W.J. (1978) 'An analysis of teacher union growth', *Industrial Relations*, vol. 17, no. 2, pp. 204–15

MOORE, W.J., PEARCE, D.F. (1976) 'Union growth: a test of the Ashenfelter-Pencavel model', *Industrial Relations*, vol. 15, No. 2, pp. 244–47

MOORE, W.J., RAISIAN, J. (1980) 'Cyclical sensitivity of union/nonunion relative wage effects', *Journal of Labor Research*, vol. 1, no. 1, pp. 115–32

MORAN, M. (1974) *The Union of Post Office Workers: A study of Political Sociology*, Macmillan, London

MULVEY, C. (1978) *The Economic Analysis of Trade Unions*, Martin Robertson, Oxford

NICHOLAS, A.W. (1965) 'Factions: a comparative analysis' in A.S.A. Monograph No. 2, *Political Systems and the Distribution of Power*, Tavistock, London

OTTER, C.V. (1975) 'Sweden: labor reformism shapes the system' in Barkin, S. (ed.) *Worker Militancy and its Consequences*, 1965–75, Praeger, New York

PARKER, S.R. *et al.* (1972) *The Sociology of Industry*, Allen & Unwin, London

PELLING, H. (1971) *A History of British Trade Unionism*, Penguin,

Harmondsworth

PENCAVEL, J.H. (1977) 'The distribution and efficiency effects of trade unions in Britain', *British Journal of Industrial Relations* vol. XV, no. 2, pp. 137–56

PEPER, B. (1975) 'The Netherlands: from an ordered harmonic to a bargaining relationship' in Barkin, S. (ed.) *Worker Militancy and its Consequences 1965–75*, Praeger, New York, pp. 118–53

PHELPS BROWN, E.H. (1957) 'The long-term movement of real wages' in Dunlop, J.T. (ed.), *The Theory of Wage Determination*, Macmillan, London

PHELPS BROWN, E.H. (1962) *The Economics of Labour*, Yale U.P., New Haven

PHILLIPS, A.W. (1958) 'The relation between unemployment and the rate of change of money wages in the United Kingdom, 1861–1957', *Economica*, vol. 25, pp. 238–99

PHILLIPS, G.A. (1976) *The General Strike*, Weidenfeld & Nicolson, London

PORKLETT, J.L. (1978) 'Industrial relations and participation in management in the Soviet type communist system', *British Journal of Industrial Relations*, vol. XVI, no. 1, pp. 70–85

PRICE, R., BAIN, G.S. (1976) 'Union growth revisited: 1948–1974 in perspective', *British Journal of Industrial Relations*, vol. XIV, no. 3, pp. 339–55

PURDY, D.L., ZIS, G. (1974) 'On the concept and measurement of union militancy' in Candler, D., Purdy, D.C. (eds), *Inflation and the Labour Markets*, Manchester U. P., Manchester

RAWSON, D.W. (1968) 'Unions and politics' in Matthews, P.W.D., Ford, G.W. (eds), *Australian Trade Unions*, Sunbooks, Melbourne

REDER, M.W. (1952) 'The theory of union wage policy', *Review of Economics and Statistics,* vol. 34, pp. 34–45

RICHARDSON, J.H. (1965) *An Introduction to the Study of Industrial Relations in Great Britain*, Allen & Unwin, London

RICHARDSON, R. (1977) 'Trade union growth', *British Journal of Industrial Relations*, vol. XV, no. 2, pp. 279–82

ROBERTS, B.C. (1956) *Trade Union Government and Administration in Great Britain*, Harvard U.P., Cambridge (Mass.)

ROBERTS, B.C. (1962) *Trade Unions in a Free Society*, Hutchinson, London

ROMER, S. (1967) *The International Brotherhood of Teamsters*, Wiley, New York

ROSEN, S. (1975) 'The United States: a time for reassessment' in

Barkin, S. (ed.), *Worker Militancy and its consequences*, 1965–75 Praeger, New York

ROSS, A.M., HARTMAN, P.T. (1960) *Changing Patterns of Industrial Conflict*, Wiley, New York

Royal Commission on Trade Unions and Employers' Association, (1968) 1965–68 *Report* HMSO, London Cmnd. 3623

RUBLE, B. (1979) 'Dual functioning trade unions in the USSR', *British Journal of Industrial Relations*, vol. XVII, no. 2, pp. 241–55

SAMUELSON, P.A., SOLOW, R.A. (1960) 'Analytical aspects of anti-inflation policy', *American Economic Review*, vol. 50, pp. 177–94

SAYLES, L.R. (1958) *Behaviour of Industrial Work Groups: Prediction and Control*, Wiley, New York

SAYLES, L., STRAUSS, G. (1953) *The Local Union*, Harcourt Brace, New York

SCHNEIDER, E.V., (1971) *Industrial Sociology*, McGraw-Hill, London

SEGLOW, P (1978) *Trade Unionism in Television*, Saxon House, Farnborough

SEIDMAN, J., KARSH, B., TAGLIACOZZO, D. (1956) 'A typology of rank-and-file union members', *American Journal of Sociology*, vol. 4, pp. 546–53

SIEDMAN, J., LONDON, J., KARSH, B., TAGLIACOZZO, D. (1958) *The Worker Views His Union*, Chicago U.P., Chicago

SELZNICK, P. (1952) *The Organisational Weapon: A Study of Bolshevik Strategy and Tactics*, McGraw-Hill, New York

SILVERMAN, D. (1970) *The Theory of Organisations*, Heinemann, London

SLICHTER, S.H. (1947) *Challenge of Industrial Relations*, Cornell U.P., Ithaca

SMELSER, N.J. (1959) *Social Change in the Industrial Revolution*, Routledge & Kegan Paul, London

SOREL, G. (1961) *Reflections on Violence*, Collier, New York

SPINARD, W. (1960) 'Correlates of trade union participation: a summary of the literature', *American Sociological Review*, vol. 25, pp. 237–44

STEIBER, J. (1967) *Governing the U.A.W.*, Wiley, New York

STOREY, J. (1976/77) 'Workplace collective bargaining and managerial prerogatives', *Industrial Relations Journal*, vol. 7, no. 3, pp. 40–55

STURMTHAL, A. (ed.) (1966) *White Collar Trade Unions*, Illinois U.P., London

SUMMERS, C. (1952) 'Union democracy and union discipline', Proceedings of New York Universities Fifth Annual Conference on Labor, Matthew Bender, New York

SYKES, A.J.M. (1967) 'The cohesion of a trade union organisation' *Sociology*, vol. 1, no. 2, pp. 141–63

TAFT, P. (1958) 'International affairs of unions and the Taft-Hartley Act' *Industrial and Labor Relations Review*, vol. II, no. 3, pp. 354–55

TAFT, P., ROSS, P. (1980) 'American labor violence: its causes, character and outcome', in Graham, H.E., Gurr, T.R. (eds), *Violence in America*, Bantam, New York

TANNENBAUM, A.S., KAHN, R.L. (1958) *Participation in Union Locals*, Row & Paterson, Evanston (Illinois)

TANNENBAUM, F. (1964) *The True Society: A Philosophy of Labour*, Cape, London

TAYLOR, R. (1978) *Labour and the Social Conflict*, Fabian Tract 458, Civic Press, Glasgow

TERRY, M. (1977) 'The inevitable growth of informality' *British Journal of Industrial Relations*, vol. XV, no. 1, pp. 76–90

THOMAS, R.L., STONEY, P.J.M. (1970) 'A note on the dynamic properties of the Hines inflation model', *Review of Economic Studies*, vol. 37, pp. 286–94

THOMSON, A.W.J. (1979) 'Trade unions and the corporate state in Britain' *Industrial and Labor Relations Review*, vol. 33, no. 1, pp. 36–54

TOWERS, B. (1978) *British Incomes Policy*, Occasional Papers in Industrial Relations, Universities of Leeds and Nottingham

TROTSKY, L. (1977) 'Marxism and trade unionism' in Clarke, T., Clements, L. (eds) *Trade Unionism Under Capitalism*, Fontana, Glasgow

TURNER, H.A. (1962) *Trade Union Growth, Structure and Policy*, Allen & Unwin, London

UNDY, R. (1978) 'The devolution of bargaining levels and responsibilities in the Transport and General Workers' Union, 1965–75' *Industrial Relations Journal*, vol. 9, no. 3, pp. 43–56

Unofficial Reform Committee (1973) *The Miners' Next Step: Being a Scheme for the Reorganisation of the Federation*, Pluto

WALKER, K.F. (1966) 'White collar unionism in Australia', in Sturmthal, A. (ed.), *White Collar Trade Unions*, Illinois U.P., London

WARNER, M. 'Industrial conflict revisited', in Warner, M. (ed.), *The Sociology of the Workplace*, Allen & Unwin, London

WARNER, M., DONALDSON, L. (1971) 'Dimension of organisation

in occupational interest associations: some preliminary findings', Third Joint Conference in Behavioural Science and Operational Research, London

WEBB, S.&B. (1896, 1924) *The History of Trade Unionism*, Longmans, London

WEBB, S.&B. (1920) *Industrial Democracy*, Longmans, Green & Co., London

WESTERGAARD, J., RESLER, H. (1975) *Class in a Capitalist Society*, Heinemann, London

WILDERS, M.G., PARKER, S.R. (1975) 'Changes in workplace industrial relations, 1966–72', *British Journal of Industrial Relations*, vol. XIII, no. 1, pp. 14–22

WILKINSON, R.K., BURKITT, B. (1973) 'Wage determination and trade unions', *Scottish Journal of Political Economy*, vol. 20, pp. 101–121

WILSON, G.K. (1979) *Unions in American National Politics*, Macmillan, London

WOODCOCK, G. (1977) 'Syndicalism defined' in Woodcock, G. (ed.) *The Anachist Reader*, Fontana, Glasgow

INDEX

Acts
    Combination Acts (1799), (1800), 20
    Conspiracy and Protection of
        Property (1875), 24
    Employment Protection (1975), 150
    Factory (1961), 149
    Industrial Relations (1971), 87, 132,
        137, 143, 151, 153, 164
    Landrum Griffin (1959), 152
    Munitions of War (1915), 151
    Right of Association and Negotiation
        (1936) (Sweden), 47
    Taft Hartley (1947), 70, 126, 152
    Terms and Conditions of
        Employment (1959), 150
    Trade Boards (1909), 149
    Trade Disputes (1906), 20, 151
    Trade Unions (1871), 24, 151
    Trade Unions (1913), 21, 151
    Wages Council (1945), 149
    Wagner (1935), 154
Adams, R., 72
Adams, R.J., 45–50
AFL/CIO, 3, 5, 126, 127, 171
Allen, V.C., 17, 24, 67–77, 135, 136
Amalgamated Association of Cotton
    Spinners, 54, 55
Amalgamated Engineering Union, 6, 61
Amalgamated Society of Engineers, 10
Amalgamated Society of Engineers,
    Machinists, Smiths, Millwrights
    and Pattern Makers, 10
American Federation of Labour, 10, 20,
    126, 171
Anderson, P., 138, 139

Associated Society of Locomotive
    Engineers and Fireman, 173

Bain, G.S., 17, 21, 22, 28, 33, 34,
    44—9, 170
Banks, J.A., 18, 26, 27, 66, 67, 78, 94
Barbash, J., 65
Barkin, S., 162
Bergman, J., 91
Bevin, E., 25, 76, 77
Blackburn, R., 38
Brandini, P.M., 91
Broomwich, L., 62
Brown, E.C., 16
Brough, I., 159
Bullock Committee, 177
Burkitt, B., 116
business unionism, 123

Cameron, G.C., 96
Canadian Labour Congress, 3
capitalism, 16–18, 23
Chamberlain, N.W., 105, 114
Child, J. 67, 78
Clegg, H.A., 1, 65, 72, 86, 106, 108,
    128, 132, 154, 159, 177, 178
clerks, 38–41, 43
closed shop, 69, 70
Coates, K., 94
co-determination (W Germany), 178
Cole, G.D.H., 61, 86, 130
Coleman, J.R., 62
collective bargaining, 1, 86–100,
    104–14, 157–66
Committee for Industrial Organisation,
    20, 126, 171

Conditions of Employment and
    National Arbitration Order 1940,
    151
Conféderation générale du Travail, 6,
    13, 126, 128
Conservative Party, 164
corporatism, 162–66
Coser, L., 141
cost-push shcool, 115, 116
Cousins, F., 124
Crompton, R., 43, 44
Crouch, C., 162, 166
Cyriax, G., 61, 66, 70

Dahrendorf, R., 141, 174
Davies, H.B., 19, 20
demand-pull school, 116–18
Demery, D., 111
democracy in unions, 53–78
Democratic Party, 127
DGB, 5, 6
Donovan Commission, 66, 86–8, 97
Dubin, R., 142

Edelstein, J.D., 65
Eldridge, J.E.T., 71, 96
Elliott, F., 32
Elsheikh, F., 21, 22, 28
employment trends, 31–4
Engels, F., 133

factory councils (Italy), 134, 135
Fair Wages Resolutions, 149, 156
Fatchett, D.J., 159, 160
Finley, J.E., 72–4
Flanders, A., 65, 70, 86, 88, 152, 153
foremen, 95
Fox, A., 74, 88, 142
functionalism, 13–16

General and Municipal Workers Union,
    7, 8, 37, 65, 177
General Strike, 1926, 131
General Builders' Association, 106
Giugni, G., 91
Goldstein, J., 60, 61, 63–5, 71
Goldthorpe, J.H., 61
Gompers, S., 126
Gramsci, A. 134, 135
Grand National Consolidated Trade
    Union, 26

Gunwicks, 106, 175
Guérin, D., 132
guild socialism, 130–2

Hall, B., 62, 70
Harbison, F.H., 142, 174
Hartman, P.T., 3, 174
Hawthorne Studies, 93, 143
Heath, E., 156
Hill, S., 93–5, 99
Hines, A.G., 115, 116
Hinton, J., 86
Hoffer, J., 62, 75
Howells, J.M., 72
Hughes, J., 69–71
human relations school, 143
Hyman, R., 137, 159

incomes policies, 154–7
Independent Labour Party, 123
industrial conflict, 87, 89–92, 114, 172,
    174, 175
industrial democracy, 177–9
Industrial Syndicalist Education
    League, 129
Industrial Workers of the World, 129
industrialisation, 13–16, 23
inflation, 114–19
In Place of Strife, 87, 137, 151, 153
International Typographical Union,
    58–60, 63–5
iron law of oligarchy, 57

Jackson, D., 115
Jamieson, S., 3
joint consultation, 178
Johnson, H.G., 112
Joint Industrial Councils, 107, 108
Jones, J., 98, 99, 172, 177

Kahn, R.L., 61
Kahn Freund, O., 151
Kalbitz, R., 90
Kelsall, R.K. 39
Kendall, W., 71, 72, 125
Kerr, C., 31, 62, 142
Keynes, J.M., 109
Killick, A.J., 72
Kalaja, J., 178
Korpi, W., 91, 92

Labour Party, 124, 158, 159, 164, 171, 172
Labour Party (Australia), 125
Labour Representation Committee, 124
Leiserson, W.M. 62
Lenin, V.I., 18, 133, 134
Lenski, G.E., 40
Lester, R.A., 174
Lewis, H.G., 110
Lewis, J.L., 72, 74
Liberal Party, 123
Lipset, S.M., 58–60, 63–5, 70, 74 140, 141
LO (Sweden), 7
local bargaining, 86–100, 108
Lockwood, D., 38–40, 94
Loveridge, R., 34, 67, 41, 78
Lumley, R., 37, 41
Lupton, T., 95
Luxemberg, R., 134

McCarthy, W.E.J., 66, 70
McGrath, C.P., 70
McNabb, R., 111
Malatesta, E., 128
Mann, T., 129, 130
Martin, R., 65, 66
Matignon Agreement, 20
marxism, 17, 18, 23, 57, 58, 128, 133–9, 159
Marx, K., 133
Metal Workers' Union (W Germany), 5, 6
Michels, R., 55–60, 64, 65, 74, 75, 176
Mayo, E., 143
Mieszkowski, P., 112
Miller, D., 99
Mills, C Wright, 62, 74, 75, 139, 140
Miners Federation of Great Britain, 123, 129, 130, 131
Miners' Next Step, 129
Miners, Wake up, 129
Moore, W.J., 22, 42, 112
Moran, M., 71, 75
Muller-Jentsch, W., 91

National and Local Government Officers Association, 37
National Association of Manufacturers, 105
National Building Guild, 131

National Economic Development Council, 155
National Incomes Commission, 155
national income, 109–14
National Transport Workers Federation, 129, 130
National Union of Bank Employees, 46
National Union of Miners, 6, 61
National Union of Railwaymen, 130, 173
new model unions, 10, 27, 122
new unionism, 10, 11
Nicholas, A.W., 66
Nixon, R., 157

Oakeshott, R., 61, 66, 70
oligarchy, 56, 57, 63, 64
Osborne Judgement, 20
Owen, R., 26

Parker, S.R., 66
Pearce, D.F., 22
Pelling, H., 129, 130
Pencavel, J.H., 110
Peper, B., 181
Phelps Brown, E.H., 111
Phillips, A.W., 117
Phillips, G.A., 131
Phillips Curve, 117
political parties, 123–7
polyarchy, 66, 67
Price, R., 17, 21, 33, 34, 48, 49
prosperity theory, 19, 20
Pardy, D.L., 116

Quinn & Leatham, 20, 124

Raisian, J., 112
Reder, M.W., 111, 112
Republican Party, 127
Resler, H., 137, 138
Richardson, R., 22
Roberts, B.C., 61, 62
Ross, A.M., 3, 174, 175
Ross, P., 105
Royal Commission on Trade Unions (1867), 24, 27

Samuelson, P.A., 117
Sankey Commission, 130, 131
Sayles, L., 61, 95
Scanlon, H., 172

Schweiker, R., 127
Seglow, P., 39
Sheffield Outrages, 24
shopfloor bargaining, 86–100, 139, 165
shop stewards, 87, 88, 91, 92, 97, 98,
    139, 165
Silverman, D., 67
size of enterprise, 17
Slitcher, S.H., 70
Smelser, N.J., 16
Social Democratic Party (Germany), 56
Social Contract, 157–62, 179
Solow, R.A., 117
Sorel, G., 129
Strauss, G., 61
Stoney, P.J.M., 116
strikes, 87, 89–92, 114, 172, 174, 175
Summers, C., 62
Sykes, A.J.M., 95
syndicalism, 128–32

Taff Vale Railway Company v
    Amalgamated Society of Railway
    Servants, 20, 124
Taft, P., 105, 175
Tannenbaum, F., 15, 61
Taylor, R., 159
Teamsters' Union, 5, 62, 75
Terry, M., 88, 89, 95
Thomas, R.L., 116
Thomson, A.W.T., 157, 166, 179
Topham, T., 94
Towers, B., 155, 156
Trade Unions
    in Australia, 1, 2, 5, 11, 14, 22, 35,
        37, 42, 122, 125, 153, 154
    in Austria, 35
    in Belgium, 1, 2, 35, 89, 90
    in Canada, 1, 2, 3, 6, 16, 21
    in Denmark, 35, 92
    in France, 1, 2, 4, 6, 13, 19, 20, 33,
        35, 37, 122, 126, 128, 129, 132
    in Germany (West), 1, 2, 5–7, 11, 13,
        14, 19, 25, 33, 35, 37, 90, 91,
        99, 122, 126, 165, 173, 178
    in Ireland (Republic), 1, 2
    in Italy, 1, 2, 35, 89, 91, 122, 125,
        126
    in Netherlands, 1, 2, 35, 92, 96, 97,
        160, 161
    in New Zealand, 1, 2
    in Norway, 1, 2, 35, 161, 162
    in Poland, 17
    in Sweden, 1, 2, 5–7, 22, 35, 46–9,
        90–2, 97, 162
    in United Kingdom, 1–8, 10, 11,
        14–17, 19–22, 24–8, 33–7, 46,
        70, 71, 122–32, 138, 139,
        152–4, 159–60, 163, 164,
        170–6
    in USA, 1–7, 10–12, 14, 17, 20, 22,
        34–37, 42, 70, 71, 92, 122,
        126, 127, 153, 154, 171, 176
    aims, 1
    craft, 5
    definition, 1
    effect on earnings 109–14
    general, 6
    and governments, 148–67
    growth of 10–28
    industrial 5, 6
    and inflation, 114–19
    influence of, 1
    internal government, 6–8
    leaders, 53–78, 139, 140, 165, 171,
        172, 176
    membership, 1, 3, 11–14, 17, 21,
        22, 33–7, 110–12
    occupational, 6
    and political action, 127–32
    political implications, of, 133–44
    political objectives of, 122, 123
    and political, parties, 123–7, 171,
        172
    size, 45, 176
    and social policy, 157–62
    structure, 5, 6
    and unemployment, 114–19
    white collar, 31–50
Trades Union Congress, 4, 38, 43, 131,
    132, 157–60, 164, 166
Transport and General Workers' Union,
    5–8, 25, 26, 37, 60, 61, 63, 64,
    71, 76, 77, 97–9, 177
Tropp, A, 39
Tolpuddle Martyrs, 27
Triple Alliance, 130
Trotsky, L, 134
Turner, H.A., 63–5, 115

unemployment, 114–19
union democracy, 53–78

Union of Post Office Workers, 75
Union of Shop Distributive and Allied
    Workers, 71
United Mineworkers' Union (USA), 62,
    72–4
Undy, R., 97–9
Unofficial Reform Committee, 129
Upper Clyde Shipbuilders, 100

Wages Councils, 149, 150
wages drift, 86
Walker, K.E., 42
Warner, M., 67, 74, 78
Webbs, S. & B., 1, 2, 15, 24–7, 53–6
welfare unionism, 123

Westergaard, J., 137, 138
white collar workers, 31–50, 107
Whittingham, W.M., 159, 160
Whitley Committee, 107, 108
Wilkinson, F., 115
Wilkinson, R.K., 116
Wilson, G.K., 127
Wilson, H., 124
Woodfield, A.E., 72
Woolman, L., 19
workers' councils (Yugoslavia), 178

Yabloski, J., 62

Zis, G., 116